"China and the US are locked in a struggle for international primacy, and the result of this contest will shape the world order for generations to come. Kishore Mahbubani captures the complexity of this battle with the measured nuance and clear insight it deserves. Not to be missed."

—IAN BREMMER, president of the Eurasia Group
and author of *Us vs. Them*

"Kishore Mahbubani's *Has China Won?* is a serious contribution: reviewing strategic wisdom from Kennan to Kennedy, asking provocative, even heretical questions about China's rise, and counseling a world safe for diversity."

—GRAHAM ALLISON, Douglas Dillon Professor of Government,
Harvard University, and author of *Destined for War:
Can America and China Escape Thucydides's Trap*

"Kishore Mahbubani has deep experience in diplomacy and international relations, an highly developed relatively rare ability to think strategically in complex settings, and a unique capacity (by virtue of his life story) to connect with and respect multiple civilizations and their values. These skills, insights, and experience are on full display in his new book, *Has China Won?* A provocative title, but a little misleading. In fact, he analyzes in an even-handed way the scenarios that could play out in the emerging rivalry between China and the USA. His assessment of the biases and mistakes on both sides is both brutal and crucial. It will take most readers out of their comfort zone, and that is part of its strength. There are many insights, but at the core is the proposition that the outcome over time will depend mainly on the capacity (or its absence) on both sides to understand and respect deep differences in civilizations that are built over hundreds and even thousands of years, ones that lead to varying governance structures and relative values with respect to individual freedoms, social and political stability, and more; in other words seeing the worlds through the eyes of the other. That said there is a wide range of common interests on which to build. Notwithstanding the title of the book, it is fairly clear by the end that in Mahbubani's view, either everyone (not just China and the USA) wins or no one wins. It is an important book at a crucial moment in history."

—MICHAEL SPENCE, recipient of the 2001 Nobel
Memorial Prize in Economic Sciences

"*Has China Won?* is a provocative title. In his latest book, Kishore Mahbubani explains why this is in fact the wrong question to ask. Despite rising resentment and mutual misperception, both the United States and China ultimately know that war between them will be cataclysmic. In this revelatory new book, Mahbubani appeals to the deeper rationality of both great powers, arguing that the greatest challenge of our times will be to answer the question of whether humanity has won. Both American and Chinese readers will benefit from Mahbubani's wisdom."

—GEORGE YEO, former minister of foreign affairs, Singapore

"Americans should heed Kishore Mahbubani's astringent advice, unwelcome as it may be: cast away illusions about eternal US primacy and exceptional virtue protected by high walls. Instead, Washington should adopt a long-term international strategy anchored in balance and cooperation; reestablish sound internal leadership and governance; win friends abroad instead of driving allies away; avoid over-commitment; and express moral modesty. Military power is not the most important weapon in the Arsenal of Democracy."

—DAVID M. LAMPTON, professor emeritus, Johns Hopkins
School of Advanced International Studies, and
Oksenberg-Rohlen fellow Freeman Spogli Institute,
Asia-Pacific Research Center, Stanford University

"Kishore Mahbubani has long extolled what the West taught the rest of the world and how many parts of Asia, including China and India, have benefited from what they have learned. Yet no one seems more surprised at what China has learned from the US than the United States itself, which now sees China purely as a rival that threatens its global primacy. Mahbubani asks pointedly: What did China do to deserve this? He has gone further than ever before to challenge his readers to think of the consequences if the rivalry is allowed to grow unchecked."

—WANG GUNGWU, university professor, National University of Singapore

"Kishore Mahbubani has a remarkable ability to see through the complacent orthodoxies that lead great nations astray. *Has China Won?* identifies the myths and mistakes that are undermining Chinese and American relations with each other and the world, and it offers both countries candid and clear-eyed advice for how to do better in the future. Leaders in Beijing and Washington will not like everything he has to say, but they would do well to pay close attention to it anyway. And so should you."

—STEPHEN M. WALT, Robert and Renée Belfer Professor of International Affairs, Harvard University

"We need to know how China thinks and sees itself in the world, whether we see them as our friends, as our adversary, or somewhere in between. There is no better guide for westerners to the Asian worldview than Kishore Mahbubani. He shares the wealth of his knowledge and experience in this vitally important book."

—LAWRENCE H. SUMMERS, former treasury secretary and former president, Harvard University

"Kishore Mahbubani has written an excellent and important book on much the biggest question in international affairs: How will the relationship between the US and China evolve? Humanity desperately needs these superpowers to co-operate. It seems more likely to have ceaseless friction between them. If it is the latter, argues Mahbubani, it is quite likely that the US will end up at a severe disadvantage, not so much because of China's inherent superiority, but rather because of US mistakes, not least a failure to grasp the Chinese reality."

—MARTIN WOLF, Chief Economics Commentator *Financial Times*

HAS CHINA WON?

The Chinese Challenge to American Primacy

KISHORE MAHBUBANI

PublicAffairs

NEW YORK

To my mother-in-law
Adele
who exemplifies American generosity with her own special graciousness

---

PublicAffairs
Hachette Book Group
1290 Avenue of the Americas, New York, NY 10104
www.publicaffairsbooks.com
@Public_Affairs

Printed in the United States of America
First Edition: April 2020

Published by PublicAffairs, an imprint of Perseus Books, LLC, a subsidiary of Hachette Book Group, Inc. The PublicAffairs name and logo is a trademark of the Hachette Book Group.

The Hachette Speakers Bureau provides a wide range of authors for speaking events. To find out more, go to www.hachettespeakersbureau.com or call (866) 376-6591.

The publisher is not responsible for websites (or their content) that are not owned by the publisher.

Library of Congress Cataloging-in-Publication Data
Names: Mahbubani, Kishore, author.
Title: Has China won? : the Chinese challenge to American primacy / by Kishore Mahbubani.
Other titles: Chinese challenge to American primacy
Description: First edition. | New York : PublicAffairs, 2020. | Includes bibliographical references and index.
Identifiers: LCCN 2019045550 | ISBN 9781541768130 ; (hardcover) | ISBN 9781541768123 ; (ebook)
Subjects: LCSH: China—Relations—United States. | United States—Relations—China. | China—Economic conditions—20th century. | United States—Strategic aspects. | China—Strategic aspects.
Classification: LCC D740.4 .M3115 2020 | DDC 327.51073—dc23
LC record available at https://lccn.loc.gov/2019045550

ISBNs: 978-1-5417-6813-0 (hardcover), 978-1-5417-6812-3 (ebook),
978-1-5417-5867-4 (international)

LSC-C

10 9 8 7 6 5 4 3 2

CONTENTS

CHAPTER 1

INTRODUCTION

ONE THING IS CERTAIN.

The geopolitical contest that has broken out between America and China will continue for the next decade or two. Although President Donald Trump launched the first round in 2018, it will outlast his administration. The president has divided America on all his policies, except one: his trade and technological war against China. Indeed, he has received strong bipartisan support for it, and a strong consensus is developing in the American body politic that China represents a threat to America. General Joseph Dunford, chairman of the Joint Chiefs of Staff, has said that "China probably poses the greatest threat to our nation by about 2025."* The summary of America's 2018 National Defense Strategy claims that China and Russia are "revisionist powers" seeking to "shape a world consistent with their authoritarian model— gaining veto authority over other nations' economic, diplomatic, and

---

* Ryan Browne, "Top US General: China Will Be 'Greatest Threat' to US by 2025," CNN, September 27, 2017, https://edition.cnn.com/2017/09/26/politics/dunford-us-china-greatest-threat/index.html.

security decisions."* Christopher Wray, the FBI director, has said, "One of the things we're trying to do is view the China threat as not just a whole-of-government threat, but a whole-of-society threat . . . and I think it's going to take a whole-of-society response by us."† Even George Soros, who spent millions trying to prevent Trump from being elected, has praised Trump on China. He has said: "The greatest—and perhaps only—foreign policy accomplishment of the Trump administration has been the development of a coherent and genuinely bipartisan policy toward Xi Jinping's China."‡ He also added that it was right for the Trump administration to declare China "a strategic rival."

Yet, even though the American establishment has, by and large, enthusiastically supported Trump on China, it is curious that no one has pointed out that America is making a big strategic mistake by launching this contest with China without first developing a comprehensive and global strategy to deal with China.

The man who alerted me to this was one of America's greatest strategic thinkers, Dr. Henry Kissinger. I still remember vividly the one-on-one lunch I had with him in a private room in his club in midtown Manhattan in mid-March 2018. On the day of the lunch, I was afraid that it would be canceled as a snowstorm was predicted. Despite the weather warning, he turned up. We had a wonderful conversation over two hours. To be fair to him, he didn't exactly say that America lacked a long-term strategy toward China, but that was the message

---

* Summary of the 2018 National Defense Strategy of the United States of America: Sharpening the American Military's Competitive Edge, https://dod.defense.gov/Portals/1/Documents/pubs/2018-National-Defense-Strategy-Summary.pdf.

† Michael Kranz, "The Director of the FBI Says the Whole of Chinese Society Is a Threat to the US—and That Americans Must Step Up to Defend Themselves," Business Insider, February 13, 2018, https://www.businessinsider.sg/china-threat-to-america-fbi-director-warns-2018-2.

‡ George Soros, "Will Trump Sell Out the U.S. on Huawei?," Wall Street Journal, September 9, 2019, https://www.wsj.com/articles/will-trump-sell-out-the-u-s-on-huawei-11568068495.

he conveyed over lunch. This is also the big message of his own book, *On China*.

By contrast, America thought hard and deep before it plunged into the Cold War against the Soviet Union. The master strategist who formulated America's successful containment strategy against the Soviet Union was George Kennan. The strategy was first publicly spelled out in the famous essay he wrote in *Foreign Affairs* under the pseudonym Mr. X, derived from his "long telegram" written in February 1946. Kennan wrote this when he was serving in the critical post of director of the Policy Planning Staff in the State Department, whose key mission is long-term strategic planning.

The director of policy planning in the State Department from September 2018 to August 2019 was Professor Kiron Skinner of Carnegie Mellon University. In a public panel discussion on April 29, 2019, she revealed that in response to the resurgence of China, her department was still trying to work out a comprehensive strategy to match the one spelled out by her predecessor, Kennan.

When I served in the Singapore Foreign Service, I was also assigned to write long-term strategy papers for the Singapore government. The big lesson I learned from Singapore's three exceptional geopolitical masters (Lee Kuan Yew, Goh Keng Swee, and S. Rajaratnam) was that the first step to formulate any long-term strategy is to frame the right questions. If one gets the questions wrong, the answers will be wrong. Most importantly, as Rajaratnam taught me, in formulating such questions, one must always "think the unthinkable."

In this spirit of "thinking the unthinkable," I would like to suggest ten areas that provoke questions that the policy planning staff should address. Having met George Kennan once in his office in the Institute of Advanced Study in Princeton, New Jersey, in the late 1990s, I believe that he would favor confronting head-on the toughest issues that lie ahead.

THE BIG TEN

1. With 4 percent of the world's population, America's share of the global GDP was close to 50 percent at the end of World War II. Throughout the Cold War, the GDP of the Soviet Union never came close in size to that of America, reaching only 40 percent that of America's at its peak.[*] Could America's GDP become smaller than China's in the next thirty years? If so, what strategic changes will America have to make when it no longer is the world's dominant economic power?

2. Should America's primary goal be to improve the livelihood of its 330 million citizens or to preserve its primacy in the international system? If there are contradictions between the goals of preserving primacy and improving well-being, which should take priority?

3. In the Cold War, America's heavy defense expenditures proved prudent as they forced the Soviet Union, a country with a smaller economy, to match America's military expenses. In the end, this helped to bankrupt the Soviet Union. China learned a lesson from the collapse of the Soviet Union. It is restraining its defense expenditures while focusing on economic development. Is it wise for America to continue investing heavily in its defense budget? Or should it cut down its defense expenses and its involvement in expensive foreign wars and instead invest more in improving social services and rejuvenating national infrastructure? Does China want America to increase or reduce its defense expenditures?

4. America did not win the Cold War on its own. It formed solid alliances with its Western partners in NATO and cultivated key

---

* Robert O. Work and Greg Grant, *Beating the Americans at Their Own Game: An Offset Strategy with Chinese Characteristics*, Center for a New American Society, 2019, https://s3.amazonaws.com/files.cnas.org/documents/CNAS-Report-Work-Offset-final-B.pdf?mtime=20190531090041.

third world friends and allies, like China, Pakistan, Indonesia, and Egypt. To preserve these close alliances, America kept its economy open to its allies and generously extended its aid. Above everything else, America was known for its spirit of generosity in the Cold War. The Trump administration has announced an America First policy and threatened to impose tariffs on key allies like the EU and Japan and third world friends like India. Can America build up a solid global coalition to counterbalance China if it also alienates its key allies? Was America's decision to walk away from the Trans-Pacific Partnership (TPP) a geopolitical gift to China? Has China already mounted a preemptive strike against a containment policy by engaging in new economic partnerships with its neighbors through the Belt and Road Initiative (BRI)?

5. The most powerful weapon that America can use to bring its allies and adversaries into line and conform to its wishes is not the US military but the US dollar. The US dollar has become virtually indispensable for global trade and financial transactions. In this regard, it serves as a global public good servicing the interdependent global economy. Since foreign banks and institutions cannot avoid using it, America has been able to indulge in extraterritorial application of its domestic laws and impose huge fines on foreign banks for violating its domestic laws on trading with Iran and other sanctioned countries. American adversaries like North Korea and Iran were also forced to the negotiating table because of crippling financial sanctions. American sanctions on these countries worked best when they were supported and endorsed by multilateral institutions, like the UN Security Council, whose decisions are binding on UN member states. Under the Trump administration, America has switched from multilateral to unilateral sanctions and weaponized the dollar to use against its adversaries. Is it wise to weaponize a global public good and use it for unilateral ends? Right now, there are no practical alternatives to the US dollar. Will that always be

the case? Is this the Achilles' heel of the American economy that China can pierce and weaken?

6. In developing a strategy against the Soviet Union, Kennan emphasized that it was vital for Americans to "create among the peoples of the world generally the impression of a country" that was successful domestically and enjoyed a "spiritual vitality."* Professor Joseph Nye described this as American soft power. From the 1960s to the 1980s, American soft power soared. Since 9/11, America has violated international law and international human rights conventions (and became the first Western country to reintroduce torture). American soft power has declined considerably, especially under Trump. Are the American people ready to make the sacrifices needed to enhance American soft power? Can America win the ideological battle against China if it is perceived to be a "normal" nation rather than an "exceptional" one?

7. General H. R. McMaster, President Trump's national security adviser from 2017 to 2018, has said that at the end of the day, the struggle between America and China represented the struggle between "free and open societies and closed authoritarian systems."† If this statement is correct, all free and open societies should feel equally threatened by the Chinese Communist Party. Of the world's three largest democracies, two are Asian: India and Indonesia. Neither the Indian nor Indonesian democracies feel threatened in any way by Chinese ideology. Neither do most European democracies feel threatened. Unlike the Soviet Union, China is not trying to challenge or threaten American ideology. By treating the new China challenge as akin to the old Soviet strategy, America is making the classic strategic mistake of fighting tomorrow's war with yesterday's strategies. Are American strategic thinkers capable

---

* Mr. X (George Kennan), "The Sources of Soviet Conduct," *Foreign Affairs*, July 1947, 581.
† Munk Debates, Toronto, May 9, 2019.

of developing new analytical frameworks to capture the essence of the competition with China?

8. In any major geopolitical competition, the advantage always goes to the party that can remain rational and cool-headed over the party that is driven by emotions, conscious or unconscious. As Kennan wisely observed, that "loss of temper and self-control" is a sign of weakness. But are America's responses to China driven by reason? Or by subconscious emotions? The Western psyche has long harbored a deep, unconscious fear of the "yellow peril." Kiron Skinner pointed out that the contest with China was with a power that was "non-Caucasian." In so doing, she put her finger on what is driving the emotional reactions to China. In the politically correct environment of Washington, DC, is it possible for any strategic thinker to suggest such a politically incorrect but truthful point without getting politically skewered?

9. Sun Tzu, one of China's greatest strategic masters, once advised: "If you know the enemy and know yourself, you need not fear the result of a hundred battles. If you know yourself but not the enemy, for every victory gained you will also suffer a defeat. If you know neither the enemy nor yourself, you will succumb in every battle."* Does America know its Chinese rival? For example, is America making a fundamental error of perception when it views the CCP as a Chinese *Communist* Party? This would imply that the soul of the CCP is embedded in its communist roots. Yet, in the eyes of many objective Asian observers, the CCP actually functions as the "Chinese *Civilization* Party." Its soul is not rooted in the foreign ideology of Marxism-Leninism but in the Chinese civilization. The most important job for a strategic thinker is to try to step into the mind of the adversary. So here's a test: What percentage of a Chinese leader's mind is preoccupied with Marxist-Leninist ideology

---

* Sun Tzu, *The Art of War*, trans. Lionel Giles (M.A. Pax Librorum, 2009), first published in 1910, https://www.paxlibrorum.com/books/taowde/.

and what percentage with the rich history of Chinese civilization? The answer would probably surprise many Americans.

10. Henry Kissinger in *On China* emphasized that Chinese strategy was guided by the Chinese game of *wei qi* (围棋), not Western chess. In Western chess, the emphasis is on finding the fastest way to capture the king. In *wei qi*, the goal is to slowly and patiently build up assets to tip the balance of the game in one's favor. The emphasis is on long-term strategy, not short-term gains. So is China slowly and patiently acquiring assets that are progressively turning the strategic game in China's favor? Interestingly, America has made two major efforts to thwart two long-term moves by China to gain advantage. Both failed. The first was the Obama administration's attempt to prevent its allies from joining the Chinese-initiated Asian Infrastructure Investment Bank (AIIB) in 2014–2015. The second was the effort by the Trump administration to prevent its allies from participating in the Chinese-initiated BRI. Is America setting aside enough resources for the long-term competition? Does American society have the inherent strength and stamina to match China's long-term game?

The goal of raising these questions is to stimulate a strategic debate, think the unthinkable, and dissect and understand the many complex dimensions of the US-China geopolitical contest that will unravel in the coming decade. One of the goals of this book is to promote hard-headed, rational thinking on an inevitably complex and shifting subject.

One fundamental question that any American strategic thinker must pose before plunging into a major geopolitical contest is one that gets at the scale of risk involved. In short, can America lose? The thought seems inconceivable. Both in physical and moral terms, America has long seen itself as the strongest nation. The American economy, and consequently its military, has been the strongest in the world for over a century. Its natural advantage of occupying a lightly populated and resource-rich continent, combined with the innovativeness and vigor of American institutions (especially its free markets, its rule of law, and its universities) and the American people, have convinced America that no nation can come close to its level of ingenuity and productivity.

In the moral dimension, to most Americans, the idea that a free and open society like America, the world's strongest democracy, could lose a contest against a closed communist society like China is inconceivable. Americans are prone to believe that good always triumphs over evil and that no political system is inherently as good as the one envisaged by the founders of the republic. This may partially explain the increasing demonization of China in recent years. The more China is portrayed as an evil actor (especially in violating American expectations that China would progressively open up and become a democratic society as it engaged America), the easier it has become for Americans to persist in the belief that they would eventually triumph against China, no matter the odds.

America also prides itself on being a rational society. In many ways, it is. It is heir to the great story of Western civilization with its foundation in reason and logic. The scientific revolution that boosted Western civilization enabled its domination. With the advantage of a vibrant market, the strongest universities, and the most highly educated elites in the world, America assumed that no society could compete with it in the critical domains of economic and military strengths, intellectual ingenuity, and moral supremacy.

Americans also assumed that since they had the most open society on the planet, the various mechanisms of this open society would alert America if it took a major wrong turn. Sadly, this has not happened in recent decades. Most Americans are unaware that the average income of the bottom 50 percent of their population has declined over a thirty-year period.* This didn't happen because of one wrong turn. As this book will document, America has turned away significantly from some of the key principles that defined social justice in American society. America's greatest political and moral philosopher in recent times has been John Rawls. Through his works, he tried to distill the wisdom of the philosophy of the great European philosophers, which America's Founding Fathers learned from. Unfortunately, many Americans are unaware how much they have turned away from some key founding principles.

Similarly, few Americans are aware that the world has changed in many critical dimensions since the heyday of American power in the 1950s. In 1950, in PPP (purchasing power parity) terms, America had 27.3 percent of the world's GDP, while China had only 4.5 percent.† At the end of the Cold War, in 1990, a triumphant moment, America had 20.6 percent and China had 3.86 percent. As of 2018, it has 15 percent, less than China's (18.6 percent).‡ In one crucial respect, America has already become number two. Few Americans are aware of this; fewer still have considered what it means.

Even more critically, the global context in which the US-China rivalry will be played out will be very different from that of the Cold War. The world has become a more complex place. It is clear that America remaining the preeminent world power, while not impossible, is going to become more and more unlikely unless America adapts to the new world that has emerged.

---

* Danny Quah, "The US Is, Indeed, the Exceptional Nation: Income Dynamics in the Bottom 50%," Lee Kuan Yew School of Public Policy, January 2019, http://www.dannyquah .com/Quilled/Output/2019.01-Danny.Quah-Income-Dynamics-in-the-Bottom-50.pdf.

† Angus Maddison, "Table B–20. Shares of World GDP, 20 Countries and Regional Totals, 0–1998 A.D.," in *The World Economy: Volume 1: A Millennial Perspective; Volume 2: Historical Statistics* (Paris: OECD, 2006), 263.

‡ World Bank, "GDP, PPP (current international $)—United States, China, World," 1990–2018, World Bank International Comparison Program database, https://data .worldbank.org/indicator/NY.GDP.MKTP.PP.CD?locations=US-CN-1W.

In the arena of civilizational dynamism, the world is returning to something like a historic balance among different human civilizations. For over two hundred years, Western civilization vastly outperformed the rest of the world, allowing it to overturn the historical precedent; from the year 1 to 1820, China and India were always the largest civilizations in terms of economic strength. The past two hundred years have therefore been an aberration.

One reason the West can no longer dominate the world is that the rest have learned so much from the West. They have imbibed many Western best practices in economics, politics, science, and technology. As a result, while many parts of Western civilization (especially Europe) seem exhausted, lacking drive and energy, other civilizations are just getting revved up. In this respect, human civilizations are like other living organisms. They have life cycles. Chinese civilization has had many ups and downs. It should be no surprise that it is now returning in strength. Having survived over two thousand years, China has developed strong civilizational sinews. Professor Wang Gungwu has observed that while the world has had many ancient civilizations, the only ancient civilization to fall down four times and rise again is China. As a civilization, China is remarkably resilient. The Chinese people are also remarkably talented. As the Chinese look back over two thousand years, they are acutely aware that the past thirty years under CCP rule have been the best thirty years that Chinese civilization has experienced since China was united by Qin Shi Huang in 221 BCE. For most of the past two thousand years, the large pool of brainpower available in the Chinese population was not developed under the imperial Chinese system. During the past thirty years, for the first time in Chinese history, it has been tapped on a massive scale. Cultural confidence, which the Chinese have had for centuries, combined with what China has learned from the West have given Chinese civilization a special vigor today. A Chinese American psychology researcher from Stanford University, Jean

Fan, has observed after visiting China in 2019 that "China is changing in a deep and visceral way, and it is changing fast, in a way that is almost incomprehensible without seeing it in person. In contrast to America's stagnation, China's culture, self-concept, and morale are being transformed at a rapid pace—mostly for the better."* If an index could measure the relative strength and resilience of different human civilizations based on their real performance over two thousand years, Chinese civilization might rank number one. The extraordinary vigor of Chinese civilization today is not unique. Other Asian civilizations are also thriving because the West has taught the world well and shared its example widely.†

I can confidently speak about the civilizational vigor of the many different societies in Asia as the result of an unusual cultural quirk. I have cultural connections with diverse societies in Asia, where half of humanity lives, all the way from Tehran to Tokyo. I was born to two Hindu Sindhi parents in Singapore in 1948. As a result, I am connected with over a billion Hindus in South Asia. Nine of the ten Southeast Asian states have an Indic cultural base too. When I see stories from the Ramayana and Mahabharata—so much a part of my childhood—performed in Southeast Asia, I feel my connection to them. Over 550 million people live in this Southeast Asian Indic space. My parents left Pakistan in 1947 because of the painful partition between Hindu India and Islamic Pakistan. As a child, I learned to read and write the Sindhi language with its Perso-Arabic script. My name, Mahbubani, also comes from an Arabic-Persian word, *mahboob*, which means "beloved." Hence, when I visit the Arabic or Iranian cultural spheres, I can also feel a cultural connection with them. When I visit Buddhist temples in China, Korea, and Japan, I can also feel the tug of cultural affinity. Buddhism, which has roots in Hinduism,

---

* Jean Fan, "The American Dream Is Alive in China," *Palladium Magazine*, October 11, 2019, https://palladiummag.com/2019/10/11/the-american-dream-is-alive-in-china/.
† Kishore Mahbubani, *Has the West Lost It?: A Provocation* (London: Penguin, 2018), 36–46.

originated in India. My mother would take me to pray in Buddhist temples, as well as Hindu temples, when I was young.

This personal connection with a remarkably wide range of Asian societies, as well as my ten years as an ambassador to the United Nations (UN), has convinced me that in the realm of international affairs, the texture and chemistry of the world have also changed in a way that most Americans are unaware of. One hundred ninety-three nation-states are members of the UN. One simple question we should ask is which country—China or the United States—is swimming in the same direction as the majority of the other 191?

Most Americans assume that America's policies and aspirations abroad are naturally in harmony with the rest of the world, since America has provided leadership to the rest of the world for decades. After World War II, America did set the broad directions for the liberal international order (which should be more appropriately called the "rules-based international order"). The main global multilateral institutions, including the UN, the World Trade Organization (WTO), the International Monetary Fund (IMF), and the World Bank, were all created at the height of American power. They reflect American values. In terms of cultural identity, they are Western in orientation, not Asian or Chinese. Yet, despite the fact that they entrench Western values and priorities, in recent years America has been walking away from these institutions, while the rest of the world, especially China, has been walking toward them.

In short, it is far from certain that America will win the contest. China has as good a chance as America of emerging as the dominant influence in the world. In fact, many thoughtful leaders and observers in strategically sensitive countries around the world have begun making preparations for a world where China may become number one.

Yet, just as it has been a strategic mistake for American thinkers to take success for granted, it would be an equally colossal strategic mistake for China to assume the same. Despite the many advantages

China has in size and civilizational resilience, it would be unwise for Chinese leaders to underestimate the underlying strengths of the American economy and society. China paid a price in recent years for becoming unwisely arrogant after the global financial crisis of 2008–2009 (which should more accurately be titled the Western financial crisis) rocked the Western economies. At the time of the Lehman Brothers crisis, the much-vaunted American financial system looked as though it was on the ropes. Unwisely, Chinese leaders began to make dismissive statements about America. Ten years later, America has bounced back.

Hence, if I were a senior Chinese leader advising President Xi Jinping, I would strongly urge Xi to overestimate rather than underestimate America's strengths. And if I were asked to draft a memo to President Xi on America's great strengths, I would write the following:

MEMO TO COMRADE XI JINPING: PREPARING FOR THE GREAT STRUGGLE WITH AMERICA

JANUARY 1, 2020

In twenty years, we will mark the two hundredth anniversary of the most humiliating period in China's history. The people of China were forced by the British to accept opium as payment for our valuable tea. As Comrade Xi has said, "with the Opium War of 1840, China was plunged into the darkness of domestic turmoil and foreign aggression; its people, ravaged by war, saw their homeland torn apart and lived in poverty and despair."[*] We were weak. We suffered a hundred years of humiliation until Chairman

---

[*] Xi Jinping, "Secure a Decisive Victory in Building a Moderately Prosperous Society in All Respects and Strive for the Great Success of Socialism with Chinese Characteristics for a New Era," delivered at the 19th National Congress of the Communist Party of China, October 18, 2017.

Mao said at the founding ceremony of the People's Republic of China that "the Chinese people have stood up."*

Today, we are strong. No power can humiliate China. We are well on the road to national rejuvenation. At the opening of the 19th National Congress of the CPC, Comrade Xi inspired us by reminding us that "the theme of the Congress is: Remain true to our original aspiration and keep our mission firmly in mind, hold high the banner of socialism with Chinese characteristics, secure a decisive victory in building a moderately prosperous society in all respects, strive for the great success of socialism with Chinese characteristics for a new era, and work tirelessly to realize the Chinese Dream of national rejuvenation."†

Yet we now also face the biggest challenge to China's rejuvenation. We had hoped that the "beautiful country" (America) would continue to remain sleeping as China rose. Unfortunately, it has now woken up. We must prepare ourselves for the next few decades of intense struggle before we achieve our goal of national rejuvenation.

It would be a huge strategic mistake for us to underestimate the great strengths of America. The Chinese people fear chaos. It is the one force that in the past brought China to its knees and brought misery to the Chinese people. Clearly, America is suffering chaos now. President Donald Trump has been a polarizing and divisive figure. American society has never been as divided since the Civil War of 1861–1865.

---

* Xinhua, "From 'Standing Up' to Rejuvenation: New China after 65 Years," People's Daily Online, English version, October 2, 2014, http://en.people.cn/n/2014/1002/c90882-8790595.html.

† Xinhua, "Full Text of Xi Jinping's Report at 19th CPC National Congress," China Daily, updated November 4, 2017, http://www.chinadaily.com.cn/china/19thcpcnationalcongress/2017-11/04/content_34115212.htm.

Chaos should be a sign of weakness. Yet for America, it is a sign of strength. The chaos is a result of the people arguing loudly and vociferously over the direction that America should take. And the people argue loudly because they believe that they, not the government, are the owners of the country. This sense of ownership of the country creates a tremendous sense of individual empowerment among the American people. Chinese culture values social harmony over individual empowerment. American culture is the opposite.

This sense of individual empowerment has enabled American society to produce some of the most powerful individuals on planet earth. In many societies, the tall nail that stands out is hammered down. A Chinese saying is: "A tall tree catches the wind" (*shù dà zhāo fēng*, 树大招风)—a person in a high position is liable to be attacked. In America, the tall tree is worshipped. Hence, the most admired and respected Americans are successful individuals like Bill Gates of Microsoft, Steve Jobs of Apple, Jeff Bezos of Amazon. Even Mark Zuckerberg and Elon Musk remain admired figures, even though their companies, Facebook and Tesla, are facing a lot of criticism. No society has as powerful an ecosystem as America for producing strong individuals. Our society cannot replicate this great strength of America. China stood up again after a hundred years because of a towering figure like Mao Zedong. American society produces many Mao Zedongs.

The second great strategic advantage of America is that it has access to humanity's best and brightest. China's population of 1.4 billion is four times bigger than America's. In theory, China can tap into a wider pool of talent among its population than America can. However, as Lee Kuan Yew wisely pointed out, America has the ability to attract the best talents from anywhere in the world. Unlike most countries, America willingly accepts foreign-born people as their own if they succeed in America. Hence, in recent years, many of the chief executive officers of major companies have been foreign-born US citizens, including Indra Nooyi of PepsiCo, Sundar Pichai of Google, Satya Nadella of Microsoft, and Andy Grove of Intel. It's not a disadvantage to be foreign born. By contrast, no major Chinese company or institution is run by a foreign-born individual.

The third great strategic advantage of America is its strong institutions. While American society believes in and encourages individual empowerment, it does not rely on strong individual leaders. Instead, it relies on strong institutions to protect society. The founders of the American republic were truly brilliant in drafting a constitution that provided for checks and balances. The democratically elected president and Congress have a lot of power. But their powers are also checked by other institutions like the world's freest media and the US Supreme Court. When the Supreme Court declared that President Donald Trump's ban on Muslims was unconstitutional, Trump could *not* use the military to overthrow the Supreme Court (as many presidents in many countries have done). In America, the rule of law is stronger than the government of the day.

The strength of American institutions and rule of law explains why the whole world has faith in the American dollar. This faith in the American dollar underlies its status as the dominant global reserve currency, giving it the "exorbitant privilege" of printing money to sustain its fiscal and current account deficits. In recent years, America has also used the

US dollar as a powerful weapon to sanction or put pressure on other countries. China does not have this weapon.

Our economy used to be one-tenth the size of that of America. Now it is over 60 percent.[*] Our country also trades more with the rest of the world than America does. We take up 10.22 percent of world total imports and 12.77 percent of world total exports,[†] compared to the US share of 13.37 percent of world imports and 8.72 percent of world exports.[‡] Yet, when it comes to global trade transactions, the dollar still makes up 41.27 percent of all transactions, whereas the renminbi (RMB) makes up 0.98 percent.[§]

Why is this so? This happens because countries and individual wealthy people have faith in the dollar. The RMB cannot replace the dollar in global financial transactions because to achieve this, we would have to make the RMB a fully convertible currency. It is not possible for our economy to do that anytime soon. Hence, the dollar will remain supreme for many decades to come.

The fourth great strategic advantage of America is that it has the best universities in the world. Throughout the long history of humanity, the most successful societies have always been those that fostered diverse schools of thought. In China's most creative period, many schools of thought emerged simultaneously: Confucian, Taoist, Legalist. Today,

---

[*] International Monetary Fund, *World Economic Outlook 2018* (Washington, DC: IMF, 2018).

[†] "China," World Trade Organization, 2017, http://stat.wto.org/CountryProfile/WSDB CountryPFView.aspx?Country=CN.

[‡] "United States of America," World Trade Organization, 2017, http://stat.wto.org /CountryProfile/WSDBCountryPFView.aspx?Country=US.

[§] SWIFT, *RMB Internationalisation: Where We Are and What We Can Expect in 2018*, https://www.swift.com/resource/rmb-tracker-january-2018-special-report.

America leads the world in fostering diverse views. The American universities have created the most powerful intellectual ecosystems in the world. This culture of challenging and criticizing conventional wisdom in turn generates creativity and innovation. Hence, in field after field, America produces more Nobel Prize winners than any other country. At one stage, in the 1980s, Japan appeared as though it could produce a more successful economy than America. Yet, even at the height of its success, it produced relatively few Nobel Prize winners. American universities are populated with hundreds of Nobel laureates.

These great universities serve another critical purpose for America. They provide the conduits through which the best minds in the world are attracted to live and work in America. These great universities, including Harvard, Yale, Stanford, and Columbia, do not look at the nationality or ethnic group of a person when hiring faculty. They will pick the best minds, no matter where they come from. Few universities in the world can match the top American universities in attracting and retaining global talent. The only country that can someday have a bigger population than China is India. China will not be able to attract the best talent from India. America has done so and will continue to do so. This will someday create a symbiotic relationship between India and America. The two biggest competitors that China may have to deal with in the future, America and India, may come together and work together. We must work hard now to prevent this from happening.

The fifth great strategic advantage, which also explains the extraordinary success of its universities, is that America is also part of a great civilization, the Western civilization.

From the beginning of human history, our civilization was on par with many European civilizations. Indeed, we invented more products than they did, like gunpowder, the compass, paper, and printing.* Yet, our civilization fell behind the West after it experienced the great Renaissance, the Enlightenment, and finally the Industrial Revolution. All this led to the great century of humiliation after the Opium War of 1840. It would therefore be a strategic mistake to underestimate the strength and vibrancy of Western civilization.

Being a member of the great Western civilization confers many benefits to the people of America. It gives them great cultural confidence, just as our people get cultural confidence from being members of our great civilization. However, America is not the only member of this civilization. The great countries of Europe, as well as Australia, Canada, and New Zealand, are also members. Hence, in any geopolitical competition, America will not be alone. There is great trust among all the members of Western civilization, especially among the Anglo-Saxon members of the Five Eyes intelligence community (Australia, Canada, New Zealand, the United Kingdom, and the United States). As the geopolitical competition heats up between our two countries, the other members of the West will help America, directly or indirectly.

In conclusion, as we begin our great struggle with America, the biggest strategic mistake we could make is to underestimate its power and strength. This country came out of nowhere two hundred and fifty years ago. It is much

---

* "Four Great Inventions of China," Embassy of the People's Republic of China in Antigua and Barbuda, November 12, 2013, http://ag.china-embassy.org/eng/zggk/t1098061.htm.

younger than us. Yet, despite its youth or perhaps because of it, it is one of the most dynamic societies ever created in human history. Let us prepare ourselves for the greatest geopolitical contest ever seen. We will have to win this contest if we are to achieve our historic goal of complete national rejuvenation by 2049.[*]

This memo may be fictional, but I believe it accurately captures the actual perceptions of America among the Chinese elite. They genuinely respect the great strengths that America has. Even the founder of Huawei, Ren Zhengfei, has publicly declared his respect of America, even though his daughter has been arrested and his company has been battered by America. As a result, the Chinese leaders will make a massive effort to avoid, as long as possible, an all-out geopolitical contest with America. It is a paradox of the great geopolitical contest that will be played out between America and China in the coming decades that it is both inevitable and avoidable. It is inevitable because many of the policymakers who will make the tactical decisions that will drive this contest are possessed by a psychology that sees all competition among great powers as a zero-sum game. Hence, if China steps up its naval deployments in the South China Sea, a neighboring sea, the US Navy will see it as a loss and step up its presence in the region. Yet, as I hope to show, there is no fundamental conflict of interest between the United States and China in keeping the international waterways safe for freedom of navigation. In fact, China has a greater interest in freedom of navigation than America does.

One key goal of this book is to blow away the thick fog of misunderstanding that has enveloped the Sino-American relationship, to enable both sides to better understand—even if they cannot approve of—each other's core interests.

---

[*] Song Wei, "Xi Thought Leads to Chinese Dream," *China Daily*, updated January 2, 2018, http://www.chinadaily.com.cn/a/201801/02/WS5a4ac774a31008cf16da487a.html.

Better understanding will not necessarily lead to peace and harmony. On purely ideological grounds, any American administration must appear sympathetic to the demonstrators in Hong Kong clamoring for more rights. American public opinion demands that the United States support the demonstrations. However, any shrewd American administration should also balance public opinion with a sound understanding of the core interests of Chinese leaders. A Chinese leader who appears to be soft on territories that were once seized from China at China's greatest moment of weakness in the nineteenth century will be condemned by his own people and quickly removed from office.

It is my hope, therefore, that, on completion, a reader of this book will develop a better understanding of the deeper dynamics driving both sides. This book also makes room for a possibly optimistic conclusion. If we believe that we live in an age of reason, where public policies are driven by hardheaded, rational calculations and a geopolitical understanding of each other's core interests, it is possible for both sides to work out long-term policies that will prevent them from moving inexorably toward a painful and unnecessary clash.

There is one important statistic that both American and Chinese leaders should be consistently aware of: 330 million people live in America and 1.4 billion in China. These are big numbers, but the combined population of America and China (1.7 billion) still makes up less than 25 percent of the world's population. Many of the remaining 75 percent of the population have now come to understand and accept that humanity lives in a small, connected, and imperiled planet that we all depend on. Hence, there will be little tolerance from the rest of the world of extreme or irrational measures adopted by either America or China.

In the Declaration of Independence, America's Founding Fathers demanded that the American people show a "decent respect for the opinions of mankind." If ever there was a time to heed such advice, it is now. The world is a complicated place. This book will draw out the complexity and also recommend how it can be managed.

To get to the happy destination of this optimistic conclusion, we first have to travel through unhappy territory. Hence, this book will begin by analyzing the major strategic mistakes made by China and America. Many of the painful observations made here may cause discomfort to both Chinese and American readers alike. Yet, the only way for China and America to learn to work together is to understand where both sides have gone wrong. And so this is where our journey will begin.

CHAPTER 2

CHINA'S BIGGEST STRATEGIC MISTAKE

C HINA'S BIGGEST STRATEGIC MISTAKE WAS TO ALIENATE SEV- eral major constituencies in America, without thinking through the consequences of doing so. Professor Susan Shirk, one of America's most prominent sinologists, observed that when President Trump announced his trade war against China, no one spoke up in defense of China: "With US and China at the precipice of a truly adversarial relationship, no group has really stepped forward to defend US-China relations, much less defend China. Not businesses, not China scholars, and certainly no one in Congress."* By contrast, in the 1990s, when efforts were made to take away China's most-favored-nation (MFN) status, several business communities protested.

China's alienation of the American business community is surprising. In theory, since the American business community can make, and has

---

* Susan Shirk, "Ep. 9: Overreach and Overreaction: The Crisis in US-China Relations," videotape, 2019 Annual Public Lecture, Center for the Study of Contemporary China, Penn Arts & Sciences, February 7, 2019, https://cscc.sas.upenn.edu/podcasts/2019/02 /07/ep-9-overreach-and-overreaction-crisis-us-china-relations-susan-shirk.

made, huge profits in China, they should be the strongest advocates of good US-China relations. American businessmen and businesswomen have no ideological agenda. They are interested only in the bottom line of their companies. All they want is easy access to the large Chinese market to increase their sales and profits. Indeed, many American companies have profited from China. Yet, despite that, virtually no American company defended China against Trump's assault. What went wrong? The story is complicated. To understand this alienation of the American business community, it's useful to begin with a few success stories of American companies in China, like Boeing, General Motors (GM), and Ford.

Boeing has benefited greatly from the Chinese market. It has sold over two thousand planes* to China, and its revenue from China has soared "ten-fold from $1.2 billion in 1993 to $11.9 billion in 2017, or from 5.7% to 21% of Boeing's total revenue from commercial planes."† In November 2018, Boeing announced that "China's commercial fleet is expected to more than double over the next 20 years. Boeing forecasts that China will need 7,690 new airplanes, valued at $1.2 trillion, by 2038."‡ Quite naturally, Boeing has made huge profits from China and also created many jobs for American workers. Equally importantly, the demand from China helped Boeing to ride through rough markets, as indicated in the following report: "The China market became even more strategically important to Boeing as a global economic recession in the early 1990s forced the company to slash production and reduce its workforce. Amid the economic gloom, business held up in China, as Boeing received an aircraft order worth $9 billion in 1990 and delivered

---

* Boeing, "Boeing Delivers Its 2,000th Airplane to China," Boeing press release, November 30, 2018, http://investors.boeing.com/investors/investor-news/press-release-details /2018/Boeing-Delivers-Its-2000th-Airplane-to-China/default.aspx.
† Neil Thomas, "For Company and for Country: Boeing and US-China Relations," US-China Case Studies, MacroPolo, February 26, 2019, https://macropolo.org/boeing-us -china-relations-history/.
‡ Boeing, "Boeing Delivers Its 2,000th Airplane to China."

its 100th plane to China in 1992 and its 200th just two years later. By 1993, China bought one-sixth of the planes Boeing sold."[*]

Boeing has only one serious global large-scale competitor, Airbus, so its success in the Chinese market is not surprising, unlike the success of American auto companies in China. American auto companies are *not* among the most competitive in the world. American auto companies fared so badly against their Japanese competitors in the home US market in the 1980s that even an avowed free marketer who abhorred state intervention, President Ronald Reagan, had to twist the arms of the Japanese to agree to a voluntary export restraint. If Reagan had been faithful to his free-market ideology, he should have allowed Japanese car makers unrestricted access to American consumers, and if he had, the American auto companies could well have crashed and burned.

So why have the relatively uncompetitive American automobile companies done so well in China? Their success is more remarkable and much more improbable than Boeing's. GM, in particular, is a success story. GM sold 3.64 million vehicles in China in 2018,[†] and China accounted for 42 percent of GM's sales in 2017. A 2013 *Forbes* report and Tufts University's Jonathan Brookfield have both identified a common reason for GM's success in China: its joint ventures with local producers. As *Forbes* noted, "Local partnerships are very important for every company that expands its overseas presence. This is especially true in China, where local partners have close ties to the Communist Party—which determines who will be in what business and for how long."[‡] Brookfield also observed that GM's partnership with Shanghai

---

[*] Thomas, "For Company and for Country."

[†] GM, "GM Set for a Record of over 20 Launches in China in 2019," Corporate Newsroom, General Motors, January 7, 2019, https://media.gm.com/media/cn/en/gm/news .detail.html/content/Pages/news/cn/en/2019/Jan/0107_sales.html.

[‡] Pano Mourdoukoutas, "How General Motors Wins the Minds and Wallets of Chinese Consumers, *Forbes*, October 1, 2018, https://www.forbes.com/sites/panosmourdou koutas/2013/10/11/how-general-motors-wins-the-minds-and-wallets-of-chinese -consumers/#59706f51386f.

Automotive Industry was key to the former's "long-term success in China": "The deal was significant enough that then-Vice President Al Gore and Chinese Prime Minister Li Peng presided over the signing ceremony of the 50/50 joint venture in 1997, and by 1999, Shanghai GM was selling Buicks as fast as it could make them."[*]

Given the failure of these companies to penetrate other globally competitive auto markets, why did they succeed in China? The most credible reason for their success in the Chinese market is that the Chinese government made a policy decision not to rely only on European and Japanese car makers to provide cars for the Chinese people. Given the complicated and often fraught relationship between China and Japan, Chinese reliance on Japanese cars would have been politically untenable. Hence, it would not be surprising if the Chinese government tilted the playing field in the auto market to provide special advantages to American auto companies.

As a result of the Chinese government's decision to give space to American cars, GM and Ford have made huge profits there, generating more profits from their sales in China than their American sales. CNN reported on February 7, 2017: "China is now GM's largest market. Sales growth there lifted it to volume it never achieved when it was the world's biggest automaker. GM recorded its fourth straight year of record sales even as U.S. sales fell slightly, the first decline in GM's home market since 2009. The U.S. car market, which rose seven straight years to its own record, may have topped out in 2016. . . . The record sales last year lifted GM to a record operating profit of $12.5 billion, up 16%. Only seven years ago, GM suffered through a federal bailout and bankruptcy."[†] In short, China has helped one of America's most iconic companies, GM, to thrive.

---

* Jonathan Brookfield, "How Western Companies Can Succeed in China," The Conversation, October 19, 2016, https://theconversation.com/how-western-companies-can -succeed-in-china-65291.

† Chris Isidore, "GM Sells 10 Million Cars for First Time Thanks to China," CNN Business, February 7, 2017, https://money.cnn.com/2017/02/07/news/companies/gm -record-sales-profits/index.html.

Boeing and GM are among the largest manufacturing companies in American business. Since they have made huge profits from the Chinese market, they should have been among the most powerful voices calling for a positive win-win relationship between America and China. Indeed, in the early years of Sino-American engagement, the American business community remained bullish and optimistic on China. When President Bill Clinton tried to tie the renewal of China's MFN status to human rights issues in 1993, the *New York Times* reported that "many American companies [. . .] vigorously lobb[ied] the White House and Congress for an extension of China's trading privileges, pointing out that billions of dollars in exports are at stake, as well as thousands of jobs." In addition, they argued that "using trade privileges to address human rights and arms proliferation will do little to persuade the Chinese to make changes. And some executives argue[d] that selling to China can help the United States realize its policy goals."*

Another report documented how Boeing played a key role in defending China's MFN status: "[In the 1990s], as anti-engagement constituencies consolidated, Boeing and numerous other US firms played a key role in persuading Congress to uphold MFN. Boeing was notable for being the vanguard of 'corporate foreign policy' and was considered by some as the 'most China-savvy' company in the country and 'the quarterback' for these efforts. A Senate staffer remarked that Boeing 'put out the full-court press' for MFN on Capitol Hill."†

Against this historical backdrop of American businesses playing a key role in defending Sino-American relations, it is truly shocking that when President Donald Trump suddenly launched a trade war against China in January 2018, no major American business voices tried to restrain him. Indeed, virtually no American voices tried to restrain

---

* Calvin Sims, "China Steps Up Spending to Keep U.S. Trade Status, *New York Times*, May 7, 1993, https://www.nytimes.com/1993/05/07/business/china-steps-up-spending-to-keep-us-trade-status.html
† Thomas, "For Company and for Country."

Trump. Instead, Trump discovered (probably to his surprise) that he received broad and deep bipartisan support. Even leading Democrats supported him. Senator Chuck Schumer said that "when it comes to being tough on China's trading practices, I'm closer to Trump than Obama or Bush."* Congresswoman Nancy Pelosi said, "The United States must take strong, smart and strategic action against China's brazenly unfair trade policies. . . . far more is needed to confront the full range of China's bad behavior."† Even a moderate and middle-of-the-road influential commentator like Thomas Friedman weighed in with support for Trump. Friedman agreed with Trump that China has not played by the rules, writing "that's why it's a fight worth having. Don't let the fact that Trump is leading the charge distract from the vital importance of the U.S., Europe and China all agreeing on the same rules for 2025—before it really is too late."†

Strikingly, the American Chambers of Commerce in Shanghai and Beijing issued reports in 2018 detailing their grievances. The American Chamber of Commerce in Shanghai's *2018 China Business Report* said: "Survey takers believe Chinese government policies favor local companies (54.5%); 60% reported that China's regulatory environment lacks transparency, no improvement on last year; and lack of IPR protection and enforcement (61.6%), obtaining required licenses (59.5%), and data security and protection of commercial secrets (52%) remain top regulatory hindrances."

---

* Chuck Schumer, "Schumer Response to President Trump Tweet on China Trade," Newsroom, Senate Democrats, May 21, 2018, https://www.democrats.senate.gov /newsroom/press-releases/schumer-response-to-president-trump-tweet-on-china-trade.

† Nancy Pelosi, "Pelosi Statement on Trump Administration's New Tariffs on China," News, Congresswoman Nancy Pelosi, California's 12th District, May 22, 2018, https:// pelosi.house.gov/news/press-releases/pelosi-statement-on-trump-administration -s-new-tariffs-on-china.

‡ Thomas L. Friedman, "The U.S. and China Are Finally Having It Out," *New York Times*, May 1, 2018, https://www.nytimes.com/2018/05/01/opinion/america-china -trump-trade.html

The same report added that "despite the relative optimism our members feel guarded about the future. Government procurement practices still favor local companies and may become even more entrenched as Made in China 2025 and other policies institutionalize local-first purchasing. American companies in strategically important business areas experience pressure to transfer technology. These policies and practices are in turn stoking demand for reciprocity in the U.S.-China trading relationship even if our members generally oppose the use of retaliatory trade tariffs."[*]

Most damagingly, the same report pointed out how many foreign companies, including American companies, feel bullied when they do business in China. It said:

> Recent U.S.-China trade frictions have shined a light on many of the imbalances in the trading relationship, including but not limited to a lack of reciprocity in cross-border investment, China's use of state-funded industrial policies, and pressure to transfer technology as the price to participate in China's market. Few companies will publicly state that they experience such pressure, but in our survey pool, 21% of companies reported having felt such pressure, most acutely in industries China views as strategically important: Aerospace (44%) and chemicals (41%) faced notable pressure, affirming the current U.S. administration's concern about this pay-to-play tactic in technology-based industries.[†]

This strong chorus of American voices supporting Trump's accusations against China provided powerful confirmation that China had made a serious strategic mistake. So what went wrong? Was it a result

---

[*] Doug Strub et al., *2018 China Business Report: The American Chamber of Commerce in Shanghai*, AmCham Shanghai and PwC, 2018, https://www.amcham-shanghai.org/sites/default/files/2018-07/2018%20China%20Business%20Report_0.pdf.
[†] Ibid., 18.

of a high-level decision of the Chinese government to ignore the American business community? Or was it a result of a myriad of micro local decisions? There were at least three major contributing factors to this alienation: the relative political autonomy of provincial and city chiefs, the hubris China experienced after the 2008–2009 global financial crisis, and the relatively weak central leadership in the 2000s. The 2000s were a decade of exceptionally rapid economic growth. China's economy grew at an average annual rate of 10.29 percent,* and many foreign businesses made a lot of money. Hence, while they chafed at unfair practices, they were prepared to accept this pain in return for exceptional profits.

One big mistake that the central party leadership made in the 2000s was to not check carefully how the provinces and cities were treating foreign investors. Yet, even if Beijing wished to do so, there are limits to how much day-to-day control the center can impose. A well-known Chinese saying is: "The mountains are high, and the emperor is far away" (*shān gāo, huáng di yuǎn,* 山高皇帝远). For millennia, the provinces of China, even under strong emperors, have always had strong local autonomy. Often, even when a problem encountered at the provincial level was raised in Beijing, little could be done. A CEO of a major European company told me that his company had signed a binding agreement with a Chinese company allowing it to buy the Chinese company five years later at a fixed price. However, when the date arrived and the European company tried to purchase the Chinese company as agreed, the Chinese company refused to sell. Appeals to local courts and provincial authorities failed. Since the European CEO was well connected in Beijing, he tried appealing for help from the center. All his appeals failed. Instead, he was encouraged to "settle" with the Chinese company by offering a higher price, despite the supposedly binding agreement.

---

* Mean rate of real GDP growth (%) from 2000 to 2009, calculated from IMF World Economic Outlook (April 2019), https://www.imf.org/external/datamapper/NGDP _RPCH@WEO/CHN.

European chambers of commerce in China have echoed the complaints of the Americans in China. George Magnus, a research associate at the China Centre, Oxford University, describes in his 2018 book *Red Flags* how China has made a huge political mistake in ignoring the strong convictions among leading American figures that China has been fundamentally unfair in many of its economic policies: demanding technology transfer, stealing intellectual property, imposing nontariff barriers. "The US has a strong case" against China in this area,[*] as Magnus notes. He describes how China's 2006 technology blueprint aimed to "turn China into a technological powerhouse by 2020 and a global leader by 2050" by promoting "indigenous innovation," and "yet, over time and for foreign firms especially, indigenous innovation came to be associated with various forms of protectionism and favoritism for local companies, unfair trade and commercial practices, and the leveraging of Chinese technical progress on the back of imported technology either from acquisitions abroad or through foreign companies operating in China. According to a US Chamber of Commerce report, indigenous innovation came to be considered by many international technology companies as 'a blueprint for technology theft on a scale the world has never seen before.'"[†] Elizabeth Economy, of the Council on Foreign Relations, has also observed that "many American and European firms complain about intellectual property theft by Chinese companies; it registers near the top of every annual foreign chamber of commerce report ranking of challenges in doing business in China."[‡]

The second factor that could have contributed to the alienation of the American business community was the hubris that China officials

---

[*] George Magnus, *Red Flags: Why Xi's China Is in Jeopardy* (New Haven, CT: Yale University Press, 2018), 166.

[†] "China's Drive for 'Indigenous Innovation'—A Web of Industrial Policies," US Chamber of Commerce, July 27, 2010, https://www.uschamber.com/report/china%E2%80%99s -drive-indigenous-innovation-web-industrial-policies.

[‡] Elizabeth C. Economy, *The Third Revolution: Xi Jinping and the New Chinese State* (New York: Oxford University Press, 2018), 142–143.

displayed just after the 2008–2009 global financial crisis. Several foreign observers have described this well. In his book *The Party*, Richard
McGregor described what happened at the 2008 Boao Forum, China's
equivalent of the annual World Economic Forum Davos meeting. At
these meetings, the Chinese would, in the past, politely say, "This is what
you do, and this is what we do." At the 2008 Boao Forum, he says, the
tone changed. This time, the message was: "You have your own way. We
have our own way. And our way is right!" McGregor goes on to describe
the tone of the meeting:

> One by one, at the 2009 Boao forum, senior Chinese officials tossed
> aside the soothing messages of past conferences to drive this reversal
> of fortune home. The first, a financial regulator, lambasted a recent
> meeting of global leaders as "lip service." Another tore into the role
> of international ratings agencies in the financial crisis. A retired Po-
> litburo member ominously suggested the US needed to make sure it
> "protected the interests of Asian countries" if it wanted China to keep
> buying its debt.*

Gideon Rachman of the *Financial Times* describes well the mood in
Beijing after the global financial crisis in his book *Easternization*:

> In the years after the crash, Western diplomats, particularly Europeans,
> began to notice a new tone in their dealings with the Chinese. In 2011,
> a British diplomat recently returned from a trip to China told me with
> a laugh that China was the only country where he had been told, "What
> you have to remember is that you come from a weak and declining na-
> tion." Another very senior British diplomat confided that "dealing with
> the Chinese is becoming increasingly unpleasant and difficult." When
> I responded that some of his counterparts in Washington still spoke

---

* Richard McGregor, *The Party: The Secret World of China's Communist Rulers* (New York:
Harper Perennial, 2012), 18.

highly of the top Chinese officials they dealt with, the UK official responded, "There is a special tone of voice that the Chinese now only reserve for the Americans." For all China's continuing insistence that it was still a developing nation, the government in Beijing was increasingly behaving like a superpower in the making—and the only country that it still seemed to regard as a true equal was the United States.

The hubris that enveloped Beijing after the global financial crisis may also explain the somewhat reckless moves that China made in the South China Sea in the following years. China is right in saying that it did not start the process of reclaiming land around the rocks and reefs in the South China Sea. The other four claimants started this game. China had exercised great restraint for a long time. Unfortunately, it suddenly decided to sharply increase its reclamation after the global financial crisis. As a result, the anti-China voices in America found the South China Sea a useful propaganda tool to use against China.

It is also clear that these displays of arrogance in Beijing were in violation of the spirit of the advice that Deng Xiaoping had passed on to his successors: "Observe the situation calmly. Stand firm in our positions. Respond cautiously. Conceal our capabilities and await an opportune moment. Never claim leadership. Take some action" (lěng jìng guān chá, wěn zhù zhèn jiáo, chén zhuó yìng fù, tāo guāng yǎng huì, jué bù dāng tóu, yǒu suǒ zuò wéi, 冷静观察，稳住阵脚，沉着应付，韬光养 晦，决不当头， 有所作为).* Clearly, Deng was advocating modesty and humility as China rose. Unfortunately, as Chinese policymakers saw America as a fallen giant, they displayed arrogance when dealing with America in the immediate aftermath of the global financial crisis.

It is possible that this problem could have been contained if China had strong leaders, like Deng Xiaoping and Zhu Rongji, who could

---

* Economy, The Third Revolution, 188.

have reined in some of this arrogance. Unfortunately, the 2000s were also a decade of relatively weak leadership. The top Chinese leadership is clearly one of the most secretive institutions in the world, similar to the Soviet Kremlin. Yet, it is also clear that the period of Hu Jintao's rule (2003–2013) was an interregnum between the strong and disciplined leadership shown by Jiang Zemin (1993–2003) and Zhu Rongji (1998–2003) and that of Xi Jinping (2013–present). This period of relative weakness led to factionalism (led by Bo Xilai and Zhou Yongkang) and a surge of corruption. It also led to a lack of discipline in China's management of its external affairs.

What could China have done differently if it had had stronger leadership in place in the 2000s? For a start, since China had benefited a great deal from the many concessions it enjoyed for joining the WTO as a developing country in 2001, it should have slowly and steadily weaned itself from these concessions by unilaterally announcing that while, in theory, it could enjoy the privileges of being a developing country member of the WTO, in practice, it would not do so.

The most explosive period of China's growth took place after it joined the WTO in 2001. Its GDP exploded from US$1.2 trillion in 2000 to US$11.1 trillion in 2015.* China had shrewdly (and justifiably) negotiated an entry into the WTO as a developing country when its per capita income was US$2,900 in purchasing power parity or PPP† in 2000 (similar to that of Pakistan, Bhutan, Yemen, Cape Verde, Marshall Islands, and Azerbaijan). By 2015, its per capita income had grown to US$14,400.‡ In the same period, China's economy also went from being the sixth largest to the second largest in the world.

---

* World Bank, "China," The World Bank data, https://data.worldbank.org/country/china.
† World Bank, "GNI per Capita, PPP (current interntional $)—China," 1990–2018, The World Bank data, https://data.worldbank.org/indicator/NY.GNP.PCAP.PP.CD ?locations=CN.
‡ Ibid.

There is obviously something clearly unfair about the world's second-largest economy (with the world's largest pool of foreign reserves) claiming that it was as vulnerable as Chad or Bangladesh in requiring special WTO provisions to protect it. The paradox here is that even though China fought hard to enjoy the title of being a developing country member, in practice, it did not take advantage of this designation. Two economists who studied the terms and conditions of China's entry into the WTO observed the following: "Contrary to popular belief, China received hardly any of the benefits that accrue to developing countries when it became a WTO member, besides the ability to use the title 'developing country.'"* Despite this, many foreign observers believed that China was taking advantage of its developing country status. One of China's best friends in America is Hank Paulson, the former US treasury secretary. He is personally deeply committed to good ties with China. He also set up the Paulson Institute, a think tank "dedicated to fostering a US-China relationship that serves to maintain global order in a rapidly evolving world."[†]

In an anguished speech he gave at a conference in Singapore in November 2018, he explained well the international disappointment with China hiding behind WTO rules that were meant for poor developing countries: "17 years after China entered the WTO, China still has not opened its economy to foreign competition in so many areas. It retains joint venture requirements and ownership limits. And it uses technical standards, subsidies, licensing procedures, and regulation as non-tariff barriers to trade and investment. Nearly 20 years after entering the WTO, this is simply unacceptable. It is why the Trump Administration has argued that the WTO system needs to be modernized and changed. And I agree."

---

* Henry Gao and Weihuan Zhou, "China's Developing Country Status Brings It Few Benefits in the WTO," East Asia Forum, October 15, 2019, https://www.eastasiaforum.org/2019/10/15/chinas-developing-country-status-brings-it-few-benefits-in-the-wto/.
† Paulson Institute, Overview, http://www.paulsoninstitute.org/about/about-overview/.

He then went on to explain why the American business community had turned against China.

> How can it be that those who know China best, work there, do business there, make money there, and have advocated for productive relations in the past, are among those now arguing for more confrontation? The answer lies in the story of stalled competition policy, and the slow pace of opening, over nearly two decades. This has discouraged and fragmented the American business community. And it has reinforced the negative attitudinal shift among our political and expert classes. In short, even though many American businesses continue to prosper in China, a growing number of firms have given up hope that the playing field will ever be level. Some have accepted the Faustian bargain of maximizing today's earnings per share while operating under restrictions that jeopardize their future competitiveness. But that doesn't mean they're happy about it.

Even more damningly, Paulson said that Chinese firms enjoyed a better playing field outside China than the one China provided to foreign firms inside China.

> Meanwhile, Chinese firms are permitted to operate in other countries in ways that foreign firms cannot act in China itself. That exacerbates these underlying tensions. And so I do believe that China's actions and failure to open up have contributed to this more confrontational view in the United States. [...] It is not just that foreign technologies are being transferred and digested. It is that they are being reworked so that foreign technologies become Chinese technologies through an indigenization process that many of the multinational CEOs I talk to believe is grossly unfair to the innovators and dreamers at the heart of their companies.

If indeed the biggest strategic mistake of China in managing relations with America has been the unnecessary and unwise alienation of the American business community (and, to some extent, the global business community), there is one positive aspect to it. It is a strategic mistake that can be rectified. It should be possible for China to regain the goodwill and trust of the global business community.

However, before China launches a new initiative to recultivate the global business community, it should analyze why and how it made such a fundamental mistake. The Chinese government in its internal analysis of the mistakes that were made needs to be brutally honest and not shy away from tackling sensitive issues.

Here's one such: many Chinese officials are familiar with Marxist literature and its derivatives. Such literature contains many derisive views of businessmen. For example, Lenin once famously remarked that businessmen would happily sell for a profit the rope that would later be used to hang them. As an aside, let me mention that I have actually seen this happen in real life. When I served in Phnom Penh in 1973 to 1974, the government in charge was a pro-American government supported by the American military. The American military would, at great expense, fly in artillery shells to defend the capital city, Phnom Penh. The corrupt generals in the pro-American government would then immediately sell these artillery shells to middlemen who would then sell them to the Khmer Rouge, even though these artillery shells would then be fired into the city and endanger the lives of the families of these pro-American generals. In short, it is true that many businessmen can be opportunistic and corrupt.*

Yet, if the Chinese government had held such a one-dimensional Leninist view of business communities, it would have been a major mistake. Businessmen and businesswomen, if they are made to sign

---

* In 1973 and 1974, I lived in Phnom Penh, Cambodia, when it was shelled almost daily. When I asked how the Khmer Rouge obtained their supply of artillery shells, I was told this story by several knowledgeable officials.

agreements under duress, even agreements that are profitable to them, will carry in their hearts deep resentment toward Chinese officials who make them sign such agreements. This may well be true even if all the procedures are perfectly legal. Yukon Huang, a former World Bank economist who served in China for many years, has pointed out that under WTO rules, it is perfectly legitimate for a developing country like China to ask for technology transfer as a condition for investing in China. He said "under the WTO's agreements on intellectual property, developed countries are under 'the obligation' to provide incentives to their companies to transfer technology to less developed countries."[*]

Yet, even if what China was requesting was legal and legitimate, it could still be true that foreign business communities felt unfairly pressurized. If they had refused to sign agreements providing technology transfer, they would have been denied access to the larger Chinese market. To preserve access to this market, the businessmen felt that they had no choice but to agree to technology transfer. Some senior Chinese officials may indeed be surprised to hear these stories of unhappiness of Western business communities. Each time China organizes a high-level forum and invites the CEOs of major Western communities, they never fail to turn up. I have personally participated in some of these gatherings. In March 2019, a remarkably high-powered group of Western CEOs, as well as Western economists and journalists, gathered for the China Development Forum in Beijing. Well-known names like Ray Dalio, the head of one of America's largest hedge funds, Steve Schwarzman, CEO and chairman of Blackstone Group, Joseph Stiglitz, a Nobel laureate, and Martin Wolf, the *Financial Times* columnist, participated.

---

[*] Yukon Huang, "Did China Break the World Economic Order?," *New York Times*, May 17, 2019, https://www.nytimes.com/2019/05/17/opinion/trade-war-tech-china-united-states.html.

Fortunately, two former famous treasury secretaries of America, Bob Rubin and Larry Summers, were also invited. Both of them spoke candidly of the challenges American businessmen face in dealing with China.

Summers said that "substantial misunderstandings exist between the United States and China, that these misunderstandings are perhaps a consequence of policies being pursued, and that these misunderstandings carry with them very substantial risks." He added that "the United States has legitimate concerns about China's trade practices in a range of areas—from intellectual property to joint venture rules and their consequence for sharing information technology." However, he acknowledged that "the reality is that there is no credible calculation that suggests that U.S. GDP would be more than one percent higher even if China had acceded to every American economic request."

Even though some of the remarks Summers made in Beijing may have been uncomfortable for his Chinese hosts, he was sending a powerful signal to Beijing to emphasize that the continual willingness of global business VIPs to attend high-level fora in China should not be taken as a sign that all is well between China and the Western business communities. Form should not be confused with substance. The same CEOs who attend high-level gatherings in China may return to their companies to find disgruntled colleagues who remain unhappy about their business dealings with China. This is why it would be wise for China to make a high-level policy decision and launch a major effort to regain the trust and confidence of Western business communities, including the American business community.

China is a massive country. Despite the strong and effective rule of the Chinese Communist Party, it will not be easy for China to change immediately the habits and practices of over a hundred million officials who have been involved in one way or another with the management of foreign businesses in China. Many systems and processes, habits and cultures have been entrenched throughout the massive Chinese governance system for decades now. It would be completely unrealistic to believe that all these established processes and customs can be changed overnight.

To engineer a U-turn throughout the vast Chinese system, the Chinese need to first make a major philosophical decision, followed by some innovative practical steps. China needs to ask itself some tough questions: What led to a great country like China suffering a century of humiliation at the hands of smaller Western powers? Why did the Chinese economy, which was on par with the rest of the world from the year 1 to 1820, fall so far behind? Why couldn't the brilliant minds in the Chinese emperor's court discern that the world had changed dramatically?

The common cause of the massive blindness of the Chinese officials in the nineteenth century was a huge Chinese philosophical assumption that China was a great self-sufficient Middle Kingdom that did not need to engage the world. As the Chinese emperor Qianlong famously told Lord Macartney, China had everything it needed. It didn't need the rest of the world.

That painful century of humiliation finally led to China opening up. Deng made the decision on pragmatic grounds. And the opening up worked: China's economy soared. Yet, do the Chinese view this opening up as a temporary measure until China becomes strong again? Do they have a desire to return eventually to their Middle Kingdom mentality, trading with the world while remaining culturally detached from it?

When China built walls and cut off communication with the rest of the world, it fell behind. When China opened up to the world, it thrived. To guarantee its continued long-term success, China should completely abandon its two-thousand-year-old Middle Kingdom mentality and decide to become the most open society in terms of economic engagement with the rest of the world. Only such a major change of mind would enable the Chinese officials to lay out the red carpet for foreign businesses, including American businesses.

Several leading American politicians, including the former presidential candidate Marco Rubio, have initiated legislation to restrict both Chinese investments into America and transfer of American technology to China. Rubio has also made many inflammatory comments about China:

> For the last two decades, China fooled the world into believing it would embrace the rules-based international order and become a responsible stakeholder. [...] China now is trying to fool the world again by luring foreign governments to join its Belt and Road Initiative with extravagant promises of Chinese investment for their infrastructure projects.*

It would be perfectly natural for Chinese policymakers to react equally emotionally to such provocative comments. However, it would be unwise and go against so many Chinese strategic precepts, which advise calm responses to provocations. For example, Sun Tzu has provided this advice: "Disciplined and calm, to await the appearance of disorder and hubbub amongst the enemy:—this is the art of retaining self-possession." China could also heed the advice in Aesop's fable:

> The Wind and the Sun were disputing which was the stronger. Suddenly they saw a traveller coming down the road, and the Sun said: "I see a way to decide our dispute. Whichever of us can cause that traveller to take off his cloak shall be regarded as the stronger. You begin." So the Sun retired behind a cloud, and the Wind began to blow as hard as it could upon the traveller. But the harder he blew the more closely did the traveller wrap his cloak round him, till at last the Wind had to give up in despair. Then the Sun came out and shone

---

* Marco Rubio, "At Their Own Peril, Countries Embrace China," Breitbart, April 25, 2019, https://www.breitbart.com/national-security/2019/04/25/exclusive-sen-marco-rubio-at-their-own-peril-countries-embrace-china/.

in all his glory upon the traveller, who soon found it too hot to walk with his cloak on.

"Kindness effects more than severity."*

Clearly, the Chinese government will have to provide a comprehensive explanation to the Chinese people on why China will open its borders more to foreign businesses, including American businesses, when Chinese businesses were experiencing greater difficulties in foreign markets, especially America. The key point that the Chinese people need to realize is that it would serve China's long-term strategic interests for China to continue opening up its economy even while the Trump administration has been creating more difficulties for foreign businesses to either invest or export to America. Over time, this will mean more countries will be trading and investing more with China than with America. In many ways, this has already happened. Over a hundred countries trade more with China than with America. And the trend will continue. Although China is becoming less exposed to the world economically, a July 2019 McKinsey report highlights how the world's exposure to China is significantly increasing, "reflect[ing] China's increasing importance as a market, supplier, and provider of capital."†

As more countries trade more with China, the net result of this process will be to give China a major strategic advantage. Many officials in the Trump administration either openly or secretly believe the best way to slow down China's economic growth is to progressively decouple the Chinese and American economies. Yet, any American effort to decouple itself from China could well result in America decoupling itself from

---

* Aesop, "The Wind and the Sun," Aesop Fables, sixth century BCE, Bartleby.com, https://www.bartleby.com/17/1/60.html.

† Jonathan Woetzel et al., *China and the World: Inside the Dynamics of a Changing Relationship*, McKinsey Global Institute, July 2019, https://www.mckinsey.com/~/media /mckinsey/featured%20insights/china/china%20and%20the%20world%20inside%20the %20dynamics%20of%20a%20changing%20relationship/mgi-china-and-the-world-full -report-june-2019-vf.ashx.

the world. MIT president L. Rafael Reif said, "If all we do in response to China's ambition is to try to double-lock all our doors, I believe we will lock ourselves into mediocrity."* China should understand well the point he's making. China locked itself into mediocrity when it cut itself off from the world. China should therefore fully abandon its Middle Kingdom philosophical mind-set and instead engage even more with the world.

A change in the philosophical mind-set will have to be accompanied by practical steps to create a more favorable environment for foreign businesses in China. The Chinese government could issue directives to make this happen. However, even though China is a well-governed country, it would be a mistake to rely only on high-level directives. What really matters is what happens on the ground or, to quote a well-known American expression, "where the rubber meets the road." The key lies in the implementation.

On effective implementation of directives, China can still learn lessons from other countries on how to promote greater investment. Here, China could take a page from Singapore, which has the most successful business promotion agency in the world, the Singapore Economic Development Board (EDB). The success of EDB in attracting American investment is simply stunning. Even though Singapore is physically the smallest state in Southeast Asia, with only 5 million people out of the 650 million people in Southeast Asia, it has attracted more American investments than the rest of Southeast Asia combined. As of 2017, US foreign direct investment in Singapore was US$274.3 billion.† As Singapore's foreign minister Vivian Balakrishnan noted: "This represents about 80% of the total US foreign direct investment in ASEAN, which

---

* L. Rafael Reif, "China's Challenge Is America's Opportunity," *New York Times*, August 8, 2018, https://www.nytimes.com/2018/08/08/opinion/china-technology-trade-united -states.html.
† USTR, "Singapore," Office of the US Trade Representative, https://ustr.gov/countries -regions/southeast-asia-pacific/singapore.

totals around US$328 billion."* American companies have invested more in Singapore than they have in larger economies like Australia (US$169 billion),† Japan (US$129 billion),‡ India (US$45 billion),§ and South Korea (US$41 billion).¶

Singapore attracted American investments out of economic necessity. China has no such economic necessity. Its economy can grow well, even without American investments. Hence, in the case for China, it should attract American, and Western, investments out of strategic necessity. The strategic reason for doing so is to create a major stabilizer in China's relations with America and with the Western world. This is why China should, like Singapore, set up a one-stop investment agency, like the EDB, to attract and facilitate investments in China. China is a sprawling country. The tasks of managing foreign investments is left to individual provinces and cities. This creates regional disparities on how inward investments are managed. If inbound American investment is deemed to be a strategic necessity, it would be logical for China to create a superagency at the national level to ensure a level playing field for all foreign investments. Specific targets should be set for this superagency.

It would be wise for this superagency to try to get investments from as many states as possible in the United States. This would help to broaden the pro-China constituencies in America. Fortunately, even though Washington, DC, has become overwhelmed by anti-China sen-

---

* Vivian Balakrishnan, "Seeking Opportunities Amidst Disruption: A View from Singapore," edited transcript, Center for Strategic and International Studies, May 15, 2019, https://www.mfa.gov.sg/Newsroom/Press-Statements-Transcripts-and-Photos/2019/05/20190516_FMV-Washington—CSIS-Speech.

† USTR, "Australia," Office of the US Trade Representative, https://ustr.gov/countries-regions/southeast-asia-pacific/australia.

‡ USTR, "Japan," Office of the US Trade Representative, https://ustr.gov/countries-regions/japan-korea-apec/japan.

§ USTR, "India," Office of the US Trade Representative, https://ustr.gov/countries-regions/south-central-asia/india.

¶ USTR, "Korea," Office of the US Trade Representative, https://ustr.gov/countries-regions/japan-korea-apec/korea.

timent, many of the governors and legislative assemblies of individual states continue to seek out and attract Chinese investments in their states and want to enhance their ties with China. For example, Kentucky governor Matt Bevin said in May 2017: "There's a tremendous amount of capital in China that's looking for a place to be deployed, in a safe, reliable environment. The United States affords that opportunity. There is tremendous infrastructure need in this country. The two largest economies in the world and the most powerful are that of the United States and China. The idea that we would not work together seems inconceivable."[*]

Similarly, Washington state, the home of Boeing, understands well the importance of close ties with China. As a report by *The Diplomat* notes: "With China as its top export market, Washington state understands the long-term strategic impact of healthy trade relations with China on Washington's economy at the state, county, and city levels. Washington's exports to China supported 83,800 jobs in 2015, and the state has received $611 million in Chinese investment since 2000."[†]

One advantage that the Chinese have over their American counterparts is that they can look overall at the strategic big picture while making their policy decisions. If American businesses become enthusiastic again about trading with and investing in China, it would rebuild a valuable political buffer that could restrain a major downturn in US-China relations. However, the reengagement of the Western business communities will not just serve China's short-term national interests; it will also be serving its long-term national interests. Clearly, the force that has helped fuel China's rapid economic growth over the past few decades has been globalization. For most of the past few decades,

---

* Evelyn Cheng, "Forget the Tough Talk: Some US Leaders Are Courting Chinese Investment," CNBC, May 5, 2017, https://www.cnbc.com/2017/05/05/tough-talk-is-in-the-air-but-some-in-us-are-courting-chinese-money.html.
† Mercy A. Kuo, "After US-China Economic Dialogue Underwhelms, Washington State Steps Up," The Diplomat, July 25, 2017, https://thediplomat.com/2017/07/after-us-china-economic-dialogue-underwhelms-washington-state-steps-up/.

America has been the champion of globalization. This was supported by a zeitgeist in America that said that the more open the world is, the better off America would be.

Now the mood in America has turned sour. No American politician can stand up and defend globalization. It would be political suicide. Since the world needs a new champion of globalization, China can step in and fill the void, and in many ways, China has begun doing so. The speech that President Xi gave at Davos in January 2017 was a sweeping intellectual defense of the virtues of globalization. Words matter. Deeds speak more eloquently. If China emerged as the most business-friendly great economic power, it would provide a huge boost to globalization. In so doing, China would be strengthening the very force that has propelled China's spectacular economic rise.

If China emerges as the new champion of globalization, will this further alienate the American body politic away from globalization, or will it serve as a wake-up call and encourage America to champion globalization again? No one can yet be sure. However, we can predict the outcomes for countries who participate in globalization and for those who walk away from it. China's leaders now know well that the previous Chinese mind-set of building walls against the world led to China eventually collapsing. Hence, China will no longer do that. Instead, it is now Trump who wants to build a wall around America, literally and metaphorically. If he succeeds, America will eventually fall behind, and China will move ahead.

CHAPTER 3

AMERICA'S BIGGEST STRATEGIC MISTAKE

A MERICA MAY YET WIN ITS GEOPOLITICAL CONTEST WITH China, but there is no question that China has won the first round. By plunging into a major geopolitical contest, possibly the biggest ever in human history, without first working out a comprehensive long-term strategy, the Trump administration has only succeeded in diminishing America's standing in the world while, at the same time, creating space for China's influence to grow in the world.

Let there be no doubt that America lacks a comprehensive strategy on China. Two leading American strategic thinkers confirm this. Henry Kissinger, the German-born Republican former national security adviser who was behind the US outreach to China in the 1970s, and Fareed Zakaria, the Indian American CNN anchor and commentator, don't always agree about everything. Yet, they concur that, when it comes to China, America has no workable strategy. Fareed Zakaria put it like this:

The US had a comprehensive bipartisan strategy towards China from the opening in 1972 until recently—to integrate China into the world, politically, economically and culturally. But in recent years, that strategy produced complications and complexities—helped usher in a new, more powerful China that did not conform to Western expectations. In the wake of this transformation, the US has been frozen. It has not been able to conceive of a new comprehensive strategy toward the Middle Kingdom.

The contrast with how America launched its epic struggle against the Soviet Union could not be more striking. America's leading strategic thinker of that time, George Kennan, provided his fellow Americans with sound advice on how the United States should deal with serious geopolitical competition in his famous Mr. X essay in *Foreign Affairs*. Currently, the Trump administration is ignoring many elements of this advice in dueling with China.

Future American historians will undoubtedly be puzzled that so many Americans, including leading Democrats, cheered on Donald Trump when he began his trade and technology war against China. Senator Chuck Schumer, a leading Democratic senator, encouraged Trump to "hang tough on China," lamenting that "America has lost trillions of dollars and millions of jobs because China has not played fair."[*] Nancy Pelosi, Speaker of the House of Representatives, has spoken similarly, insisting, in March 2018, that "the United States must take strong, smart and strategic action against China's brazenly unfair trade policies."[†]

---

[*] Bob Fredericks, "Schumer: We Have to Be Tough on China," *New York Post*, August 1, 2019, https://nypost.com/2019/08/01/chuck-schumer-backs-trump-on-new-china-tariffs/.

[†] Nancy Pelosi, "Pelosi Statement on Trump Administration's New Tariffs on China," News, Congresswoman Nancy Pelosi, California's 12th District, May 22, 2018, https://pelosi.house.gov/news/press-releases/pelosi-statement-on-trump-administration.

This Democratic support is puzzling because many of Trump's actions, by violating many of the key precepts of Kennan's strategic advice, have actually served China's interests. There is no doubt that China's leaders have been aggravated by Trump's trade war and assault on Huawei. Yet, the Chinese leaders must also be aware that Trump has provided China many long-term dividends. Many of these dividends come from Trump and his advisers not thinking long term, like Kennan did.

America would present a formidable challenge to China if it were a united, strong, and self-confident country. Kennan emphasized this dimension in his Mr. X essay, when he argued that American power depended on its ability to "create among the peoples of the world generally the impression of a country which knows what it wants, which is coping successfully with the problems of its internal life and with the responsibilities of a world power, and what has a spiritual vitality capable of holding its own among the major ideological currents of the time."

Trump has done the opposite. He has divided and polarized America. Yet it would be unfair to blame him alone. As this book will document, America is facing severe structural challenges in the political, economic, and cultural dimensions. To outsiders, it appears that America today lacks the "spiritual vitality" Kennan was speaking about. This is a result of deep-seated economic and social problems predating Trump, which will be examined more closely in the chapter entitled "The Assumption of Virtue."

However, Trump's administration must take sole blame for following a unilateral, rather than a multilateral, approach to deal with China. He provided China a major geopolitical gift by walking away from the Trans-Pacific Partnership (TPP), a brilliant move by the Obama administration to anchor America's presence in East and Southeast Asia, which would have yielded rich, long-term dividends for the American economy. Trump has also alienated key friends and allies, including Canada, Mexico, the EU, Japan, India, and Vietnam, with his unthinking shoot-from-the-hip tweets.

At the beginning of the Cold War with the Soviet Union, America took the lead in building the world's multilateral architecture, which included the Bretton Woods system, the Marshall Plan, and NATO. Now it is China, not America, that is taking the lead in building a new multilateral architecture, including the Asian Infrastructure Investment Bank (AIIB) and the Belt and Road Initiative (BRI). America opposed both these initiatives. This didn't stop many of its key friends and allies from joining them. The UK, Germany, India, and Vietnam joined as founding members of AIIB, which is proving itself to be a better-governed institution than the IMF and the World Bank. Its standard of corporate governance is higher and more transparent.

While China projects an image of being a stable and predictable member of the global multilateral order, America, under Trump, is increasingly perceived as a chaotic and unpredictable actor. Donald Trump once famously said that "trade wars are good, and easy to win."[*] Instead, Trump's track record in this area shows that trade wars are in fact difficult to win. In the magazine *Foreign Affairs* (November/December 2019), Weijian Shan observed: "The numbers suggest that Washington is not winning this trade war. Although China's economic growth has slowed, the tariffs have hit U.S. consumers harder than their Chinese counterparts. With fears of a recession around the corner, Trump must reckon with the fact that his current approach is imperiling the U.S. economy, posing a threat to the international trading system, and failing to reduce the trade deficit that he loathes."[†]

Trump has, of course, made things worse by launching a series of chaotic and uncoordinated measures against China beginning in 2018. The first anti-China measures were the 25 percent tariffs Trump imposed on China on July 6, 2018, on a "new $50 billion list [which]

---

[*] Thomas Franck, "Trump Doubles Down: 'Trade Wars Are Good, and Easy to Win,'" CNBC, March 2, 2018, https://www.cnbc.com/2018/03/02/trump-trade-wars-are-good-and-easy-to-win.html.

[†] Weijian Shan, "The Unwinnable Trade War," *Foreign Affairs*, November/December 2019.

target[ed] even more intermediate inputs—95 percent of the products hit [were] intermediate inputs or capital equipment used largely by American-based companies dependent on imports from China."* Clearly, a tax on intermediate inputs would only undermine the competitiveness of American companies. This was unwise, but on July 6, 2018, the United States went ahead.

Did anyone in the Trump administration work out a thoughtful and well-considered strategy before launching the first round of these tariffs (which were followed by many more rounds)? The honest answer is no. An influential American friend of mine told me privately that when President Trump decided to impose tariffs on several countries, the then director of the National Economic Council, Gary Cohn, patiently tried to put across to President Trump the basics of economic theory to explain why they were not a good policy tool. All of Cohn's efforts to persuade Trump failed. Cohn finally asked why he insisted on tariffs. Trump replied: "I just like tariffs." Trump proved his point by imposing or threatening to impose tariffs on friends and foes, including the EU, Japan, Canada, Mexico, and China.

One important point needs to be stressed here. It was Americans, especially distinguished American economists, who taught the world that free trade was good and that tariffs, especially arbitrary tariffs, are bad. American economists explained that the very trade deficits that are the subject of Trump's complaints are *not* the result of unfair trading practices. They are the result of domestic macroeconomic decisions made by America. Ronald Reagan was no left-wing nut. He was a traditional American conservative. His leading economic adviser was the late Harvard professor Marty Feldstein, who explained clearly how America's trade deficit came about. He said: "foreign import barriers and exports subsidies are not the reason for the US trade deficit . . . the real reason is

---

* Chad P. Bown and Melissa Kolb, "Trump's Trade War Timeline: An Up-to-Date Guide," PIIE, September 20, 2019, https://www.piie.com/system/files/documents/trump-trade-war-timeline.pdf.

that Americans are spending more than they produce . . . blaming others won't alter that fact."* Trump has shocked the world in many ways. Even so, the world is genuinely shocked that America has elected a president who could not pass an Economics 101 undergraduate examination on international trade.

At the same time, Donald Trump may have expected China to capitulate as soon as tariffs were imposed. Anyone with a basic understanding of China and its recent history would have known that this would never have happened. Still, Chinese negotiators would have been prepared to make more generous concessions in a mutually beneficial deal, and indeed, press reports have suggested that China had agreed during trade negotiations to buy more American products by the billions of dollars. Hence, if the goal of the Trump administration had been to reduce the trade deficit with China, China would have cooperated. However, as Robert Zoellick, a US trade representative and deputy secretary of state under President George W. Bush, has pointed out, the goals of the Trump administration have never been clear.

> The US administration's current position reflects an internal division. One faction wants to decouple the American economy from China; this group favors tariffs, barriers to cross-border investment and uncertainties that would compel companies to break supply chains. The other faction seeks to change China's practices in order to boost US exports, protect intellectual property and technology, and counter discrimination against overseas investors; these actions would expand American economic ties with China. To reconcile these conflicting aims, the compromise has been to make extraordinary demands— and rely on Mr. Trump's instincts to decide whether to do a deal. . . .

* Martin Feldstein, "Inconvenient Truths about the US Trade Deficit," Project Syndicate, April 25, 2017, https://www.project-syndicate.org/commentary/america-trade-deficit-inconvenient-truth-by-martin-feldstein-2017-04.

The principal problem in the negotiation now is what America will do in return if China takes steps to open markets, buy goods, and secure US interests. For now, Washington has insisted on retaining the tariffs it imposed until Beijing delivers on its promises. US negotiators also want the right to re-impose tariffs whenever America chooses—and to prohibit Chinese retaliation.[*]

Kevin Rudd, the former prime minister of Australia, observed that, as prime minister, he would never have accepted a lopsided agreement like the one that America is trying to push through with China, even though Australia is one of America's staunchest allies.[†] As Zoellick said, "When China's politburo reviewed the prospective deal, it choked on the lack of mutual obligations. The two sides also failed to agree on Beijing's shopping list for buying US goods. To China, the terms looked unequal, raising old ghosts from 19th-century diplomacy about foreigners treating them with a lack of dignity and respect."[‡]

On the Friday of August 23, 2019, Trump exploded in anger and launched his fiercest tweets against China when the latter announced that it would proceed with its counterretaliatory measures. Without thinking through the consequences, Trump pronounced that "our great American companies are hereby ordered to immediately start looking for an alternative to China, including bringing your companies HOME and making your products in the USA." In response, Myron Brilliant, executive vice president of the US Chamber of Commerce, made the obvious point that "Trump may be frustrated with China,

---

[*] Robert Zoellick, "Donald Trump's Impulsive Approach to China Makes US Vulnerable," *Financial Times* (London), June 26, 2019, https://www.ft.com/content/e88078e8-966d-11e9-98b9-e38c177b152f.

[†] CGTN, "Kevin Rudd: If the U.S. Offered Australia What It Offered China, I Would Not Accept It Either," China Global Television Network, May 21, 2019, https://news.cgtn.com/news/3d3d774e3349444f34457a6333566d54/index.html.

[‡] Zoellick, "Donald Trump's Impulsive Approach to China Makes US Vulnerable."

but the answer isn't for US companies to ignore a market with 1.4 billion consumers."*

The chaos generated by Trump and his tweets is now par for the course. What is not par for the course is the failure of America's much vaunted system of checks and balances to save America from a mercurial and chaotic ruler. Neither the US Congress nor the fourth estate, neither the Supreme Court nor the executive branch can do anything to restrain Donald Trump. Consequently, all around the world, trust in America's institutions of governance has begun to erode.

In this regard, even though the Chinese leaders must be hugely exasperated with Donald Trump, they could, with their long view of history, also see Trump as a long-term asset, as he has single-handedly done more to reduce America's prestige and influence in the world than any other American leader has. America was generally perceived to be a reliable partner by its closest allies. This sense of trust in America has diminished considerably. The worst-case scenario for China would have been a reenactment of the containment policy that America has successfully used against the Soviet Union. Under Trump, the chances of this happening are practically zero. Even after he leaves office, the next president will not be able to restore the trust in America that Trump has eroded.

It would be truly unwise for any American to underestimate the erosion of trust in America. Many of America's best friends have warned America to take it seriously. The famed *Financial Times* commentator Martin Wolf, who once wrote that he had inherited his father's "fiercely pro-American" attitude,[†] has declared that "under Trump, America has

---

* Washington Post, "President Trump Calls on American Companies to Cut Ties with China, Intensifying Trade War," PennLive Patriot News, August 23, 2019, https://www .pennlive.com/business/2019/08/president-trump-calls-on-american-companies-to -cut-ties-with-china-intensifying-trade-war.html.

† Martin Wolf, "How We Lost America to Greed and Envy," *Financial Times* (London), July 17, 2018, https://www.ft.com/content/3aea8668-88e2-11e8-bf9e-8771d5404543.

become a rogue superpower."* Prior to the August 2019 G7 Summit in Biarritz, Edward Luce, another influential *Financial Times* columnist, similarly quipped that "if [Trump] can make it through a French weekend without accelerating the demise of the west—offering to buy a chunk of Europe, for example—that would be a victory of sorts."†

No society is invulnerable. Every society has its own weaknesses. This is why the erosion of global trust in America is so dangerous. It could in turn expose the area of America's maximum vulnerability, indeed, its Achilles' heel: the dollar. The US dollar is currently well protected by a complex global financial system, which in turn generates a sense of invulnerability. Yet, a core vulnerability remains. More than most countries, America can afford to live beyond its means (although financial globalization has enabled some countries with strong domestic institutions and good macroeconomic fundamentals, like Australia and Canada, to also sustain prolonged periods of current account and fiscal deficits). Domestically, the US government spends more than it collects in income. This creates a fiscal deficit. Internationally, America imports more goods than it exports. This creates a trade deficit. How does America pay for these twin deficits? It borrows money. This is not abnormal. Many countries, not unlike many domestic households, borrow money. At some point, when they can no longer borrow money, they face a crunch. This is what happened to Greece. It had to cut its expenditures drastically so that it could continue to receive funds from overseas. In the past few decades, many countries have had to endure extreme pain when their international borrowings became too much: Argentina in 2001, Mexico in 1982, Russia in 1998, Thailand in 1997,

---

* Martin Wolf, "The US-China Conflict Challenges the World," *Financial Times* (London), May 21, 2019, https://www.ft.com/content/870c895c-7b11-11e9-81d2 -f785092ab560.

† Edward Luce, "The Next Stop on Donald Trump's End-of-Diplomacy Tour," *Financial Times* (London), August 2, 2019, https://www.ft.com/content/66cc66b6-c45f -11e9-a8e9-296ca66511c9.

Iceland in 2008, Greece in 2010. As a result, their populations suffered a severe drop in standards of living.

However, unlike these other countries, America can fund its twin deficits and pay for its excess expenditures by printing Treasury bills. The US Treasury only has to pay for the cost of paper. In return for handing out pieces of paper, the rest of the world sends real money (hard-earned cash) to buy the US Treasury bills. For example, Chinese workers have to work hard to produce low-cost goods to export to the rest of the world. These exports receive hard-earned dollars, which the Chinese government converts to yuan to pay to the workers. What does the Chinese government do with these hard-earned dollars? It uses many of these to buy US Treasury bills. The US Treasury then uses these dollars from China to pay for excess government expenditures. For the record, the largest purchasers of US Treasuries are China ($1.113 trillion), Japan ($1.064 trillion), Brazil ($306.7 billion), the United Kingdom ($300.8 billion), and Ireland ($269.7 billion).* As a result of this, when the US government cannot pay for the twin deficits, it can simply print money (i.e., paper) to pay for these excess expenditures. And why does the rest of the world buy these pieces of paper (US dollars)? One key reason is that most of world trade is carried out in US dollars. Hence, when China buys Argentinian beef, it pays Argentina with US dollars. When Argentina buys Chinese cell phones, it pays with US dollars. This makes the US dollar indispensable for the global economy. Hence, it functions as the global reserve currency.

Many American economists are aware of the enormous benefits that American people get from the US dollar serving as the global reserve currency. In June 2019, Ruchir Sharma wrote: "Reserve currency status had long been a perk of imperial might—and an economic elixir. By generating a steady flow of customers who want to hold the currency, often in the form of government bonds, it allows the privileged

---

* US Department of Treasury, "Major Foreign Holders of Treasury Securities" (chart), October 16, 2019, https://ticdata.treasury.gov/Publish/mfh.txt.

country to borrow cheaply abroad and fund a lifestyle well beyond its means." Sharma adds: "And for nearly a century now this privilege has helped to keep US interest rates low, making it possible for Americans to buy cars and homes and, in recent decades, run large government deficits that they could not otherwise afford." There are two key phrases in the quotes above. America can afford to "fund a lifestyle well beyond its means" and "run large government deficits that they could not otherwise afford."

Sharma wrote his article in response to suggestions by Donald Trump and Elizabeth Warren that America should consider devaluing its currency to become more competitive. He warned that this would be very dangerous because "America is not an emerging country. It's an unrivalled financial superpower, a position built in large part on hard-won trust in the dollar, which is an enduring source of American power and prosperity."

The key word that Sharma has used is *trust*. The world has been happy to use the US dollar as the global reserve currency because they trusted the US government to make the right decisions on the US dollar that would take into consideration the economic interests not only of the 330 million American people but also of the remaining 7.2 billion people outside America who also rely on the US dollar to fund their international transactions. This trust is a key pillar of the resilience of the US dollar as a global reserve currency.

In recent decades, this trust has begun to erode because America has occasionally used the privilege of having the global reserve currency as a weapon against other countries. Here are two examples of how the US dollar has been weaponized; both involve American efforts to isolate Iran. In 2012, a British bank, Standard Chartered, was fined $340 million because it had used the US dollar to finance a trade transaction with Iran. This fine clearly represented an extraterritorial application of American domestic laws. As a British bank, Standard Chartered had broken no British laws. Neither had it violated any sanctions imposed by the UN Security Council. Yet, the dominance of the US dollar in international financial transactions enabled America to punish a British firm for breaking American laws—a clear weaponization of the US dollar.*

In recent years, the US government has imposed even heftier fines on non-American banks for working with countries like Iran, Cuba, and Sudan. For example, BNP Paribas SA was fined US$8.9 billion in 2015. As a result, many countries that had trusted the US dollar now find it to be a double-edged sword, cutting the fingers of whoever holds it. This creates an obvious incentive to reduce dependence on the US dollar, which could eventually precipitate a fall in global demand for US dollars, crippling the United States' ability to finance its twin deficits. Donald Trump has recently created an additional incentive for moving away from the US dollar through his calls to devalue the dollar. As the former French president Valéry Giscard d'Estaing said, this is an "exorbitant privilege" that Americans enjoy. Americans should be grateful that the rest of the world is funding this exorbitant privilege. Trump is unappreciative. He is punishing the countries that are conferring this privilege to America. The rest of the world is genuinely bewildered, wondering why America is taking steps that could in the long run jeopardize this privilege.

The most dangerous thing that Donald Trump has done is to create a strong incentive for other countries to stop relying on the US dollar as the dominant global reserve currency. In particular, by pulling out of the Joint Comprehensive Plan of Action (JCPOA), which six countries, namely America, the UK, France, Germany, Russia, China, and Iran, had agreed to, he has forced the other participating countries to find an alternative way of trading with Iran. Here it is important to mention a critical point of international law. Many Americans support

---

* I wrote about this topic in "What Happens When China Becomes No. 1?," *Straits Times* (Singapore), April 24, 2015, https://www.straitstimes.com/opinion/what-happens -when-china-becomes-no-1.

Trump's struggle against Iran because it is seen as a struggle between good (America) and evil (Iran). However, in walking away from the JCPOA, it is America that is violating international law.

The JCPOA was agreed on by Iran and the five permanent members of the UN plus Germany on July 14, 2015, and endorsed by UN Security Council Resolution 2231, adopted on July 20, 2015.[*] When an agreement is endorsed by the UN Security Council, it becomes a binding agreement that all states have to comply with. Indeed, as a permanent member of the UN Security Council, America is under an even greater obligation to abide by its rules as it has always insisted that all countries must abide by the binding decisions of the UN Security Council.

The Trump administration didn't just walk away from the JCPOA. It also announced that it would impose sanctions on any country that continued to trade with Iran on the basis of these agreements. The "legal" route that the Trump administration took to punish countries for trading with Iran was by sanctioning their use of the US dollar in these cross-border payments.

This created a legal dilemma for the other five signatories of the Iran agreement. Under international law, their companies were allowed to trade with Iran. However, if the companies trading with Iran used the US dollar to do so, these companies would have had to pay massive fines in American courts. To solve this legal dilemma, France, Germany, and the UK decided to set up the Instrument in Support of Trade Exchanges (INSTEX), "a new channel for non-dollar trade with Iran to avert U.S. sanctions."[†] In reality, INSTEX would not have any major effect on trade with Iran: most major global companies do more

---

* ACA, "The Joint Comprehensive Plan of Action (JCPOA) at a Glance," Fact Sheets & Briefs, May 2018, Arms Control Association, https://www.armscontrol.org/factsheets /JCPOA-at-a-glance.
† John Irish and Riham Alkousaa, "Skirting U.S. Sanctions, Europeans Open New Trade Channel to Iran," Reuters, January 31, 2019, https://www.reuters.com/article /us-iran-usa-sanctions-eu/european-powers-launch-mechanism-for-trade-with-iran -idUSKCN1PP0K3.

trade with America than with Iran and would not dare to go against the Trump administration, which could be harsh and punitive toward any companies dealing with Iran.

However, in symbolic terms, INSTEX represents a huge shift in the international system. For the first time, three major allies of America (France, Germany, and the UK) have created an alternative to the US dollar-based payment system. It could one day serve as a model for two future potential adversaries of America (China and Russia) to set up an alternative global channel of payments that would bypass and undercut the global role of the US dollar. Equally importantly, France, Germany, and the UK have announced that they "are also working to open INSTEX to economic operators from third countries." Representatives of China and Russia were also present at this meeting.* In short, a small wedge has been put into one of America's global strategic assets, the global reserve currency status of the US dollar.

More ominously for America, some influential voices are now saying that the world should stop using the US dollar as the global reserve currency. Mark Carney, governor of the Bank of England, in a speech at the annual Jackson Hole gathering of central bankers in the United States in August 2019, cast a critical eye on the predominance of the US dollar in the international monetary system. He noted that "the dollar represents the currency of choice for at least half of international trade invoices (around five times greater than the US's share in world goods imports, and three times its share in world exports) and two-thirds of both global securities issuance and official foreign-exchange reserves." Further, Carney asserted that the world's

---

* Helga Maria Schmid, chair, "Statement Following the Meeting of the Joint Commission of the Joint Comprehensive Plan of Action," Vienna, Austria, June 28, 2019, https://eeas .europa.eu/headquarters/headquarters-homepage/64796/chairs-statement-following -28-june-2019-meeting-joint-commission-joint-comprehensive-plan_en.

reliance on the dollar "won't hold"* and that it is imperative that an international monetary system is built that is "worthy of the diverse, multipolar global economy that is emerging."†

Former IMF chief economist Maurice Obstfeld also observed that other countries used to be "less concern[ed]" about America's control of the global monetary system "when the US was viewed as a responsible leader of the world economy." However, that status quo is now changing, as the actions of American leaders become far less predictable.‡

Both Carney and Obstfeld are expressing a point of view that is growing in popularity around the world. This sentiment is perfectly reasonable. Countries all around the world see no reason why their trade with other countries (besides America) and their economic growth should be imperiled by unilateral American policies premised on the use of the dollar as a weapon. Here too America could undermine its own long-term interests by weaponizing the US dollar. The economic historian Barry Eichengreen recently said as much when he warned that "the more the Trump administration uses the dollar as a weapon, the stronger the incentive for other governments to invest in alternatives, and the faster this movement will be."§ Perhaps nothing will come from

---

* Carney reasoned that the ubiquity of the US dollar means that even countries that have few direct trade links with the United States are implicated by movements in that currency. They face, therefore, no option but to self-insure by hoarding dollars to preempt capital flight, resulting in excess savings and lower global growth.

†Mark Carney, governor of the Bank of England, "The Growing Challenges for Monetary Policy in the Current International Monetary and Financial System," speech given at the Jackson Hole Economic Symposium, Wyoming, August 23, 2019, https://www .kansascityfed.org/~/media/files/publicat/sympos/2019/governor%20carney%20speech %20jackson%20hole.pdf?la=en.

‡ Brendan Greeley, "Central Bankers Rethink Everything at Jackson Hole, *Financial Times* (London), August 25, 2019, https://www.ft.com/content/360028ba-c702-11e9-af46 -b09e8bfe60c0.

§ Barry Eichengreen, "How Europe Can Trade with Iran and Avoid US Sanctions," Project Syndicate, March 12, 2019, https://www.project-syndicate.org/commentary/europe -instex-trade-with-iran-avoid-trump-sanctions-by-barry-eichengreen-2019-03?barrier =accesspaylog.

this small wedge created by INSTEX. The US dollar could continue to reign supreme over the coming decades. However, it doesn't take a strategic genius to figure out that it is not in America's long-term interest to jeopardize one of its largest global strategic assets (the US dollar) by using it to extract small gains from one relatively small country, Iran. The strategic competition with China is going to be a long-term game, not a short-term one. By creating a dent in global trust in the US dollar, America is putting a pebble in its own running shoe, just as the race with China is about to become more competitive. This is what happens when America fails to develop a comprehensive global strategy to deal with the return of China. As Fareed Zakaria observes, "INSTEX is a warning sign, the canary in the coal mine. The United States' closest allies are working hard to chip away at a crucial underpinning of U.S. global power."*

If the acceptance of the US dollar as a global reserve currency allows the American people to live beyond their means, it would be wise for American policymakers to consider the long-term implications of this dependency. Here, a wise policymaker would have to balance two equally important but conflicting truths. First, in the short term, there is no threat to the US dollar serving as the global reserve currency. Second, in the medium to long term, the US dollar will inevitably lose its status as the dominant global reserve currency. Given the equal validity of these conflicting truths, what should a wise American policymaker do? Create incentives for countries to move away from the US dollar as the global reserve currency to accelerate the end of this role? Or to create incentives for countries to use the US dollar as long as possible, as it enables Americans to live beyond their means?

The answer is obviously the latter. This makes it surprising that all recent American administrations have been piling on incentives for the

---

* Fareed Zakaria, "America Squanders Its Power," *Washington Post*, June 13, 2019, https://fareedzakaria.com/columns/tag/dollar.

rest of the world to walk away from the US dollar so that they would not be imperiled by unilateral American sanctions. In the near future, there is no danger that the Chinese renminbi (RMB) can replace the US dollar. As Eswar Prasad said:

> Although China's rapidly growing economy and its dynamism are enormous advantages that will help promote the international use of its currency, its low level of financial market development is a major constraint on the likelihood of the renminbi attaining reserve currency status. Moreover, in the absence of an open capital account and convertibility of the currency, it is unlikely that the renminbi will become a prominent reserve currency, let alone challenge the dollar's status as the leading one. A huge gulf still exists between China and the U.S. in the availability of safe and liquid assets, such as government bonds. The depth, breadth, and liquidity of U.S. financial markets will serve as a potent buffer against threats to the dollar's preeminent status. I anticipate that the renminbi will become a competitive reserve currency within the next decade, eroding but not displacing the dollar's dominance.[*]

However, even though the RMB will certainly not replace the US dollar as a global reserve currency in the near future, this does not mean that China cannot explore other means of reducing global dependence on the US dollar. It's hard to believe that if a majority of the world's population begins to lose trust in the US dollar, no other alternative could be found.

With modern technology, it may be possible to create new alternatives that would not have been viable before. One admittedly speculative example will illustrate this point. The primary role that the US dollar

---

[*] Eswar S. Prasad, *The Dollar Trap: How the U.S. Dollar Tightened Its Grip on Global Finance* (Princeton, NJ: Princeton University Press, 2014), 261.

plays in, say, the trade between China and Argentina is to provide a measure of the relative value of Argentinian beef against the relative value of Chinese cell phones. If the main purpose of the US dollar is to measure the relative value of these two commodities, there is no reason why an alternative unit of measuring relative value could not be created.

This is where technology can help, in particular, blockchain technology. Blockchain technology has been used to create alternative cryptocurrencies like Bitcoin, Litecoin, Ethereum, and Monero. Facebook also announced in June 2019 the launch of its own cryptocurrency, Libra. While I am no blockchain expert, the sharp rise in popularity of cryptocurrencies and the investment of large firms like Facebook in developing blockchain-based currencies suggests that it may eventually provide a sound, practical, and invulnerable way of measuring relative values. So far no countries have used alternative blockchain technology currencies to trade with one another because, ultimately, they don't trust these currencies.

This is where China can step in. It can set up an alternative unit of measuring relative value, a sort of alternative currency, based on blockchain technology. A sufficient number of countries would trust this alternative vehicle when and as they trust China to be an impartial arbiter in international issues. Many Americans would doubt this statement. However, there is empirical evidence to back this up. When China launched the BRI, America opposed it. In theory, most countries should have backed away from joining the BRI. In practice, most countries joined. As of April 2019, 125 countries had signed agreements with China on the BRI.* This provides a clear indication that most countries would also trust a new blockchain technology currency that is ultimately backed by China.

When I first started writing the paragraphs on cryptocurrencies in July 2019, I had no information on what if anything China was go-

---

* "China Signs 197 B&R Cooperation Documents with 137 Countries, 30 Int'l Organizations," November 15, 2019, *Xinhua*, www.xinhuanet.com/english/2019-11/15/c_138558369.htm.

ing to do in this sensitive area. If I could have an intuition that China could do more with blockchain technology, it would not be surprising for Chinese officials to reach the same conclusion. As it happened, on August 11, 2019, at an event held by the China Finance 40 Forum—an independent think tank specializing in policy research on economics and finance—in Yichun, Heilongjiang, deputy director of the People's Bank of China (PBOC)'s payments department, Mu Changchun, said that the PBOC is "close" to issuing its own cryptocurrency.* Mu conveyed the PBOC's intention that the currency, like other digital currencies, would replace cash in circulation but, unlike decentralized blockchain-based currencies, afford Beijing greater control over its financial system. As such, the PBOC will retain exclusive control of the ledger.† Even more significantly, on October 24, 2019, President Xi Jinping announced that the development of blockchain technology would now become a high priority of the Chinese government. During a meeting with top Communist Party leaders, President Xi said: "The application of blockchain technology has been extended to sectors including digital finance, Internet of Things, smart manufacturing, supply chain management and digital asset trading, and the world's major countries are stepping up efforts in planning blockchain technology development."‡ That same month, China passed a cryptography law aimed at "facilitating the development of the cryptography business and ensuring the security of cyberspace and information." Reuters reported that the law was passed as China "gears up to launch its own digital currency" and that "the law states that the state encourages and supports the research

---

* "China Says Its Own Cryptocurrency Is 'Close' to Release," *Straits Times* (Singapore), August 13, 2019, https://www.straitstimes.com/business/banking/china-says-its-own-cryptocurrency-is-close-to-release-0.

| Bloomberg News, "China Preparing to Launch Its Own 'Cryptocurrency,'" Al Jazeera, August 12, 2019, https://www.aljazeera.com/ajimpact/china-preparing-launch-cryptocurrency-190812093909567.html.

‡ Xinhua, "Xi Stresses Development, Application of Blockchain Technology," October 25, 2019, Xinhuanet, http://www.xinhuanet.com/english/2019-10/25/c_138503254.htm.

and application of science and technology in cryptography and ensures confidentiality."* Countries may not necessarily keep their long-term savings and foreign currency reserves in this new China-backed digital currency; however, they would trust it for the purpose of trading goods and services. If China succeeds in creating an alternative blockchain technology currency, a country like India, a friend of America, could use this blockchain technology currency if it wishes to import oil from Iran and not worry about sanctions from America. In short, the weaponizing of the US dollar has created a powerful global incentive to create an alternative currency for global trading purposes.

Many American policymakers would not be alarmed by this development as the total size of global trade financed by US dollars is dwarfed by the size of global financial transactions based on US dollars. This is true. Nonetheless, it would be wise for Americans to get alarmed if China attempts to create such a new blockchain currency. Most Americans are familiar with Jenga, a block-stacking game. Sometimes all it takes to bring down a complex construction is to remove one block.

The role of the US dollar in financing global trade may well be the critical block that is sustaining the global reliance on the US dollar globally. Once this block is gone, the complex international system based on the US dollar could come tumbling down, rapidly or slowly. Significantly, three months after I had written these words in mid-2019, a newspaper column was published by Niall Ferguson, Henry Kissinger's biographer. Ferguson observed that the "digital payment systems established by Alibaba (Alipay) and Tencent (WeChat Pay) have grown explosively. One emerging market at a time, China is building a global payments infrastructure. Right now, the various systems are distinct national versions of the Chinese original. But there is no

---

* Ben Blanchard, "China Passes Cryptography Law as Gears Up for Digital Currency," Reuters, October 26, 2019, https://www.reuters.com/article/us-china-lawmaking /china-passes-cryptography-law-as-gears-up-for-digital-currency-idUSKBN1X600Z.

technical reason why the systems could not be linked internationally. Indeed, Alipay is already being used for cross-border remittances. If America is stupid, it will let this process continue until the day comes when the Chinese connect their digital platforms into one global system. That will be D-Day: the day the dollar dies as the world's No. 1 currency and the day America loses its financial sanctions super-power."* By saying this, Ferguson has also clearly identified that the global acceptance of the US dollar as a reserve currency is indeed the Achilles' heel of America.

When the dollar is no longer the dominant global reserve currency, the biggest victims would be American financial institutions, as a lot of their revenues and profits come from the global acceptance of the US dollar. Frankly, no living person can predict the consequences to the global financial system if the US dollar is no longer used to finance global trade transactions. The system is far too complex and interconnected.

As I have explained in this chapter, the American people receive enormous financial benefits from the US dollar serving as the global reserve currency, including the "exorbitant privilege" of sustaining long-term fiscal and current account deficits. Trump is dead wrong when he said on July 2, 2019, that China has had a "big advantage" over America in trade for many years.[†] Trump implied that the Chinese people have been fleecing the American people by enjoying massive trade surpluses. In reality, the American people have been fleecing the Chinese people because they have been paying for Chinese products with money printed on paper. Realistically, Americans should expect a reduction in their standard of living if they can no longer print money to pay for Chinese products. Secondly, well over 90 percent of global financial transactions

---

* Niall Ferguson, "America's Power Is on a Financial Knife Edge," September 15, 2019, Niall Ferguson, http://www.niallferguson.com/journalism/finance-economics/americas-power-is-on-a-financial-knife-edge.
† "Any Deal with China Must Favour US: Trump," *Straits Times* (Singapore), July 3, 2019, A10.

take place in US dollars. Trillions are traded daily. A large part of the fees for these transactions go to American banks, which is why even though America enjoys a trade deficit in goods, it enjoys a trade surplus in services.

No sensible strategist would risk these enormous benefits for the paltry benefits of punishing one relatively small country, like Iran. Yet, this is exactly what America has been doing. It should be abundantly clear that the cavalier use of the US dollar as a weapon provides a perfect illustration of the danger of America not having a comprehensive long-term strategy for managing the rise of China. America is potentially sacrificing massive global benefits that flow from the US dollar remaining as the global reserve currency for the meager benefits of punishing, for example, Iran. Quite naturally, this provides China a clear long-term competitive advantage, as the Chinese leaders have been very disciplined and focused in sticking to their long-term strategy. Hence, it is not unreasonable to ask, as the title of this book does, has China won?

The fundamental question that still needs to be answered in this chapter is: Who is responsible for the lack of comprehensive long-term strategy to deal with China? Many Americans, especially Democrats, independents, and liberals, would like to blame Trump for this lack of strategy. Certainly, Trump has behaved in a wild and reckless manner in his dealings with the world. Yet, the failure to devise a long-term strategy is the result of a deeper structural flaw in how Americans view the world, a flaw that affects Americans on both the left and the right.

After over a century of dominating the world, especially after the end of the Cold War forty years ago, no American leader has posed a simple question to the American people: Does America need to make strategic and structural adjustments, both in its domestic and international policies, to cope with a different world? As a keen watcher of American politics, I am struck by how few leading figures have suggested that

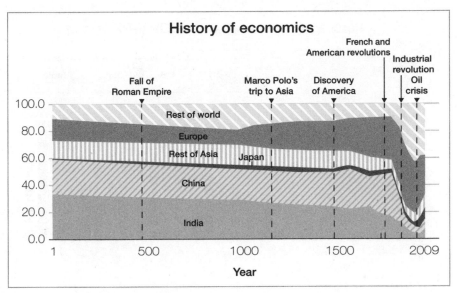

CHART 1. History of Economics (Designed by Patti Issacs)

America should do a fundamental reboot of its strategic thinking and consider whether a fundamental change of direction is needed.

The absence of such a question surfacing in the American discourse is particularly striking because it is obvious that America needs to change course fundamentally. History has turned a corner, and whenever this happens, all nations have to adapt and adjust. Indeed, most nations have begun to do so. America is the exception.

How has history turned a corner? The best way to answer this question is to take a longer view of history. Look at Chart 1.

From the year 1 to 1820, the two largest economies were always those of China and India. Only in the last two hundred years did Europe, followed by America, surpass them. Viewed against the backdrop of two thousand years of world history (i.e., the "big picture"), the past two hundred years of Western (including American) domination have been a major aberration. Hence, it is perfectly natural to see the return of China and India bring this aberration to an end. What is surprising,

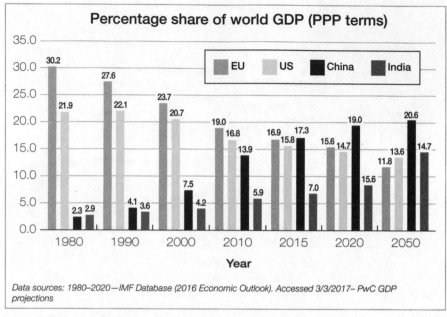

CHART 2. Percentage Share of World GDP (Designed by Patti Issacs)

indeed even shocking, is how fast China, India, and the rest of Asia have bounced back. Please see Chart 2.

If you compare the tabulation of relative economic shares in 1980 against the tabulation in 2020, we can see how dramatically history has turned a corner in recent decades. In these decades America has refused to make any strategic or structural adjustments to this major turn in history. Indeed, to put it bluntly, America has continued in a straight line on autopilot, while the rest of the world is changing course.

Future historians may compare this failure to adjust to another such historical failure—that of the Qing dynasty mandarins in nineteenth-century China who failed to realize that the rise of the West meant that China had to change course. They didn't. As a consequence, China experienced a lot of trauma for a century or so. It was Asia's greatest living historian, Professor Wang Gungwu, who alerted me to this. He told me that my descriptions of the failures of the West, including America, to strategically adjust to a new world reminded him "of the confident mandarins of late Qing China who dismissed the possibility of a new world emerging that could challenge their superior system."

America today is in a much stronger position than the Qing dynasty was. No great power would dare to trample on American soil in the way that the Western powers did on China's soil in the nineteenth century. America will not be held hostage by gunboat diplomacy. Yet, there are other kinds of shocks that could prove painful over the long term. One of the greatest mistakes made by great powers throughout history has been to assume that they were invulnerable, especially when they are at the peak of their power. There is no doubt that many American strategic thinkers make this assumption, which is why few of them (apart from a few scholars like Stephen Walt and John Mearsheimer) recommend any major strategic adjustments.

This failure to make strategic adjustments may also explain the structural domestic challenges faced by American society. Over the past thirty years, inequality has exploded in America, as shown in Chart 3. While the average income of the bottom 50 percent has stagnated, the average income of the top 1 percent has grown astronomically.

The economists are still debating the root causes for this sharp increase in inequality. The causes are complex. Nonetheless, the stagnation of wages of the bottom 50 percent must have been caused in part by the injection of millions of low-wage Chinese workers into the global economic system. As explained by the eminent Western economist Joseph Schumpeter, all this has led to "creative destruction," including loss of competitiveness and jobs in America. Clearly, after encouraging the entry of China into the WTO in 2001, American leaders should have thoughtfully prepared for the structural impact of this event on the American economy and society. Sadly, no leader suggested this. American workers were left alone to cope with this structural shock.

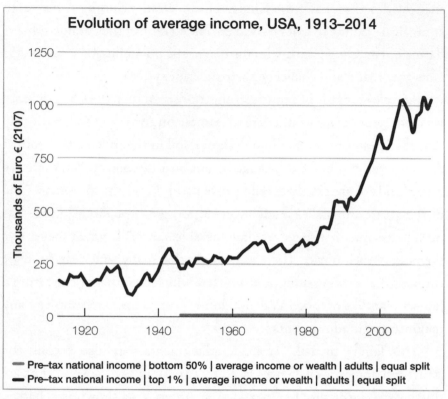

Evolution of average income, USA, 1913–2014

Y-axis: Thousands of Euro € (2107) — 0, 250, 500, 750, 1000, 1250

X-axis: 1920, 1940, 1960, 1980, 2000

— Pre–tax national income | bottom 50% | average income or wealth | adults | equal split
— Pre–tax national income | top 1% | average income or wealth | adults | equal split

CHART 3. Evolution of Average Income, United States, 1913–2014* (Designed by Patti Issacs)

Many European countries spend 1 to 3 percent of their GDP to retrain their workers. America spends 0.24 percent.[†] This failure to take care of American workers led to an inevitable populist backlash, resulting ultimately in the election of Donald Trump. Negative consequences always flow from the failure to make strategic adjustments when the world changes significantly.[‡]

---

* World Inequality Database, "Income Inequality, USA, 1913–2014" (chart), https:// wid.world/country/usa/.

† OECD, "Public Spending on Labour Markets," Organisation for Economic Development and Co-operation, 2000–2017, https://data.oecd.org/socialexp/public-spending -on-labour-markets.htm.

‡ Kishore Mahbubani, "How the West Can Adapt to a Rising Asia," TED Talk, April 2019, https://www.youtube.com/watch?v=dsJWs6Z6eNs.

Can America make a U-turn and now make strategic adjustments to this new phase of history? In theory, democratically elected governments should be more flexible and adaptable than rigid and sclerotic Communist Party governments, as in the former Soviet Union and in contemporary China. Sometimes, however, practice is the opposite of theory. Some aspects of American society have become as rigid and ossified as Qing dynasty China.

To deal with the long-term challenge from China effectively, Americans first need to ask themselves some simple questions: What are the deep assumptions about the world that Americans take for granted? Which assumptions remain valid in the new world, and which need to be questioned? Challenging deeply held assumptions is never easy or comfortable. But it would be unwise for Americans to ignore events and attempt to remain in their comfort zones when the world that is coming will inevitably force them, sooner or later, to step outside their comfort zones. What follows are some deeply held American assumptions that deserve questioning.

The first assumption is that America will remain the number one economy forever. Indeed, this could well happen if Chinese society falters or if the Chinese economy gets caught in a middle-income trap. Yet, if one assumes that the Chinese people are as smart and capable as their fellow Asian neighbors, there is no reason why the Chinese economy cannot accomplish what Singapore, Japan, or South Korea have achieved. China's per capita income is now about US$18,000. If China were to eventually achieve the per capita income of Singapore (where 75 percent of the population is ethnic Chinese), its GDP would balloon to $141 trillion, in purchasing power parity terms. By contrast, America's GDP is now $20 trillion.[*] Clearly, the prospects of China having a bigger economy than America are realistic.

---

[*] World Bank, "World Bank Open Data," The World Bank data, https://data.worldbank.org.

It would therefore be logical to question the widely held assumption that America will be the number one economy forever. It would also be wise for American society to begin debating America's place in the world and how its domestic policies should adapt to this new world. Leading American figures should discuss these issues in the media. Since America is, in theory, one of the world's most open societies, it should be easy to propose this admittedly difficult subject for debate.

In practice, however, it would be suicidal for any American politician to do so. One of America's most thoughtful recent presidents was Bill Clinton. After he left office, he said in a speech in Yale in 2003 that America should prepare itself for a world where America was no longer the sole superpower. One of his close associates was Strobe Talbott, who also served as his deputy secretary of state from 1994 to 2001. Talbott asked Clinton why he gave the speech. Clinton replied that he "wanted to build a world for our grandchildren to live in where America was no longer the sole superpower, for a time when we would have to 'share the stage.'"* Yet, as Talbott explains in his book, even though Clinton knew that America would someday become number two, his "political instincts told him it would be inviting trouble to suggest that the sun might someday set on American pre-eminence."† So Clinton gave the speech only after he left office.

I know, too, from personal experience that American politicians won't say publicly that America may become number two. In January 2012 I chaired a high-level panel discussion on the future of American power. Four distinguished Americans were on the panel: Republican senators Saxby Chambliss (Georgia) and Bob Corker (Tennessee), and Democrats Michael Froman (deputy assistant to the president and deputy national security adviser for international economic affairs) and Nita M. Lowey (congresswoman in New York). When I suggested that

---

* Strobe Talbott, *The Great Experiment: The Story of Ancient Empires, Modern States, and the Quest for a Global Nation* (New York: Simon and Schuster, 2009), 329.
† Ibid., 330.

America could one day become the number two economy, none of the four distinguished panelists could agree with me publicly.

This personal experience made me aware that despite its openness, America has its own sacred cows. One such sacred cow is that America is number one and will be number one forever. This creates a very difficult problem for any American leader or leader-in-waiting. If America is going to work out a thoughtful and comprehensive strategy to adapt to a new world, this strategy will have to rest on realistic assumptions about the future. One realistic assumption is that America will become number two. It is suicidal for American society to punish politicians who speak about such inevitable realities. If American politicians can't speak these truths publicly, this will in turn prevent them from suggesting new strategies for America to adapt.

The assumption of staying number one forever is not the only sacred cow in American discourse. An equally strong assumption is the belief that American society is inherently virtuous, both in its domestic and international behavior. As Stephen Walt, a Harvard professor, has said, this assumption is sadly not true. When 330 million Americans out of a global population of 7.5 billion people see themselves as an inherently virtuous people (and, therefore, in some ways superior to the rest of the human race, indeed as an exceptional nation), while the remaining 7.2 billion people on planet earth (living in states that are both friendly and unfriendly to America) do not share America's assumption about itself, this obviously creates a dangerous intellectual divide between America and the world. And if American thought leaders work out a comprehensive global strategy for America on the assumption that America is perceived by the world to be an inherently virtuous society, wouldn't this comprehensive strategy be flawed from its very inception?

Perhaps, at the end of the day, this may be the fundamental explanation for the lack of a new comprehensive long-term American strategy to deal with the new world of the twenty-first century. Any realistic and credible strategy would have to question deeply held assumptions in the

American psyche. Since it would be both psychologically and politically difficult to surface these assumptions for questioning, it would be safer for politicians to keep on suggesting that all America needs to do is to keep doing what it has been doing before and do it well, to keep America as number one. This is also the assumption behind Trump's MAGA (Make American Great Again) goal: to neither reinvent America nor confront dangerous American illusions, all the while pursuing an increasingly unilateralist path. In short, America will continue on autopilot. If America keeps doing this, it will, effectively, present China with a geopolitical gift and allow China to eventually win a geopolitical contest that American blundered into without first working out a thoughtful, comprehensive, and long-term strategy.

CHAPTER 4

IS CHINA EXPANSIONIST?

O NE WELL-ACCEPTED "FACT" ABOUT XI JINPING IS THAT HE reneged on his promise not to militarize the South China Sea islands. In December 2016, the *Wall Street Journal* reported: "For a man who stood at the White House in September 2015 and promised not to militarize the South China Sea, Xi Jinping is sure doing a lot of militarizing."* In two articles for the *Washington Post*, John Pomfret wrote that "China routinely makes commitments that it does not keep. Just remember Xi's 2015 promise to then-President Barack Obama not to militarize the islands it created in the South China Sea"† and again that Xi "broke his promises to President Barack Obama not to militarize the

---

* Thomas Shugart, "China Arms Its Great Wall of Sand," *Wall Street Journal*, December 15, 2016, https://www.wsj.com/articles/china-arms-its-great-wall-of-sand-1481848109.

† John Pomfret, "A China-U.S. Truce on Trade Only Scratches the Surface of a Broader Conflict," *Washington Post*, December 3, 2018, https://www.washingtonpost.com /opinions/2018/12/03/china-us-truce-trade-only-scratches-surface-broader-conflict /?utm_term=.0e6e9a186448.

seven Chinese-made islands in the South China Sea."* *The Economist* was perhaps the most forthright in its accusation of Xi's broken promise, declaring in April 2018: "Less than three years ago, Xi Jinping stood with Barack Obama in the Rose Garden at the White House and lied through his teeth. [. . .] China absolutely did not, Mr. Xi purred, 'intend to pursue militarisation' on its islands."†

If Xi had indeed made such a promise and reneged, it would only go to confirm a widespread belief in the West that China has become aggressive and expansionist. It would also confirm a belief that the Chinese are being perfidious and deceptive when they claim that China will rise peacefully. So what is true?

Few Americans can claim to know China as well as Ambassador Stapleton Roy. Born in China, a fluent Mandarin speaker, Roy also served as the American ambassador to China from 1991 to 1995 and has stayed exceptionally well informed on US-China relations. He explained what happened: In a joint press conference with President Obama on September 25, 2015, Xi Jinping had proposed a more reasonable approach on the South China Sea. Xi had supported full and effective implementation of the 2002 Declaration on the Conduct of Parties in the South China Sea, signed by China and all ten ASEAN members; had called for early conclusion of the China-ASEAN consultations on a Code of Conduct for the South China Sea; and had added that China had *no intention* of militarizing the Spratlys, where it had engaged in massive reclamation work on the reefs and shoals it occupied. Roy said that Obama missed an opportunity to capitalize on this reasonable proposal. Instead, the US Navy stepped up its naval patrols. China responded by proceeding with militarization.

---

* John Pomfret, "How the World's Resistance to China Caught Xi Jinping Off Guard," *Washington Post*, December 21, 2018, https://www.washingtonpost.com/opinions/2018/12 /21/how-worlds-resistance-china-caught-xi-jinping-off-guard/?utm_term=.105ab7ca5227.
† "China Has Militarised the South China Sea and Got Away with It," *The Economist*, June 21, 2018, https://www.economist.com/asia/2018/06/21/china-has-militarised -the-south-china-sea-and-got-away-with-it.

In short, Xi did not renege on a promise. His offer was effectively spurned by the US Navy. The big question is how an untruth becomes accepted as a fact by well-informed, thoughtful Western elites. And this is not easy to answer. Having observed closely over several decades how untruths about China get generated and accepted widely, I have come to the conclusion that they are produced by a unique ecosystem that involves the best intelligence services of the world and the best newspapers of the world.

It is an Anglo-Saxon ecosystem and it involves the Five Eyes club, which brings together the intelligence services of America, Australia, Canada, New Zealand, and the United Kingdom. There is a high degree of trust among these five Anglo-Saxon countries. Intelligence is therefore shared with great confidence. From time to time, these intelligence services share information with leading Western newspapers.

Major Western newspapers are bold and largely independent. No government has the power to control their reporting. Indeed, they often stand up to and confront their governments with inconvenient facts. As a result, when they report stories, a high degree of credibility (justifiably) is associated with them. All of them boldly proclaim that their goal is to report the truth, not serve as propaganda vehicles, like *Pravda* in the former Soviet Union or the *People's Daily* in China. These claims of independent reporting are absolutely correct and fully justified.

Yet, it is also true that these newspapers must rely on government sources for some of their stories, including intelligence services like the Five Eyes network. Many of these stories are credible. For example, it is a fact that Xi did offer to not militarize the Spratly Islands in the South China Sea (and for the record, he did not offer to demilitarize the Paracel Islands, which are disputed with Vietnam only). It is also a fact that the Chinese military did subsequently step up its activities in the Spratly Islands. The missing unreported "fact" is that the US Navy provoked the latter reaction. For obvious reasons, this fact was not shared by the Five Eyes network.

In April 2018, I was included in an unusual delegation that was invited to visit Beijing. The delegation comprised the veteran *Washington Post* editorial writer Carl Bernstein, the historian Niall Ferguson, the *New York Times* columnist Tom Friedman, the *Financial Times* columnist Martin Wolf, and me. We were given high-level access in Beijing. Among others, we met Liu He, the chief trade negotiator in the US-China trade talks, Lou Jiwei, the former finance minister, and Zhou Xiaochuan, the former governor of the Central Bank. After leaving Beijing, all of us wrote about our visit. Some were more critical of China's policies; others less so. However, all of us tried to explain China's point of view.

China, historically, has been clumsy at explaining or defending its points of view. Given the rigidities of the Chinese political system, it is hard to find a good spokesman who can, with humor and sharp insights, explain the Chinese perspective effectively. One surprising exception to this rule is Ren Zhengfei, the founder of Huawei. He has spoken directly to many leading Western media outlets, including CNN, MSNBC, Bloomberg TV, Time, CBS, and BBC. He speaks with great authority and clarity, using direct and striking language. By contrast, many official Chinese spokesmen use slogans.

Yet, if China were to try to make a case that it is inherently not a militaristic power, it would have many strong arguments to deploy. The first argument is historical. If Chinese civilization is inherently militaristic, this militaristic streak, especially the desire to conquer and subjugate other territories, would have surfaced long ago. Over the past two thousand years, China has often been the single strongest civilization in the Eurasian landmass. If China was inherently militaristic, it would have and should have conquered territories overseas, as the European powers did. Future historians will, for example, marvel at the fact that even though Australia is geographically close to China, it was physically occupied and conquered by far more distant British forces. Indeed, had James Cook sailed directly, it would have taken him at least ninety days to reach Australia's Botany Bay, having departed from Plymouth Dockyard in August of 1768; counterfactually, were he instead to have sailed from China, he would have found himself ashore in just under thirty days.*

This Chinese reluctance to conquer Australia and other overseas territories is not because China always lacked a navy. Before the Portuguese and Spanish began the ruthless European policies of colonizing the world in the sixteenth century, the Chinese had by far the strongest navy in the world. At the start of the fifteenth century, nearly a hundred years before Christopher Columbus tried to find a route to the so-called Spice Islands, China sent out seven naval expeditions, under the remarkable leadership of Admiral Zheng He, a legendary Chinese figure. He traveled as far as Africa on ships that were far larger in size than the Portuguese or Spanish vessels: "The stars of the Chinese fleet were the treasure ships—sweeping junks, several stories high, up to 122 meters long and 50 meters wide. In fact they were about four times bigger than the 'Santa Maria,' the ship Columbus sailed to America on behalf of the Spanish crown."†

Along the way, he did get into military battles. For example, in his voyages between 1409 and 1411, he "captured King Alagak-Konara (亞烈苦奈兒) of Ceylon and chose Yapanaina (耶巴乃那) to be the king instead," and in his voyages between 1413 and 1415, he "captured Sekandar, (蘇幹剌) king of Sumatra (Atcheh) and then installed a new king."‡

---

* Cook, of course, did not sail directly to Australia, charting as he did the greater part of the South Pacific Ocean. These figures were generated by inputting the estimated speed (six knots) of Cook's eighteenth-century vessel, the HMS *Endeavor*, into the S&P Global Platts sea route calculator.

† Andreas Lorenz, "Hero of the High Seas," *Der Spiegel*, August 29, 2005, https://www.spiegel.de/international/spiegel/china-s-christopher-columbus-hero-of-the-high-seas-a-372474-2.html.

‡ Hsu Yun-Ts'iao, "Notes Relating to Admiral Cheng Ho's Expeditions," in ed. Leo Suryadinata, *Admiral Zheng He and Southeast Asia* (Singapore: ISEAS, 2005), 124–135.

Yet, quite remarkably, China did not conquer or occupy any over-seas or distant territories. Singapore's former foreign minister George Yeo remarked that "throughout Chinese history, the Chinese have been averse to sending military forces far away. . . . In the 8th century, at the peak of China's development during the Tang Dynasty, they had an army near the Fergana Valley in Central Asia, when the Abbasids were moving eastwards. They clashed. In the famous battle of Talas, the Abbasids defeated the Tang army, and the Chinese never crossed the Tianshan Mountains again in their history."[*]

Professor Wang Gungwu of the National University of Singapore identifies the Han Chinese people as essentially agrarian. They spread through all the land areas of China where they could find good agricul-tural soil. As soon as they encountered the hostile steppes or the rugged mountain regions, they turned back. Similarly, the Han people didn't be-lieve in going overseas. Most of China's territorial expansion, like Inner Mongolia or Xinjiang or the rugged mountain regions, took place when China was ruled by "foreign" dynasties, like the Yuan (1279–1368) and Qing (1644–1911). The story of Tibet is more complex. Tibet was first conquered by China under the Mongols in 1244, but "enjoy[ed] con-siderable autonomy under Yuan Dynasty."[†] In the many centuries since this initial conquest, struggles have ensued over Tibet's domination by the different Chinese governments, from the Qing to the republican government. It was only in 1950 that Tibet was formally incorporated into the People's Republic of China. China's claims over Tibet therefore come with a highly contested history. This is a simplification of a rich and complex Chinese history, but the significant grain of truth is that for most of the past two thousand years, the Han Chinese have not

---

[*] George Yeo, "A Continuing Rise of China," *Business Times* (Singapore), October 30, 2019, https://www.businesstimes.com.sg/opinion/thinkchina/a-continuing-rise-of-china.

[†] "Tibet Profile: Timeline," BBC News, November 13, 2014, https://www.bbc.com/news/world-asia-pacific-17046222.

been militarist or expansionist, despite the many wars they have fought, most of which were within China.

The relatively peaceful streak of the Han Chinese people is brought out when their behavior is compared with some of their neighbors. One of the most powerful and terrifying imperialist expansions in human history was carried out by China's immediate neighbors in the North, the Mongols. Led by the brutal and dynamic Genghis Khan, these relatively small Mongolian tribes (far smaller in population than the Chinese people) conquered not just China but almost all of Asia, becoming also the only East Asian force to threaten an invasion of Europe. Yet the more powerful Chinese empire never emulated this conquering example of its neighbors.

The Mongols conquered and ruled China itself for over a century. In a piece for the Asia Society, Jean Johnson writes that "Genghis Khan moved his troops into the quasi-Chinese Chin-ruled north China in 1211, and in 1215 they destroyed the capital city. His son Ogodei conquered all of North China by 1234 and ruled it from 1229 to 1241. Genghis Khan's grandson, Kublai Khan, defeated the Chinese Southern Song in 1279, and for the first time all of China was under foreign rule. In 1271 Kublai Khan named his dynasty Yuan which means 'origin of the universe.' The Yuan dynasty in China lasted from 1279 to 1368."[*] As a result, there was massive cross-fertilization between Mongolian and Chinese culture. In this process, the Mongols could have transferred their militaristic culture into the software of Chinese civilization. Instead, the opposite happened. The Chinese progressively civilized their Mongol rulers, and while Kublai Khan fought wars with China's neighbors, he made no effort to conquer the world like Genghis Khan tried to do.

What was the powerful antimilitary DNA of Chinese civilization that eventually infected Mongol rulers? It probably goes back to

* Jean Johnson, "The Mongol Dynasty," Asia Society, https://asiasociety.org/education/mongol-dynasty.

Confucius. The Chinese have long had a saying that "just as good iron is not transformed into a nail; a good man is not made into a soldier." At several points in the *Analects*, Confucius cautions against people who only have the strength of soldiers. In one dialogue:

> Zilu said, "Does the *junzi* [君子] prize valor?" The Master said, "The *junzi* gives righteousness the topmost place. If a *junzi* had valor but not righteousness, he would create chaos. If a small person has valor and not righteousness, he becomes a bandit.*

In another dialogue:

> Zilu said, "Master, if you were put in charge of the three army divisions, then whom would you wish to have with you?" The Master said, "Those who fight tigers with their bare hands, wade across rivers, and are willing to die without regret—I would not want their company. I would certainly want those who approach affairs with fearful caution and who like to lay careful plans for success."†

In contrast to American culture, where there is a strong built-in reverence for the man in uniform, Chinese culture has revered scholars more than soldiers, even though there are military figures who are celebrated in folklore and literature for their patriotism and loyalty. Overall, there is an even greater reverence for the man who is skilled in both, encapsulated in the idea of 文武双全 (*wén wǔ shuāng quán*), that is, someone who is both a fine scholar and soldier. One harsh fact needs to be spelled out clearly here. In recent decades, America's first option when confronted with a strategic challenge has been to use a military option. The Chinese avoid military options, as Henry Kissinger explained:

---

* Confucius, "The Analects of Confucius," trans. Robert Eno, 2015, https://chinatxt .sitehost.iu.edu/Resources.html.

† Ibid.

[The] foundations [of China's distinctive military theory] were laid during a period of upheaval, when ruthless struggles between rival kingdoms decimated China's population. Reacting to this slaughter (and seeking to emerge victorious from it), Chinese thinkers developed strategic thought that placed a premium on victory through psychological advantage and preached the avoidance of direct conflict.*

Kissinger has accurately distilled the essence of the advice given by China's master strategist Sun Tzu, who once said: "All warfare is based on deception. . . . Pretend inferiority and encourage his arrogance. . . . For to win one hundred victories is not the acme of skill. To subdue the enemy without fighting is the acme of skill." This does not mean that the Chinese are incapable of fighting wars. Over the past two thousand years, they have fought many wars with many neighbors, especially when they were ruled by foreign dynasties, and they have gradually expanded their territory to occupy vast spaces. Just as one can argue about the legitimacy of the American occupation of Texas and California, one can also argue about the legitimacy of the Chinese occupation of Tibet, Xinjiang, and Taiwan. However, just as it would be politically suicidal for any American president to suggest that Texas and California be returned to Mexico, it would also be suicidal for any Chinese leader to suggest that Tibet, Xinjiang, and Taiwan be abandoned by the Chinese state. These are some hard political realities that cannot be changed.

Although China has occupied some neighboring territories, it has also learned to live in peace with many of its neighbors with whom it has fought many wars, including four wars with Myanmar, two wars with the Japanese, three wars with the Koreans, and seven wars with the Vietnamese. Indeed, it is quite remarkable that China has accepted the independence of Vietnam because Vietnam was occupied by China for one thousand years, from 111 BCE to 938 CE.

---

* Henry Kissinger, *On China* (New York: Penguin, 2011), 25.

The Chinese have also learned the art of losing wars gracefully, if its neighbor accepts the ritual of apologizing to the Chinese emperor for defeating an invading Chinese army. This was brought home clearly to me when I delivered a lecture in Columbia University in 1985 on Vietnam's relations with its neighbors. During this lecture, I said that while the Vietnamese had from time to time defeated invading Chinese armies, they had always, thereafter, sent emissaries to Beijing bearing tributes to "apologize" for having defeated the Chinese invaders. I argued that the real mistake that Vietnam made in 1979 was not defeating China but failing to apologize to China for defeating it. To my surprise, three Vietnamese diplomats who were seated in the front row nodded in agreement when I said this.

As China becomes more and more powerful, it will, like all great powers, assert its power and influence. Just as America's neighbors in Latin America had to adapt and adjust to American power as it exploded in the late nineteenth century, China's neighbors will also have to adapt and adjust. But China will not resort to military means as its first expression of power. This is why Graham Allison wisely reminded his fellow Americans to be careful in wishing that China would be more like us:

> Americans enjoy lecturing Chinese to be "more like us." Perhaps they should be more careful what they wish for. Historically how have emerging hegemons behaved? To be more specific, how did Washington act just over a century ago when Theodore Roosevelt led the US into what he was supremely confident would be an American century? [. . .] In the decade that followed his arrival in Washington, the US declared war on Spain, expelling it from the Western Hemisphere and acquiring Puerto Rico, Guam, and the Philippines; threatened Germany and Britain with war unless they agreed to settle the disputes on American terms; supported an insurrection in Colombia to create a new country, Panama, in order to build a canal; and declared itself the

policeman of the Western Hemisphere, asserting the right to intervene whenever and wherever it judged necessary—a right it exercised nine times in the seven years of TR's presidency alone.[*]

The long two-thousand-year record of Chinese history clearly shows that China is fundamentally unlike America as it is reluctant to use the military option first. It is also fundamentally different from America in another regard. It does not believe that it has a "universal" mission to promote Chinese civilization and encourage everyone else in humanity to emulate it. Americans fundamentally believe that they should stand for universal values and sincerely believe that the world would be a better place if the rest of humanity absorbed and implemented American values. Hillary Clinton said in a 2016 speech:

> When we say America is exceptional, it [...] means that we recognize America's unique and unparalleled ability to be a force for peace and progress, a champion for freedom and opportunity. Our power comes with a responsibility to lead, humbly, thoughtfully, and with a fierce commitment to our values. Because, when America fails to lead, we leave a vacuum that either causes chaos or other countries or networks rush in to fill the void.[†]

The Chinese believe the opposite. They believe that only Chinese can be Chinese in culture, values, and aesthetics. I have long lived in a Chinese-majority society of Singapore. None of my Chinese friends would have expected me to become like them, even if I were fluent in the language and adopted Chinese customs habitually.

---

[*] Graham Allison, *Destined for War: Can America and China Escape Thucydides's Trap?* (Boston: Houghton Mifflin Harcourt, 2017), 89–90.

[†] Daniel White, "Read Hillary Clinton's Speech Touting 'American Exceptionalism,'" *Time*, August 31, 2016, updated September 1, 2016, https://time.com/4474619/read -hillary-clinton-american-legion-speech/.

This "universalizing" streak of American culture may explain why America has gotten involved in so many military conflicts. Both Gaddafi of Libya and Assad of Syria were and are deeply flawed rulers. Yet, America is several thousand miles away from Syria and Libya. It has no vital national interests in either country. But because of its universalizing vision, it felt a moral obligation to get involved militarily. The Chinese are genuinely puzzled by this. Why get involved in foreign military conflicts when it doesn't serve one's own national interests?

The Chinese are even more puzzled that America has allowed its involvement in unnecessary Middle East conflicts to undermine its more fundamental national interests. Such involvements have drained resources and taken away the possibility of using the same resources to improve the lives of relatively poor Americans instead. The Chinese are privately delighted because each unnecessary involvement in a Middle Eastern conflict reduces American ability to deploy resources against China. Having seen the folly of wasteful American military involvements, the Chinese have learned one wise lesson: refrain from getting involved in unnecessary fights. It is not an accident that China has not fought a major war in forty years and has not fired a bullet across its borders in thirty years. This lack of military action reflects both a powerful civilizational impulse and a deeply pragmatic view of power.

Having carefully refrained from using military options for over four decades, the Chinese are genuinely bewildered by the American portrait of China as an inherently aggressive, militaristic, and expansionist power. As a result of this strong conviction that China is becoming militarily aggressive, the American security establishment, including the Department of Defense, the National Security Council, and the FBI, has concluded that China is now a direct threat to America. In September 2019, the Department of Defense reported the remarks of undersecretary of defense for policy John C. Rood as saying that "it is not an exaggeration to say China is the greatest long-term threat to the U.S. way of life, but China also poses the greatest challenge to the Defense Department."* A month later, Vice President Pence made several remarkable allegations that China's military behavior has become "increasingly provocative" over the past year, arguing that China has "regularly menace[d]" and "strong-arm[ed]" its ASEAN neighbors in the South China Sea, while provoking Japan in the East China Sea and using the BRI to "establish footholds in ports around the world, ostensibly for commercial purposes, but those purposes could eventually become military."† A well-known scholar on China, Robert Sutter of George Washington University, has said: "There is now a remarkable whole of government anti-China stance which I have not seen in the last 50 years in Washington."‡

These expressions of alarm about China in the military sphere are getting more strident. When Patrick Shanahan took over as acting defense secretary on January 1, 2019, a news report quoted an anonymous defense official: "While we are focused on ongoing operations, Acting Secretary Shanahan told the team to remember China, China, China."§

In the deeply polarized political atmosphere of Washington, DC, in early 2019, it was almost impossible to get a broad-based political consensus on any topic. Yet, even in this deeply polarized environment, a strong consensus developed among the American political, security,

---

* Terri Moon Cronk, "China Poses Largest Long-Term Threat to U.S., DOD Policy Chief Says," US Department of Defense, September 23, 2019, https://www.defense.gov/explore /story/Article/1968704/china-poses-largest-long-term-threat-to-us-dod-policy-chief-says/.
†"Remarks by Vice President Pence at the Frederic V. Malek Memorial Lecture," Conrad Hotel, Washington, DC, October 24, 2019, https://www.whitehouse.gov /briefings-statements/remarks-vice-president-pence-frederic-v-malek-memorial-lecture/.
‡ Daljit Singh, How Will Shifts in American Foreign Policy Affect Southeast Asia? (Singapore: ISEAS, 2019), 4.
§ Zhenhua Lu, "'China, China, China': Trump's New Pentagon Chief Patrick Shanahan Sets US Defence Priorities," South China Morning Post, January 3, 2019, https:// www.scmp.com/news/world/united-states-canada/article/2180451/china-china -china-new-pentagon-chief-patrick.

and intellectual establishments, involving both Democrats and Republicans, that China had emerged as an aggressive military competitor to the United States.

Above all else, America is known to be a rational society, with many competing points of view debated all the time. Yet in Washington, DC, today, it is virtually impossible to make the case that China is not a military threat to America. Any objective future historian will see this reality much more clearly. It is plain to see that defensiveness—in the form of securing China's national borders and sovereignty—is the emphasis of contemporary Chinese military policy. This defensive line of thinking is evident in China's defense white paper, published in July 2019, which emphasizes "safeguard[ing] . . . national sovereignty and territorial integrity" as part of its "defensive" national defense policy.*

Kevin Rudd, who has a deep knowledge of China's history, has explained well the emphasis on defensive postures in China's strategic thinking. He writes:

> Neighboring states occupy a particular place in China's strategic memory. Historically, they've been the avenue through which China's national security has been threatened, resulting in successive foreign invasions—from the Mongols in the north in the 12th century, to the Manchurians in the northeast in the mid-17th century, to the British, French, the Western imperial powers including the United States, and then the absolute brutality of the Japanese occupation from the east. In Chinese traditional strategic thought, this has entrenched a deeply defensive view of how to maintain China's national security. But Chinese historiography also teaches that purely defensive measures have not always succeeded. The failure of the Great Wall of China to provide security from foreign invasion is a classic case in

---

* "China's National Defense in the New Era," State Council Information Office of the People's Republic of China, Beijing, July 24, 2019, http://english.www.gov.cn/archive /whitepaper/201907/24/content_WS5d3941ddc6d08408f502283d.html.

point. For these reasons, modern Chinese strategic thinking has explored different approaches. First and foremost, through political and economic diplomacy, China wishes to secure positive, accommodating, and, wherever possible, compliant relationships with all its neighboring states.

Citing Chinese initiatives like the BRI and Shanghai Cooperation Organization, Rudd concludes that "the strategic imperative is clear: to consolidate China's relationships with its neighboring states. And by and large, this means enhancing its strategic position across the Eurasian continent, thereby consolidating China's continental periphery."[*]

In other words, what American thinkers have labeled Chinese expansionism is more accurately explained by China's obsession—informed by its long and painful history of subjugation and invasion—with securing its borders by "consolidat[ing] [its] relationships with its neighboring states."

Moreover, although China has fought countless wars with Japan, Korea, Myanmar, and Vietnam, the prospects of any such war breaking out in the next few decades are virtually zero as well. Why? Since all the immediate neighbors have lived next to China for thousands of years, they have long developed sophisticated and subtle instincts on how to manage a rising China. And the Chinese elite (unlike the American elite) have a deep understanding of their long history with their neighbors. There will be many back-and-forths between China and its neighbors, accompanied by all kinds of sophisticated and subtle shifts. But there will not be wars.

The one exceptional trigger for a war involving China is Taiwan. Most of the time, the Chinese leaders have a lot of policy flexibility.

---

* Kevin Rudd, *The Avoidable War: Reflections on U.S.-China Relations and the End of Strategic Engagement* (New York: Asia Society Policy Institute, January 2019), https://asiasociety.org/sites/default/files/2019-01/The%20Avoidable%20War%20-%20Full%20Report.pdf.

There are no strong domestic lobbies to worry about. But the one issue where the Chinese leaders cannot bend and compromise is Taiwan. Any Chinese leader, including Xi Jinping (despite all his power), could be removed if he is perceived to be weak on Taiwan. Why is Taiwan so fundamental to China? There is a very simple explanation. Every Chinese knows the century of humiliation that China suffered from the Opium War to 1949. Nearly all the historical vestiges of this century of humiliation have been removed or resolved, including Hong Kong and Macau.

Only one remains: Taiwan. It was Chinese territory until China was forced to hand it to Japan after the humiliating defeat in the Sino-Japanese War of 1894–1895. The Chinese have been disappointed by the Western powers several times on Taiwan. At the end of World War I, when China thought it had worked with the Western powers, it initially received assurance from America and the British that Taiwan would be returned to China at the Versailles Peace Conference. As Rana Mitter reports: "Under the treaty [of Versailles], Germany had to give up its territories on Chinese soil, along with all its other colonies around the world. The Chinese assumed that the territories would be restored to the young republic, as a reward for the efforts of the nearly 100,000 Chinese workers who had been sent to the Western Front in Europe to assist the British and French. But the territories were awarded instead to Japan. The Western Allies turned out to have made simultaneous secret agreements with both China and Japan in order to bring them both in on the Allied side."* China felt enormously deceived by the West at this conference. The failure to return Shandong triggered the massive protests that broke out on May 4, 1919. The May Fourth Movement holds a special place in Chinese memories.

This history has taught the Chinese not to accept Western assurances. Any move by America or any other Western power to support, directly or indirectly, the secession of Taiwan from China brings back

* Rana Mitter, *Forgotten Ally: China's World War II, 1937–1945* (New York: Houghton Mifflin Harcourt, 2013).

this historical memory. It provokes a strong, powerful, and virulent national reaction, which boxes in any Chinese leader who may be trying to look for room to maneuver. America cannot claim that it doesn't understand the significance of Taiwan. It was clearly the hottest issue to resolve when Nixon and Kissinger began the process of reconciliation with China. Many clear understandings were reached between America and China. The most explicit understanding reached was that Taiwan and China belonged to one country. The 1972 joint communique stated: "The U.S. side declared: The United States acknowledges that all Chinese on either side of the Taiwan Strait maintain there is but one China and that Taiwan is a part of China. The United States Government does not challenge that position. It reaffirms its interest in a peaceful settlement of the Taiwan question by the Chinese themselves."* Since both Taipei and Beijing agree that Taiwan and China belong to the same country, it is also erroneous for any American to claim that Beijing's claims on Taiwan are proof that China is an expansionist, aggressive nation. The Chinese desire to reunite Taiwan with the mainland represents a restitution, not an expansion.

The most fundamental question that America has to ask itself is a simple one: Does it consider itself legally bound by the clear agreements that it has reached with China on Taiwan? Most Americans believe that America is an inherently law-abiding country that both respects and abides by explicit treaties and agreements it has signed. In practice, America has walked away from treaties and agreements it has signed. There is only one reason why this happens. As the strongest country on planet earth, America can walk away from any legal agreement or treaty and not face any consequences. No force can make America abide by its legal obligations.

In the past, until as recently as 2001 (before 9/11 happened), America's primary impulse and instinct was to respect international

---

* "The Joint U.S.-China Communique, Shanghai," February 27, 1972, https://photos
.state.gov/libraries/ait-taiwan/171414/ait-pages/shanghai_e.pdf.

agreements. Thomas Franck documented this in *The Power of Legitimacy Among Nations*, by describing how the US Navy refrained from boarding a vessel in 1988 even though it was found to be carrying illicit nuclear materials:

> Early in 1988, the U.S. Defense Department became aware of a ship approaching the Gulf with a load of Chinese-made Silkworm missiles en route to Iran. The Navy believed the delivery of these potent weapons would increase materially the danger to both protected and protecting U.S. ships and the Defense Department therefore, quite cogently, argued for permission to interdict the delivery. The State Department, however, countered that such a seizure on the high seas, under the universally recognized rules of war and neutrality, would constitute aggressive blockade tantamount to an act of war against Iran. The U.S., if it enforced a naval blockade, would lose its purchase on brokering peace as a neutral. In the event, the delivery ship with its cargo of missiles was allowed to pass. Deference to systemic rules had won out over tactical advantage in the internal struggle for control of U.S. policy.*

Post-9/11, most of these self-restraints have disappeared.

The Trump administration is clearly the most extreme American administration in ignoring all legal obligations that follow from international treaties and agreements. John Bolton, Trump's former national security adviser, has said explicitly: "It is a big mistake for us to grant any validity to international law even when it may seem in our short-term interest to do so—because, over the long term, the goal of those who think international law really means anything are those who want to constrict the United States." Before his resignation, Bolton led the charge within the Trump administration to ignore or violate previous

---

* Thomas M. Franck, *The Power of Legitimacy Among Nations* (Oxford, UK: Oxford University Press, 1990), 3–4.

agreements that America had reached with China and Taiwan. In an op-ed for the *Wall Street Journal* in January 2017, Bolton argued that "it is high time to revisit the 'one-China policy' and decide what America thinks it means, 45 years after the Shanghai Communiqué."[*] In response, Ted Galen Carpenter, a senior fellow in security studies at the Cato Institute, wrote in *The National Interest* in June 2019:

> Before [Bolton's] current stint in government service, he pushed for highly dangerous and provocative policies. He urged the United States to establish formal diplomatic relations with Taiwan and even advocated moving U.S. military forces from Okinawa to Taiwan. Either measure would cross a bright red line as far as Beijing is concerned and would likely trigger PRC military action to prevent Taiwan's permanent political separation from the mainland. Having someone with those views holding a crucial policy post and sitting just a few doors down from the Oval Office greatly increases the likelihood of a further boost in U.S. support for Taiwan, despite the risk of war with China.[†]

Bolton is no fool. He knew that many of his words and actions on Taiwan riled China. There is a real danger that Bolton or someone like him may initiate or trigger a series of actions that could force China to take military action across the Taiwan Strait. I deliberately used the words *force China to take military action* because a Chinese leader who is seen to be weak on Taiwan becomes politically vulnerable. To protect his political position, he may be left with no choice but to act. George Kennan provided his fellow Americans some wise advice on the need

---

[*] John Bolton, "Revisit the 'One-China Policy': A Closer U.S. Military Relationship with Taiwan Would Help Counter Beijing's Belligerence," *Wall Street Journal*, January 17, 2017.
[†] Ted Galen Carpenter, "Forget the U.S.-China Trade War: Is a Conflict over Taiwan the Real Threat?," *The National Interest*, June 8, 2019, https://nationalinterest.org/feature/forget-us-china-trade-war-conflict-over-taiwan-real-threat-61627.

to avoid provocations when he made the case for containment of the Soviet Union: "such a policy has nothing to do with outward histrionics: with threats or blustering or superfluous gestures of outward 'toughness.' While the Kremlin is basically flexible in its reaction to political realities, it is by no means unamenable to considerations of prestige. Like almost any other government, it can be placed by tactless and threatening gestures in a position where it cannot afford to yield even though this might be dictated by its sense of realism."* Bolton seems to disagree: he has engaged in tactless and threatening gestures toward China.

Many Americans naturally believe that America is behaving responsibly on Taiwan because it is the main guarantor against an outright military invasion of Taiwan. This is true. Yet it is also true that it is the people of Taiwan who will suffer if American actions provoke military responses from China. If America's goals on Taiwan are truly noble, if it wants to protect the Taiwanese people, and if, in the long run, America wants to see the gradual emergence of a democratic China, it should allow the continuation of the only democratically run Chinese society in the world, which is Taiwan. (Note: Singapore does not qualify for this description since it is a multiethnic society, not a Chinese society.) The best way to preserve the democratic system in Taiwan is for America to leave Taiwan alone. It should also forcefully indicate that it will not support Taiwanese independence. This is the tough love message that President George W. Bush sent to the then Taiwanese leader, Chen Shui-bian, who was flirting with independence. And this tough love message worked.

Might China invade Taiwan unilaterally and without provocation? There are two major constraints on China. The first is the Taiwan Relations Act, passed by the US Congress on January 1, 1979. It explicitly says that it is the policy of the United States "to maintain the capacity of

---

* Mr. X (George Kennan), "The Sources of Soviet Conduct," *Foreign Affairs*, July 1947.

the United States to resist any resort to force or other forms of coercion that would jeopardize the security, or the social or economic system, of the people on Taiwan," and "the United States will make available to Taiwan such defense articles and defense services in such quantity as may be necessary to enable Taiwan to maintain a sufficient self-defense capability."* The second is that it is actually in China's national interest to allow the continuation of a social and political laboratory to indicate how a Chinese society functions under a different political system. There is a convergence of Chinese and American interests here. China could learn long-term lessons from Taiwan on how Chinese people cope with democracy. It is also in America's long-term interests to have a well-functioning democratic society in Taiwan.

In short, if political wisdom, rather than short-term tactical games, dominates Chinese and American decision making on Taiwan, both sides could agree on Taiwan retaining its autonomy. Strong American discouragement of Taiwanese independence movements will help to reduce tension across the Taiwan Straits. Reduced tension across the Taiwan Straits will also help to reduce the pressure on the Chinese leaders to accelerate the reunification of Taiwan with China.

Sometimes, simple metaphors can help to draw out contrasting strategies. Imagine Taiwan as an unsinkable aircraft carrier stationed within striking distance of China; then imagine it as a healthy virus that could stimulate the body politic of Chinese society.

If Taiwan is viewed as an unsinkable aircraft carrier, America should try to keep Taiwan as separate from the mainland as possible. Hence, the goal would be to accentuate the differences. Although America cannot explicitly support the voices calling for Taiwan independence (as this would be a clear violation of the agreements signed between America and China on Taiwan), it could send indirect signals indicating its sympathy for the Taiwanese voices advocating independence. It could

* Taiwan Relations Act, Public Law 96-8 96th Congress, January 1, 1979, https://photos .state.gov/libraries/ait-taiwan/171414/ait-pages/tra_e.pdf.

also work more sympathetically with the Democratic Progressive Party (DPP). Hence, when the DPP president of Taiwan requests a stopover in America en route to Latin America, America would allow it, even though these visits infuriate Beijing. America could also supply Taiwan with more advanced military weapons, even though this would violate a clear provision of its Joint Communiqué with China of August 17, 1982, which explicitly stated:

> The United States Government states that it does not seek to carry out a long-term policy of arms sales to Taiwan, that its arms sales to Taiwan will not exceed, either in qualitative or in quantitative terms, the level of those supplied in recent years since the establishment of diplomatic relations between the United States and China, and that it intends gradually to reduce its sale of arms to Taiwan, leading, over a period of time, to a final resolution.*

But if, instead, Taiwan is understood as a healthy virus, America should encourage greater contact between Taiwan and the mainland in the hope that exposure to the open and free-wheeling democracy would lead to the gradual transformation of China toward a fully fledged democracy. It would thus be in America's interests to see more links between Taiwan and China. To facilitate this, America should work more closely with the Kuomintang (KMT), rather than the DPP, as the KMT is opposed to Taiwanese independence.

In theory, China should be opposed to a policy of developing closer links with a free and democratic Taiwan as it could lead to calls for a similar political system in mainland China. It is therefore truly remarkable that all the recent governments in China have gone out of their way to both increase and facilitate greater contact between the mainland and

---

* "Joint Communiqué of the People's Republic of China and the United States of America," Embassy of the People's Republic of China in the United States of America, August 17, 1982, http://www.china-embassy.org/eng/zmgx/doc/ctc/t946664.htm.

Taiwan. As recently as 2008, there were 188,744 Taiwanese tourists visiting China and 329,204 Chinese tourists visiting Taiwan. When relations between China and Taiwan improved from 2008 to 2016, while the KMT president Ma Ying-jeou was in power, the numbers increased significantly to 3.6 million Taiwanese tourists in 2016 and a peak of 4.18 million Chinese tourists in 2015.[*]

The big breakthrough happened in 2008 when China allowed direct flights for tourists.[†] Flight times from Shanghai to Taipei (and vice versa) were reduced from five hours (excluding transit time in Hong Kong) to two hours. If Americans want to understand how relatively enlightened Chinese policies toward Taiwan have been, they should compare them with American policies toward Cuba. No American president had the courage to meet Fidel Castro when he was alive. By contrast, Xi met President Ma Ying-jeou in Singapore in 2015.

America has a strong macho culture. The leaders who are admired are the ones who appear strong and belligerent. Presidents who are seen to be weak struggle, like Jimmy Carter or Barack Obama. However, there are times when softer approaches can be more effective in protecting and promoting America's interests. A defter approach on Taiwan, rather than the approach advocated by John Bolton, is to America's advantage. This is why a stronger political consensus on Taiwan should develop in Washington, DC, to avoid forcing the Chinese to take military action on Taiwan, when they don't want to do so.

Apart from Taiwan, the other issue that has generated military tensions between America and China has been the South China Sea. Hank Paulson referred, in passing in 2018, to "a disagreement that recently brought our navies into a near-collision on the high seas." His recommendation to China was to "implement robust rules of engagement to prevent PLA Navy captains from the kind of maneuver that nearly

---

[*] "Bespoke Tours," Tourism Bureau, Republic of China, Taiwan, https://stat.taiwan.net.tw.
[†] "Direct Flights Between China and Taiwan Start," New York Times, July 4, 2008, https://www.nytimes.com/2008/07/04/business/worldbusiness/04iht-04fly.14224270.html.

resulted in a collision in the South China Sea last month."* Paulson was clearly upset that a Chinese naval vessel had carried out a dangerous naval maneuver near an American naval vessel. So far, we do not know what really happened.

However, we do know that American naval vessels routinely carry out naval patrols twelve miles off Chinese shores. Chinese naval vessels do not, so far, carry out naval patrols twelve miles off the shores of California or New York. Under international law, the US Navy (and other navies) is perfectly justified to sail twelve miles off Chinese shores. These patrols are not inherently provocative, but the manner in which these patrols are carried out can be.

America justifies its aggressive naval patrolling in the South China Sea on the grounds that it is protecting a global public good: "freedom of navigation in the high seas." The irony about this American claim is that the biggest beneficiary of the global public good that America is protecting is China. China today trades more with the rest of the world than America does. More Chinese products sail across the world than American products do. Any thoughtful, rational, and sensible observer would therefore be puzzled by an American-Chinese clash over the issue of freedom of navigation. There is a total convergence of interests between America and China on this global good when it applies in 99.99 percent of the world's oceans.

The problem occurs over less than 0.01 percent of the world's ocean surfaces. Even in the South China Sea, there is no disagreement as most of the sea lanes are open international waters through which many naval vessels cross without problem or hindrance. And of the disputed rocks and reefs in the South China Sea, China controls only a minority. Vietnam occupies between forty-nine and fifty-one outposts across twenty-seven features; by contrast, China only has twenty outposts in

---

* Henry M. Paulson Jr., "Remarks on the United States and China at a Crossroads," Paulson Institute, November 6, 2018, http://www.paulsoninstitute.org/news/2018/11/06/statement-by-henry-m-paulson-jr-on-the-united-states-and-china-at-a-crossroads/.

the Paracel Islands. Similarly, in the Spratlys, China controls eight maritime features, such as islands, reefs, and low-tide elevations, while the Philippines occupies nine and Malaysia occupies five. Taiwan controls only one outpost in the Spratlys, Itu Aba Island.* When Malaysia, the Philippines, and Vietnam began reclaiming land around their features, China decided to follow suit. However, while Malaysia, the Philippines, and Vietnam could only reclaim a few acres around their features, China could reclaim up to two thousand acres with its massive resources.

These land reclamations have triggered a problem. China has claimed that the waters up to twelve miles from its new constructed features are territorial waters. Unfortunately for China, the UNCLOS provisions on this issue are clear. Countries are not allowed to claim territorial waters around rocks and reefs, even after land has been reclaimed around them. Under international law, China is wrong to claim that the waters surrounding those features are territorial waters, and America is right in insisting that they are international waters.

The questions that then follow are: What is the best way to resolve this difference of views between America and China on the South China Sea? Is the best way to send American naval vessels to within twelve miles of these Chinese features to prove that they are international waters? Or, if international law is clearly on America's side, would it be wiser for America to take China to the world court to prove that its case is right?

President Xi Jinping tried to provide a face-saving way for both parties to deescalate the rising tensions over the South China Sea when he proposed that China would not militarize any of its reclaimed features in the South China Sea if America would not send any naval vessels to provoke the Chinese. There was a great opportunity for both sides to deescalate the issue. But America missed the chance. Will America continue to misread Chinese intentions? During the next decade or two,

---

* "Occupation and Island Building," Asia Maritime Transparency Institute, CSIS, Washington, DC, https://amti.csis.org/island-tracker.

China will probably emerge as the world's strongest power, without becoming an expansionist one. Two thousand years of Chinese history have created a strategic culture that advises against fighting unnecessary wars in distant places. The likelihood therefore is that, while China's strategic weight and influence in the world will grow significantly, it will not behave as an aggressive and belligerent military power. If the real competition between America and China will not take place in the military sphere, is it wise for America to focus on enhancing its military capabilities when the real contest will be in the nonmilitary sphere? Is it time, therefore, for Washington, DC, to change its strategic consensus on China?

CHAPTER 5

CAN AMERICA MAKE U-TURNS?

I N THE CURRENT GEOPOLITICAL CONTEST BETWEEN AMERICA and China, America is behaving like the Soviet Union, and China is behaving like America did in the Cold War.

In the Cold War, America was often supple, flexible, and rational in its decision making while the Soviet Union was rigid, inflexible, and doctrinaire. The Soviet Union became entangled in unnecessary and painful conflicts, draining its resources and spirits in international conflicts, while America, after withdrawing from the Vietnam War, stayed out of direct involvement in large-scale military conflict. The Soviet Union behaved unilaterally, ignoring international opinion, while America acted multilaterally, marshalling global opinion to its side. America kept its economy dynamic and strong while the Soviet Union's static economy drained away its resources in military expenditure.

Replace the word *America* with *China* and the words *Soviet Union* with *America* and you will get a sense of how differently America is behaving compared to its Cold War strategy. Obviously, some qualifications and nuances have to be introduced, but it is striking how powerful the comparison is.

The key argument of this chapter is that the rigidity and inflexibility of American decision making has become structurally entrenched, and this is especially visible in the way that the United States approaches military conflict. Even though it may be rational for America to make U-turns in some key areas, its rigid and inflexible decision-making procedures are preventing it.

Take defense budgets: a rational case can be made for reducing them. If an all-out war between America and China is unthinkable (both countries would be wiped out completely), and if even a brief skirmish between Americans and Chinese is unfeasible (because it would lead both sides down a slippery slope toward all-out war), it should be clear to any reasonable strategic thinker that the outcome of the looming geopolitical contest between these two powers will not be settled militarily. Hence, it is irrational for America to step up its military spending as it already has enough weapons to destroy all of China several times over. Indeed, it is rational for America to reduce its military expenditure and redirect the new resources to other critical areas, like research and development in science and technology.

The US Navy has thirteen aircraft carrier battle groups. American national security would in no way be undermined if it were to mothball one of the battle groups, or even three. This would lead to enormous savings. According to US Navy captain Henry J. Hendrix: "Carrier strike groups are expensive to buy and to operate. Factoring in the total life-cycle costs of an associated carrier air wing, five surface combatants and one fast-attack submarine, plus the nearly 6,700 men and women to crew them, it costs about $6.5 million per day to operate each strike group."[*] Similarly, a lot of other military expenses could be trimmed

---

[*] Henry J. Hendrix, *At What Cost a Carrier?* (Washington, DC: Center for a New American Security, March 2013), https://s3.amazonaws.com/files.cnas.org/documents/CNAS-Carrier_Hendrix_FINAL.pdf.

away to save money for the nonmilitary dimension of the geopolitical competition with China. Many years ago, in 2011, Fareed Zakaria warned presciently that American military expenditures had ballooned out of control:

> The Pentagon's budget has risen for 13 years, which is unprecedented. Between 2001 and 2009, overall spending on defense rose from $412 billion to $699 billion, a 70 percent increase, which is larger than in any comparable period since the Korean War. Including the supplementary spending on Iraq and Afghanistan, we spent $250 billion more than average U.S. defense expenditures during the Cold War—a time when the Soviet, Chinese and Eastern European militaries were arrayed against the United States and its allies. Over the past decade, when we had no serious national adversaries, U.S. defense spending has gone from about a third of total worldwide defense spending to 50 percent. In other words, we spend more on defense than the planet's remaining countries put together.

If America were a rational actor, it would spend less. However, it is virtually impossible for America to reduce its defense expenditures because the decision-making processes on buying weapons have become locked in. Even though the United States has deployed some of its most talented people as its defense secretaries, including Ash Carter and Jim Mattis, the sad reality is that American defense secretaries, no matter how brilliant, cannot reduce defense expenses.

Why not? Defense spending is not decided as a result of a comprehensive rational national strategy to evaluate which weapon systems America would need in its *current* geopolitical environment. Instead, weapons systems are purchased as a result of a complex lobbying system by defense contractors who have wisely allocated defense manufacturing plants to all the key congressional districts in America. Hence, the senators and representatives who want to preserve jobs in their constituencies decide which weapons systems will be produced for the US military. Winslow T. Wheeler, who worked in the Senate and in the Government Accountability Office on national security issues for thirty-one years, documents the extent of this wastefulness:

> They [the Senate Defense Subcommittee] were cutting military pay and readiness accounts so they could add to the DoD Research and Development (R&D) and the Procurement accounts. That's where the vast majority of the earmarks—rather, congressional special in-terest items—are. In R&D they added $3.9 billion to the Penta-gon's request. The account went from $91 billion to $94.9 billion. In Procurement, they added $4.8 billion to the Pentagon's request of $130.6 billion. Some of the earmarks in these accounts were huge. The controversial F-35 got over $2 billion in several earmarks, the notorious Littoral Combat Ship got $950 million, unrequested C-130s got $640 million, and so on.[*]

It is in China's national interest for this irrational and wasteful de-fense spending to continue. The more money that America spends on weapons systems that will never be used against China, the better off China will be. In short, American military expenditures are geopoliti-cal gifts to China. If American defense spending was a result of rational process, there should now be a significant U-turn involving either a clever reduction or even a simple freeze of American defense expen-ditures. However, this will not happen. Like the former Soviet Union, the current United States of America is locked into irrational processes it cannot break free from.

By contrast, Chinese hands are not tied by any defense lobbies. They will make rational long-term defense decisions to keep China secure. If

---

[*] Winslow T. Wheeler, "Those Porky Pentagon Earmarks Never Really Went Away," *The American Conservative*, January 11, 2019, https://www.theamericanconservative.com /articles/those-porky-pentagon-earmarks-never-really-went-away/.

they thought rigidly and mechanically, they would have copied America and tried to build thirteen aircraft carrier battle groups. It would be absolutely stupid for them to do so. Hence, they are focused on using the strategies adopted by a weaker military power engaged in asymmetric warfare. China spends its budget on sophisticated land-based missiles that could make US aircraft carrier battle groups utterly ineffective. An aircraft carrier may cost $13 billion to build.* China's DF-26 ballistic missile, which the Chinese media claims is capable of sinking an aircraft carrier,† costs a few hundred thousand dollars. New technology is also helping China to defend itself against aircraft carriers. Professor Timothy Colton of Harvard University told me that aircraft carriers become "sitting ducks" when they face the threat of hypersonic missiles, which are maneuverable and fly at tremendous speed, at varying altitudes.

This strategy of asymmetric warfare was actually forced upon Chinese policymakers by an American maneuver. Robert Ross documents how a crisis emerged in the Taiwan Straits in 1996: "During the ten months following [then president] Lee [Teng-hui]'s visit to Cornell, the United States and China reopened their difficult negotiations over U.S. policy toward Taiwan. The negotiations reached a climax in March 1996, when China displayed a dramatic show of force consisting of military exercises and missile tests targeted near Taiwan, and the United States responded with an equally dramatic deployment of two carrier battle groups."‡ President Bill Clinton sent two aircraft carriers to the mouth of the Taiwan Straits and threatened to send them through the

---

* Zachary Cohen, "US Navy's Most Expensive Warship Just Got Even Pricier," CNN, May 15, 2018, https://edition.cnn.com/2018/05/15/politics/uss-gerald-ford-aircraft-carrier-cost-increase/index.html.

† David Axe, "Report: China Tests DF-26 'Carrier-Killer' Missile (Should the Navy Be Worried?)," *The National Interest*, January 30, 2019, https://nationalinterest.org/blog/buzz/report-china-tests-df-26-carrier-killer-missile-should-navy-be-worried-42827; http://www.globaltimes.cn/content/1137152.shtml.

‡ Robert S. Ross, "The 1995–96 Taiwan Strait Confrontation: Coercion, Credibility, and the Use of Force," *International Security* 25, no. 2 (Fall 2000): 87–123.

Straits. This made the Chinese aware that they were defenseless against American aircraft carrier battle groups. There was only one rational response for China to make: develop the capabilities to ensure that America couldn't possibly make this threat again. Today, any American president would think twice before deciding to send aircraft carriers down the Taiwan Straits. For the Chinese military, they would appear as easy targets. The US military uses the term Anti-Access Area Denial (A2AD) to describe this Chinese strategy as being offensive. By protesting against it, they are conceding that it is effective.

The height of Chinese defense rationality is shown in their decision not to increase their stockpile of nuclear weapons. America has 6,450; China has 280. However, if 280 is enough to deter America (or Russia) from launching a nuclear strike on China, why pay for more? It was very wise of President Obama to organize four nuclear security summits and two Nuclear Non-proliferation Treaty (NPT) review conferences[*] to talk about reductions in nuclear weapons. But though he could talk about them, he didn't have the power to reduce the number of America's nuclear weapons to a rational level. Chinese leaders have that power and have wisely exercised it.

It would also be rational for the United States to reduce its involvement in costly, painful, and unnecessary conflicts. The Soviet Union was dragged down by its involvement in Afghanistan and its support of Vietnam's invasion of Cambodia in the 1980s. America was not directly involved on the ground in any major conflict then (after the Vietnam War), although it supported a lot of covert operations against Soviet proxies. This was a wise strategy.

Today, America is doing the opposite. America, not the Soviet Union, is bogged down in Afghanistan. It has spent trillions of dollars and is

---

[*] Alicia Sanders-Zakre, "Timeline: Arms Control Milestones During the Obama Administration," Arms Control Association, December 2016, https://www.armscontrol.org/ACT/2016_12/Features/Timeline/Arms-Control-Milestones-During-the-Obama-Administration.

staring at complete failure of its intervention in Afghanistan. American intervention in 2001 was justified when Osama bin Laden used Afghanistan as the base for launching the 9/11 attack on America. Virtually the whole world, including China and Russia, supported this intervention. However, if America had been supple, flexible, and rational, it would have mounted a surgical operation to remove all Al-Qaeda operatives from Afghanistan and then withdrawn. More damagingly, America didn't pursue any realistic diplomatic option to resolve the Afghan conflict.

The invasion of Iraq in 2003 was completely unjustified, either in terms of international law or of a rational calculation of America's national interests. Here, too, trillions of dollars were lost.

If America was well managed by a sharp and insightful strategic thinking class, one logical consequence of the end of the Cold War should have been a sharp reduction of American involvement in external conflicts since American involvement in many of these conflicts was a result of the geopolitical chess match against the Soviet Union. When the Soviet Union collapsed, America had won handsomely. The United States should have seized the rewards of this phenomenal victory and pulled back from its interventions in foreign conflicts. What is truly shocking is that the exact opposite happened.

John Mearsheimer has described this well in his book *The Great Delusion*:

> With the end of the Cold War in 1989 and the collapse of the Soviet Union in 1991, the United States emerged as by far the most powerful country on the planet. Unsurprisingly, the Clinton administration embraced liberal hegemony from the start, and the policy remained firmly intact through the Bush and Obama administrations. Not surprisingly, the United States has been involved in numerous wars during this period and has failed to achieve meaningful success in almost all of those conflicts. Washington has also played a central role in destabilizing the greater Middle East, to the great detriment of the

people living there. Liberal Britain, which has acted as Washington's faithful sidekick in these wars, also bears some share of the blame for the trouble the United States has helped cause. American policymakers also played the key role in producing a major crisis with Russia over Ukraine. At this writing, that crisis shows no signs of abating and is hardly in America's interest, let alone Ukraine's.[*]

The Congressional Research Service, an independent body, produced a study entitled "Instances of Use of United States Armed Forces Abroad, 1798–2018." If America had been well served by the world's largest strategic thinking establishment, this study should have shown a reduction in American interventions after 1989. This study demonstrates that in the 190 years preceding the end of the Cold War, American troops were deployed a total of 216 times, or 1.1 times per year on average. However, in the twenty-five years after the end of the Cold war, America increased its military interventions sharply and used its armed forces 152 times, or 6.1 times per year.[†]

Who made this decision? Was it a result of a comprehensive evaluation of America's global strategic priorities (as China would have done if it were in the same shoes)? Or was it a result of sheer groupthink? All the evidence suggests that it is the latter. Moreover, it's clear that the American voters do not sanction this level of aggressive entanglement abroad; many of the missions are not defined as wars, legally, and congressional oversight over the decisions to deploy troops has diminished such that presidents barely pay lip service to letting Congress debate them.

What makes this tendency toward groupthink in America truly shocking is that no country has as many well-funded strategic think

---

[*] John J. Mearsheimer, *The Great Delusion: Liberal Dreams and International Realities* (New Haven, CT: Yale University Press, 2018), 153.

[†] Congressional Research Service, *Instances of Use of United States Armed Forces Abroad, 1798–2018*, CRS report, updated December 28, 2018, https://crsreports.congress.gov /product/pdf/R/R42738/23.

tanks as America does. Indeed, no country spends as much money as America does on think tanks. The result should have been more thinking. Instead, there has been less thinking. Clearly, the role and responsibility of these strategic think tanks ought to be to exercise strategic vigilance and advise the American body politic if they believe that America is not paying attention to the emerging strategic challenges. The think tanks are highly competitive with one another. There is a full spectrum of views, from the left to the right, represented within them. The total number of Americans involved in the strategic thinking industry is enormous. The number is not confined to those working in the think tanks. Many of them also work in a huge national security apparatus, including the NSC, CIA, FBI, NSA, and so on. All these people are part of one ecosystem, as they often flow in and out of government, as administrations change in Washington, DC. Clearly, America has the largest strategic thinking industry in the world. This strategic thinking industry is in turn part of the freest society on planet earth, which rewards both bold independent views and dissent from conventional views. In theory, no society is more immune to groupthink than America is.

But groupthink has taken over Washington's approach to China. While China was rising slowly and steadily, especially in the three decades after the end of the Cold War, the American strategic establishment remained distracted and, indeed mired, in various unnecessary military interventions that served China's strategic purpose by keeping America distracted.

One scholar who has tried to understand the deeper roots from which this groupthink originates is Professor Stephen Walt of Harvard University. In his book *The Hell of Good Intentions*, Walt describes in detail how an industry has developed in Washington, DC, that profits from greater American intervention overseas and suffers losses when interventions reduce. To use a colorful Chinese expression, the "rice bowls" of the members of this industry would break if America stops intervening. This is how Walt describes the symbiotic relationship between the strategic think tanks and the lobbies of the defense industries:

> The days when a public servant such as George Marshall would decline opportunities to profit from public service are long gone. Today, a successful career in Washington—and sometimes even a badly tarnished one—can pave the way to a lucrative career in the private sector, provided one does not stray outside the "respectable" consensus.*

Walt adds the following observation:

> Threat inflation also prevails because individuals and groups with an interest in exaggerating threats are more numerous and better funded than those who seek to debunk them, and they often enjoy greater political prestige. The entire military-industrial complex has obvious incentives to overstate foreign dangers in order to persuade the body politic to give it additional resources. Hawkish think tanks get generous support from defense contractors and individuals; by comparison, groups offering less frightening appraisals are generally less well-funded and less influential.†

Many members of this large and varied strategic thinking class resent this claim. Yet, there were several instances when this groupthink clearly surfaced. The first and most obvious time was in the buildup to the Iraq War in 2003. Many leading minds in countries friendly to America, including Brazil, Egypt, France, and Germany, warned stridently that the war would be both illegal and disastrous. These warnings proved to be completely right.

---

* Stephen M. Walt, *The Hell of Good Intentions: America's Foreign Policy Elite and the Decline of U.S. Primacy* (New York: Farrar, Straus and Giroux, 2018), 109.
† Ibid., 161.

As a result of this groupthink, America spent almost a trillion dollars[*] and achieved nothing except to undermine its friends in the Gulf by enhancing Iran's influence in the region. Most importantly, China's economy grew most spectacularly in the ten years after the invasion of Iraq. The Iraq War was undoubtedly a huge strategic gift to China.

Having been burnt in Iraq and Afghanistan, the logical response of America, if it were supple, flexible, and rational, would be to walk away from getting involved in unnecessary conflicts in the Islamic world. The inability to make this U-turn demonstrates that, like the old Soviet Union, America has become rigid, inflexible, and doctrinaire. Quite amazingly, the major strategic minds inside the administration and outside continue to support American military intervention in various Islamic countries, including Libya, Syria, Yemen, Somalia, and so on.

If George Kennan were alive today, he would clearly see that America has been deeply wounded, internally and externally, by its involvements in unnecessary conflicts in the Islamic world. If the strategic priority for America is to focus on China, it should logically and rationally decide to walk away from most, if not all, its involvements in the Islamic world. The biggest geopolitical advantage America has is that it is physically far away from the Islamic world. Both the Atlantic and Pacific Oceans separate America from both ends of the Islamic arc, from Morocco to Indonesia.

One of the most important drivers of twenty-first-century human history will be the monumental struggle within this vast Islamic world, with over 1.3 billion people, to come to terms with the new modern world. There will be many ups and downs. The many countries of the world that are geographical neighbors of Islamic countries have learned how to handle and work with their Islamic neighbors carefully and

---

* Neta C. Crawford, "Costs of War," Watson Institute: International & Public Affairs, Brown University, November 14, 2018, https://watson.brown.edu/costsofwar/files /cow/imce/papers/2018/Crawford_Costs%20of%20War%20Estimates%20Through %20FY2019.pdf.

sensitively. For example, Australia handles Indonesia carefully and delicately. Thailand understands and appreciates Malaysia's sensitivities. America has not developed any such sensitivity. America is the only major world power that can afford to detach itself from this existential struggle of the Islamic world. Instead, unwisely, America has decided to meddle, directly or indirectly, in many Islamic conflicts. It is always unwise to put one's fingers into a hornet's nest. One always gets stung. It would therefore be wiser for America to completely disengage from the Islamic world. Amazingly, no major figure in America advocates this common-sensical move, although it has been wise for George Soros and Charles Koch to set up the Quincy Institute for Responsible Statecraft in 2019 with the goal of "lay[ing] the foundation for a new foreign policy centered on diplomatic engagement and military restraint."*

In the past, one strategic rationale for America's continued involvement in the Middle East, especially in the Gulf, is that it needed oil from the Arabs. Now, America exports oil. Hence, by spending millions of dollars daily to station American forces in the Gulf, the only country America is helping is China, as it is protecting oil supplies to China. Since America has no strategic gains and only strategic losses from its continued deep involvement in the Middle East, we should be seeing today the emergence of a strong consensus in Washington, DC, that the time has come for America to pull back from the Middle East.

Curiously, despite having the largest strategic thinking industry in the world, the opposite is happening. Two presidents who could not be more different are Barack Obama and Donald Trump. They agree on virtually nothing. Yet, both could see that any American involvement in Syria was pointless. Both tried to cut down America's involvements in Syria. Both should have been praised for their strategic common sense. Instead, both were vilified.

---

* Quincy Institute for Responsible Statecraft, https://quincyinst.org/.

When Obama famously decided not to bomb Syria after an alleged chemical attack in August 2013,[*] the strategic thinking class almost unanimously condemned Obama for not doing so because Obama had said that any use of chemical weapons would cross a "red line." Yet, none of these voices explained what a bombing would have achieved. Would it have removed Assad? Probably not. And if Assad had been removed, would the Syrian people have been better off or would they have suffered even greater loss of life, as the Iraqis and Libyans did after earlier Western interventions? What American national interests would have been enhanced by bombing Syria? Most importantly, given the wise advice of one of America's Founding Fathers that America should show a "decent respect for the opinion of mankind," did any leading members of this strategic thinking class notice that a vast majority of the countries of the world would have disapproved of a unilateral act of bombing?

A good indication of global sentiments toward thoughtless American interventions has been provided by a former Indian diplomat, Shyam Saran, who wrote this about Western intervention:

> In most cases, the post-intervention situation has been rendered much worse, the violence more lethal, and the suffering of the people who were supposed to be protected much more severe than before. Iraq is an earlier instance; Libya and Syria are the more recent ones. A similar story is playing itself out in Ukraine. In each case, no careful thought was given to the possible consequences of the intervention.[†]

On December 19, 2018, President Donald Trump announced that he would withdraw American troops from Syria. He should have been

---

[*] Ben Rhodes, "Inside the White House During the Syrian 'Red Line' Crisis," *The Atlantic*, June 3, 2018, https://www.theatlantic.com/international/archive/2018/06/inside-the-white-house-during-the-syrian-red-line-crisis/561887/.

[†] Shyam Saran, "The Morning-After Principle," *Business Standard* (New Delhi), June 10, 2014, http://www.business-standard.com/article/opinion/shyam-saran-the-morning-after-principle114061001300_1.html.

praised for his strategic common sense. Instead, he was attacked. One typical comment came from Charles Lister, senior fellow at the Middle East Institute, who said: "Next time the U.S. needs to challenge an imminent terror threat somewhere in the world, we'll presumably want to do so 'by, with & through,' using local partners. You think they're going to trust us now? Not a chance."*

When Lister criticized Donald Trump for abandoning the fight against ISIS forces in Syria, I wonder if he was aware that the entry of these ISIS fighters into Syria from Afghanistan, which America was supposed to be fighting, had been encouraged and facilitated by the Obama administration.[†]

When the archives are opened, future historians will confirm whether American forces were transporting ISIS fighters into Syria or fighting ISIS forces in Syria. Neither activity serves any real national interest of America. Many of my friends outside America are truly puzzled that even though no real American interests are served by America's involvement in such conflicts, there is a remarkably sharp consensus in the strategic thinking industry that America should continue to get its fingers stung in the Islamic world.

One scholar who has tried to provide some intellectual justification for America's involvement in military conflicts is Robert Kagan. He argues that the world would descend into chaos if America withdrew. His book title, *The Jungle Grows Back*, says it all. If America withdraws from the world, the world can only regress back toward becoming a jungle, dominated by primitive savagery and chaos. This is what Kagan says:

---

* Natasha Turak, "Trump Risks 'Damaging America's Reputation for the Long Term' with Syria Withdrawal, Experts Warn," CNBC, December 22, 2018, https://www.cnbc .com/2018/12/22/trump-may-be-damaging-us-credibility-with-syria-withdrawal -experts.html.
† Kishore Mahbubani, *Has the West Lost It?: A Provocation* (London: Penguin, 2018), 55–56.

What we liberals call progress has been made possible by the protection afforded liberalism within the geographical and geopolitical
space created by American power. [...] The question is not what will
bring down the liberal order but what can possibly hold it up? If the
liberal order is like a garden, artificial and forever threatened by the
forces of nature, preserving it requires a persistent, unending struggle
against the vines and weeds that are constantly working to undermine
it from within and overwhelm it from without.[*]

This book was well received. It got many positive reviews in America. Zachary Karabell wrote in the *New York Times*: "Kagan may well
overstate the role the United States can and should play going forward,
but he powerfully underscores just how tenuous the world order is and
always has been."[†] Yet none of the reviewers stated the most obvious
point about this book: it was an insult to the seven billion people who
live outside America. Kagan, in his inability to envision a civilized world
without American leadership, reveals the deeply troubling implication
of his thesis: that America is the only truly civilized society on earth—
the ineluctable bearer of a twenty-first-century "white man's burden." In
short, if America retreats, the world descends into savagery and chaos.

Will it? Fortunately, we can provide an empirical answer to this
question. Several scholars have documented at great length how
the world has never been so civilized. In *Enlightenment Now*, Steven
Pinker provides overwhelming evidence to show how the world has
progressed and become a far more civilized place than it has ever been.
As Pinker claims: "The world has made spectacular progress in every

---

[*] Robert Kagan, *The Jungle Grows Back: America and Our Imperiled World* (New York:
Alfred A. Knopf, 2018), 9–10.
[†] Zachary Karabell, "What Is America's Role in the World? Three Authors Offer Very
Different Views," *New York Times*, November 16, 2018, https://www.nytimes.com
/2018/11/16/books/review/robert-kagan-jungle-grows-back.html.

single measure of human well-being."* The subsequent chapters of his book document how the world has progressed in a stunning number of dimensions: in the increase of life expectancy, gross world product, and GDP per capita and social spending, in the spread of democracy and human rights, and in the decline of child and maternal mortality, childhood stunting, undernourishment, extreme poverty, global inequality and deaths from infectious disease, natural disasters, famine, war, and genocide—just to name a few.

Similarly, Yuval Noah Harari has also documented how the world has become more civilized. He writes:

> The last 500 years have witnessed a breathtaking series of revolutions. The earth has been united into a single ecological and historical sphere. The economy has grown exponentially, and humankind today enjoys the kind of wealth that used to be the stuff of fairy tales. Science and the Industrial Revolution have given humankind superhuman powers and practically limitless energy. The social order has been completely transformed, as have politics, daily life and human psychology.
>
> Today humankind has broken the law of the jungle. There is at last real peace, and not just absence of war. For most polities, there is no plausible scenario leading to full-scale conflict within one year. What could lead to war between Germany and France next year? Or between China and Japan? Or between Brazil and Argentina? Some minor border clash might occur, but only a truly apocalyptic scenario could result in an old-fashioned full-scale war between Brazil and Argentina in 2014, with Argentinian armoured divisions sweeping to the gates of Rio, and Brazilian carpet-bombers pulverising the neighbourhoods of Buenos Aires. Such wars might still erupt between several pairs of states, e.g. between Israel and Syria, Ethiopia and Eritrea,

---

* Steven Pinker, *Enlightenment Now: The Case for Reason, Science, Humanism, and Progress* (New York: Viking, 2018), 52.

or the USA and Iran, but these are only the exceptions that prove the rule. This situation might of course change in the future and, with hindsight, the world of today might seem incredibly naïve. Yet from a historical perspective, our very naïvety is fascinating. Never before has peace been so prevalent that people could not even imagine war.

Kagan should note the first sentence of the second paragraph: "Today humankind has broken the law of the jungle."

In one part of the world the real tropical jungle grows back quickly and fiercely. That region is Southeast Asia. This is also the best part of the world to test the proposition that the world becomes uncivilized when America stops bombing. America dropped more bombs on Southeast Asia during the Vietnam War than it did in Europe during the entire period of World War II. This how the BBC describes it: "President Obama described Laos as the most heavily bombed nation in history. Eight bombs a minute were dropped on average during the Vietnam War between 1964 and 1973—more than the amount used during the whole of World War Two. The US flew 580,344 bombing missions over Laos, dropping 260m bombs—equating to 2m tons of ordnance, with many targets in the south and north struck time and again as part of efforts to isolate Communist North Vietnamese forces."[*]

Most Americans know that the American military retreated ignominiously from Southeast Asia when its officials had to be helicoptered out of the American embassy in Saigon. After this spectacular American withdrawal and the complete cessation of American bombing, Southeast Asia should have descended into chaos. Instead, as my coauthor Jeffery Sng and I have documented in *The ASEAN Miracle*, Southeast Asia has done spectacularly well since 1975. The reasons are obviously complex. However, one key reason was that the Southeast Asians woke

---

[*] "Laos: Barack Obama Regrets 'Biggests Bombing in History,'" BBC News, September 7, 2016, https://www.bbc.com/news/world-asia-37286520.

up to realize that their own destiny would be forged by their own decisions. Southeast Asia has long been described as the Balkans of Asia. It would not have been surprising to see conflict erupt after the American withdrawal. Instead, the region became, in every sense of the word, a beacon of peace and prosperity.

The presumption underlying Kagan's book is completely wrong. Over the past few decades, the world has not been retreating into a jungle. Instead, as documented by Steven Pinker and Yuval Noah Harari, the world has never been more civilized. Consequently, if America were supple, flexible, and rational, it should take full advantage of this positive new global environment and make a U-turn away from using its military as its primary weapon in all of its external involvements. Instead of using expensive weapons systems, America should resort to old-fashioned diplomacy. Diplomacy is also much cheaper than military options.

Why diplomacy? The spectacular success of Southeast Asia after the spectacular military failure and withdrawal of America from the region should have taught American strategic thinkers a valuable lesson: sometimes the tools of diplomacy can be more effective than the most powerful military force in the world. When I served as Singapore's ambassador to the UN from 1984 to 1989, I worked closely with American diplomats to successfully gather support for ASEAN's diplomatic campaigns to reverse the Soviet-supported Vietnamese occupation of Cambodia.

This global diplomatic campaign to isolate Vietnam was a spectacular success. Vietnam withdrew from Cambodia in 1989 when the end of the Cold War and the collapse of the Soviet Union made Vietnamese occupation untenable. Since Vietnam and the ASEAN countries had been at loggerheads for over a decade following the Vietnamese invasion of Cambodia in December 1978, what should have followed, logically speaking, were decades of bitterness and hostility, akin to the bitterness and hostility between America and Iran following the Iran hostage crisis of 1979. Instead, Vietnam joined ASEAN in 1995, barely six years after withdrawing from Cambodia. It's hard to find a better example of diplomatic reconciliation in human history.

Unfortunately, even though the spectacular diplomatic success in Southeast Asia after the ignominious American withdrawal should have taught America the value of good diplomacy, there are structural reasons why America cannot focus more on diplomacy. To practice good diplomacy, you need good diplomats. To get good diplomats, you need to promise a good diplomatic career to young American diplomats, with the prospect of "the best and the brightest" diplomats being rewarded with ambassadorial postings to key capitals of the world, including Beijing and Tokyo, London and Paris, Berlin and Brussels. Instead, probably the best ambassadorial posting that a bright young American diplomat can aspire to achieve is to Bamako, the capital of Mali.

Why is this so? American ambassadorships are now for sale. The most desirable postings go to donors of presidential campaigns. Curiously, even a president like Barack Obama, who should have known better, gave out a record number of American ambassadorships to rich donors. According to the American Foreign Service Association (AFSA) in 2014, "in his second term so far, Obama has named a record number of political appointees, more than half, as compared to other recent presidents, who tend to name donors and friends to about one-third of the ambassadorial posts."* Undoubtedly, some of these donors were effective, as Jon Huntsman proved in China. However, since American presidential candidates have to raise a lot of money and since generous donors now expect to be rewarded with plum ambassadorial posts, it is virtually impossible for America to now develop a professional diplomat corps that can match what the Chinese have built. To make matters worse, even though the budget of the State Department

---

* Michele Kelemen, "More Ambassador Posts Are Going to Political Appointees," *All Things Considered*, NPR, February 13, 2014, https://www.npr.org/2014/02/12/275897092/more-ambassador-posts-are-going-to-political-appointees.

($31.5 billion) is truly miniscule compared to that of the Defense Department ($626 billion),* many American politicians are trying to squeeze it. Fareed Zakaria describes the danger of this approach:

> Since the Cold War, Congress has tended to fatten the Pentagon while starving foreign policy agencies. As former defense secretary Robert Gates pointed out, there are more members of military marching bands than make up the entire U.S. foreign service. Anyone who has ever watched American foreign policy on the ground has seen this imbalance play out. Top State Department officials seeking to negotiate vital matters arrive without aides and bedraggled after a 14-hour flight in coach. Their military counterparts whisk in on a fleet of planes, with dozens of aides and pots of money to dispense. The late Richard Holbrooke would laugh when media accounts described him as the "civilian counterpart" to Gen. David Petraeus, then head of U.S. Central Command. "He has many more planes than I have cellphones," Holbrooke would say (and he had many cellphones).†

In his brief and disastrous stint as secretary of state, Rex Tillerson tried to reduce the expenses of the State Department. This is how the *Chicago Tribune* described his work: "Most of the United States' special envoys will be abolished and their responsibilities reassigned as part of the State Department overhaul, Secretary of State Rex Tillerson told Congress on Monday, including envoys for climate change and the Iran deal. Special envoys for Afghanistan-Pakistan, disability rights and closing the Guantanamo Bay detention center will be eliminated under the plan. [. . .] Of 66 current envoys or representatives, 30 will

---

* These are 2017 figures. See Table 5.2—Budget Authority by Agency: 1976–2024, Historical Tables, Office of Management and Budget, White House, https://www.whitehouse.gov/omb/historical-tables/.

† Fareed Zakaria, "Why Defense Spending Should Be Cut," *Washington Post*, August 3, 2011, https://www.washingtonpost.com/opinions/why-defense-spending-should-be-cut/2011/08/03/gIQAsRuqsI_story.html?noredirect=on&utm_term=.17e7a8ac3d8b.

remain, a cut of 55 percent. Nine positions will be abolished outright. [...] A roughly one-third budget cut and elimination of thousands of jobs are expected."* After Tillerson left, things initially improved under Pompeo. However, this improvement was temporary. By October 2019, one of America's most seasoned diplomats, William J. Burns, observed the following: "In my three and a half decades as a U.S. Foreign Service officer, proudly serving five presidents and ten secretaries of state from both parties, I've never seen an attack on diplomacy as damaging, to both the State Department as an institution and our international influence, as the one now underway." He was referring to the "contemptible mistreatment of Marie Yovanovitch—the ambassador to Ukraine who was dismissed for getting in the way of the president's scheme to solicit foreign interference in U.S. elections."† It's hard to believe that America's diplomats will not be demoralized by such developments.

If the outcome of the rising geopolitical competition between America and China is not likely to be resolved in the military arena and is more likely to take place in the diplomatic arena, it is completely illogical for America to strengthen its military while weakening its diplomatic options. Yet this is exactly what is happening. And it will continue to happen because it is structurally impossible for America to make U-turns in areas where deep structures support vested interests.

Future historians will probably record accurately that one of the most disastrous decisions America made after the end of the Cold War was to walk away from diplomacy. Here, too, there is a simple structural reason to explain why America did so. At the end of the day, diplomacy is always about give and take and to make sensible compromises. At the end of the Cold War, America emerged as the sole superpower and

* Josh Lederman, "Tillerson to Cut More Than Half of State Department's Special Envoys," *Chicago Tribune*, August 28, 2017, https://www.chicagotribune.com/news /nationworld/politics/ct-tillerson-state-department-special-envoys-cuts-20170828 -story.html.
† William J. Burns, "The Demolition of U.S. Diplomacy," *Foreign Affairs*, October 14, 2019.

enjoyed the benefits of a brief unipolar moment in world history. As the sole superpower, America could always have its way. Unfortunately, it lost the art of making compromises with the rest of the world.

In the late 1980s, as America became more self-confident, after the emergence of Gorbachev, I was asked, as Singapore's ambassador to the UN, to chair negotiations on a document to help the poor African nations as part of the UN Program of Action for African Economic Recovery and Development (UNPAAERD). The negotiations took the normal course. Countries stated their opening positions. As usual, there were significant gaps between the positions of the donor countries, including America and the European Union, and the recipient countries, the African countries. Finally, after weeks of negotiations, with a lot of give and take (with the poor African countries making more concessions than the donors, as they had no choice), we agreed on a compromise text. On the last day, just before we were about to adopt this compromise text, the American delegation raised its hands to say that they had received fresh instructions from the US Treasury, which had suddenly discovered problems with some language in the painfully negotiated compromise text. Quite understandably, all the other countries in the room exploded in anger. However, it did not matter. America was so powerful that it could ignore the sentiments of the rest of the world.

This episode typifies another structural problem with American diplomacy. Most diplomats from most countries receive one set of instructions from their capitals. Hence, they spend most of their time negotiating with other countries. American diplomats do the opposite. They spend almost 90 percent of their time negotiating with several agencies in Washington, DC, to receive a reasonable and coherent set of instructions. After painfully negotiating with several Washington, DC, agencies, the American diplomats are left with positions that give them little room to compromise. Negotiations only succeed when countries have the flexibility to make compromises at the negotiating table. American diplomats are severely handicapped in this respect. Both absolute power and conflicting demands from domestic agencies leave American negotiators with little room for flexibility.

At the same time, there is some good news to report on the diplomatic front. Over time, many of the key agencies in Washington, DC, have developed good expertise in understanding the rest of the world. Ironically, this was revealed as a result of a leak, the WikiLeaks release of a trove of American diplomatic dispatches. After the leaks, Oxford historian Timothy Garton Ash wrote in the *Guardian* that "my personal opinion of the state department has gone up several notches.... [W]hat we find here is often first rate."*

Having worked with American diplomats over three decades when I was in the Singapore Foreign Service, I know from personal experience that the US State Department has had many outstanding diplomats. Some of the best diplomats I met in my career were American diplomats, including career diplomats like Tom Pickering, Chas Freeman, and John Negroponte. I could name many more. Clearly, there must have been an effective ecosystem of selecting and nurturing talent that resulted in the emergence of such outstanding professionals.

There is no doubt that this ecosystem has been damaged by the poor leadership of recent secretaries of state, including Rex Tillerson and Mike Pompeo. President Trump has also undermined many American governmental institutions as he has scant respect for them. Quite a few American diplomats have resigned in protest. However, the majority have stayed on. There is therefore hope that the State Department could be revived and become once again an effective diplomatic institution, if the right leadership emerges again.

American foreign policy would be significantly strengthened if the administration in office could learn the art of listening to American

* Timothy Garton Ash, "US Embassy Cables: A Banquet of Secrets," *Guardian* (Manchester, UK), November 28, 2010, https://www.theguardian.com/commentisfree/2010/nov/28/wikileaks-diplomacy-us-media-war.

diplomats and developing policies that are in harmony with the views and sentiments of the global population. In theory, this should be the easiest U-turn to make since all that the American government has to do is to listen to the advice of its own diplomats. Sadly, expert advice plays a very small role in American policymaking. All too often, domestic political considerations trump sensible diplomatic advice.

All this leads to a depressing conclusion. If America is going to respond effectively to the new geopolitical challenge from China, it needs to make some massive U-turns, including cutting down its military expenditures, withdrawing from all military interventions in the Islamic world, and stepping up its diplomatic capabilities. Yet, powerful vested interests in America will make it impossible for America to make any of these sensible U-turns.

I began this chapter with a painful comparison between America of today and the Soviet Union of yesterday. I conclude it with an even more painful comparison. Historians will probably continue debating for decades, if not centuries, on why the mighty Soviet Union, once the second-most powerful country in the world, collapsed so suddenly and spectacularly.

Many reasons can be cited and have been cited. However, there was probably one key factor that has not been fully discussed: the Soviet Union failed because none of the leaders could even conceive of the possibility of the Soviet Union failing.

There is no danger of America collapsing like the former Soviet Union. America is a much stronger country, blessed with great people, institutions, and many natural advantages. However, while America will not totally collapse, it can become greatly diminished, a shadow of itself. Any moderately realistic analyst can work out a scenario for how this could happen. Yet, many Americans are blind to such an outcome. History teaches us failure can happen if one cannot think of failing.

The sad truth is that even though many Americans have become seized by the new challenge posed by China, they cannot take the next logical step and think about how America might fail. The majority believe that America will win, no matter what happens, because it deserves to. This strong conviction that success is inevitable rests on five key assumptions.

First, America will inevitably win the geostrategic competition against China, just as it eventually won against Germany and Japan in World War II and against the Soviet Union in the Cold War. In short, the idea of America losing a struggle is inconceivable. Second, China's political and economic system is unsustainable and will collapse because all communist governments eventually fail while all democracies eventually succeed. Third, America has abundant resources and need not make any fundamental strategic adjustments or sacrifices in the competition with China. Fourth, America has a fundamentally just and well-ordered society, resting on the wise American Constitution and the rule of law, and hence, no fundamental restructuring of American society is needed in the coming contest with China. Fifth, given a choice between partnering with the beacon of freedom, the shining city on the hill (which is America), or with a Communist Party dictatorship, the majority of humanity will naturally gravitate toward partnering with America.

If Americans want to think realistically about a future in which they could become number two, they could begin by questioning all these assumptions. Indeed, it is possible that all five assumptions could prove to be false. Let's review each of them.

First, American confidence that it will defeat communist China as easily as it defeated Germany, Japan, and the Soviet Union rests on the flawed assumption that the challenges are of the same scale. Actually, America's population and resources were always superior to those of its previous adversaries. China's population is four times larger. More importantly, China's civilization is the oldest continuous civilization on the planet. America is not competing with an anachronistic Communist Party. It is competing with one of the world's oldest and strongest civilizations. And when strong and resilient civilizations bounce back, they do so with great civilizational energy and force.

Second, and related to the first point, America, unlike its competition with the Soviet Union, is not competing with the Chinese *Communist* Party (CCP). The goals of the Chinese leaders are not to promote communism globally. Instead, the Chinese leaders are focused on reviving and rejuvenating Chinese civilization. To achieve this goal of making the Chinese civilization once again one of the strongest civilizations, the leaders have recruited the best minds in China to work in the CCP. A small analogy might help to explain this critical point. When America competed with the Soviet Union, it was like Harvard University (USA) competing with an underfunded community college (USSR). However, the competition between America and China could well be characterized as that between Harvard University (China) and a midlevel state-funded university (USA). The quality of mind of Chinese policymakers today is quite amazing. Many Americans have not noticed it yet.

Third, on a per capita basis, America has far more resources than China does. However, unlike geopolitical contests in the past, future geopolitical contests will not be determined by physical resources. They will be determined by intellectual resources, especially resources resulting from investment in research and development (R&D). America's R&D budget has peaked and will decline. China's R&D budget will continue to climb. Please see Chart 4.

The president of Massachusetts Institute of Technology (MIT), Dr. L. Rafael Reif, has observed that "China has unrivaled capacity to rapidly ramp up large-scale production of advanced technology products and quickly bring innovation to market." He added, "Unless America responds urgently and deliberately to the scale and intensity of this challenge, we should expect that, in fields from personal communications to business, health and security, China is likely to become the world's most advanced technological nation and the source of the most

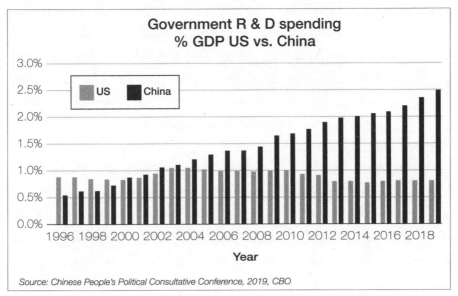

CHART 4. Government R&D Spending: Percent of GDP, United States versus China (Designed by Patti Issacs)

cutting-edge technological products in not much more than a decade."[*] If America wants its R&D budget to keep pace with that of China (which will have a bigger economy than America's within a decade or so), America will have to make some sacrifices. It will have to cut some items from its budget. Yet, as this chapter has documented, America will be unable to do so because the lobbies in Washington, DC, are deeply entrenched and cannot be overcome. Logic and common sense cannot defeat the influence of money in American politics.

Fourth, and related to the third point, America no longer has an exemplary just and well-ordered society. If John Rawls, or any Western moral philosopher of his ilk, were to examine it today, he would clearly see that America has effectively become a class-stratified society, not the middle-class society that America's Founding Fathers had worked to create as a reaction to the feudalism that the settlers had left behind in

---

[*] L. Rafael Reif, "China's Challenge Is America's Opportunity," *New York Times*, August 8, 2018, https://www.nytimes.com/2018/08/08/opinion/china-technology-trade-united -states.html.

Europe. Indeed, if the Founding Fathers were to come alive today, they would be shocked at how much real political and economic power has been seized by the American ruling elite and how little real political power has been left for the rest. The regular presidential and congressional elections don't really take away the effective power of the ruling elites. They only create the illusion that the people are in charge of their destiny; in reality, they are not.

Fifth, there was a point of time, especially from the 1950s to the 1980s, when American society seemed to outperform every other society on earth. America was then clearly a shining city on the hill. Since the end of the Cold War, America has lost both its strategic discipline and its material and moral capacity to inspire the rest of humanity.

In short, American confidence in the belief that it can never become number two rests on five flawed assumptions. The United States must revisit its confidence and consider the serious possibility of becoming the number two power. One way of understanding this possibility is to trigger a public discussion in America on how the world would look to America if and when it becomes the number two power. However, for this debate to begin, a brave American politician will have to propose it. It would of course be political suicide. Sadly, despite its traditions of encouraging open debate, in this area, America will not be broad-minded enough to tolerate an open discussion of what happens when America becomes number two. Even in the area of opening up a new subject for public discussion, America cannot make a U-turn.

CHAPTER 6

SHOULD CHINA BECOME DEMOCRATIC?

A SMALL LOOSE ROCK CAN TRIGGER AN AVALANCHE. THIS IS what happened when the National People's Congress passed the constitutional amendment to remove term limits for the office of the presidency on March 11, 2018. A wave of criticism from the Western media was heaped on Xi Jinping. *The Economist* wrote: "The decision announced on February 25th to scrap term limits for China's president, Xi Jinping, pierces the veil of Chinese politics. It reveals that, at a time when the ruling Communist Party is presenting China to the world as a modern, reliable and responsible state, capable of defending globalization, the internal political system that the party monopolizes is premodern, treacherous, inward-looking and brutal."* Meanwhile, *Time* likened this move as a return to Maoist authoritarianism: "China's return to strongman politics dredges up dark memories of the nation's tribulations under Mao Zedong, whose ill-fated Great Leap Forward

---

* "China's Leader, Xi Jinping, Will Be Allowed to Reign Forever," *The Economist*, February 26, 2018, https://www.economist.com/china/2018/02/26/chinas-leader-xi-jinping -will-be-allowed-to-reign-forever.

and Cultural Revolution cost tens of millions of lives. With reverence for Xi a necessary condition for career advancement, there's very little incentive to voice differing opinions, with the lack of vigorous policy debate a real worry for continued good governance. Today, this has possibly calamitous consequences far from China's borders given the world's number two economy remains the single largest contributor to global GDP growth."[*]

Significantly, many thoughtful and well-informed American observers of China also felt a deep sense of betrayal. Orville Schell said: "In my lifetime I did not imagine I would see the day when China regressed back closer to its Maoist roots. I am fearing that now."[†] David Shambaugh has written that "Xi's actions and the clear concentration of power in himself reveal a return to the patriarchal mode of strongman politics that was characteristic of the Mao era. While many in China recall the horrors of the Mao era, Xi has many times spoken wistfully of that period. Thus, as China has now fully moved into the 21st century as a global power, internally it has substantially regressed to an antiquated political system of 50 years ago."[‡]

There's no doubt that even well-informed observers of China, like Schell and Shambaugh, bought into the assumption held by many key members of America's foreign policy elite that continued engagement of China by America would lead to American values seeping into China and that China would gradually open up its political system and join the Western liberal mainstream. One honest policymaker who made

[*] Charlie Campbell, "'More Opposition in Mao's Time.' Why China's Xi Jinping May Have to Rule for Life," *Time*, March 12, 2018, http://time.com/5195211/china-xi-jinping-presidential-term-limits-npc/.

[†] James Fallows, "China's Great Leap Backward," *The Atlantic*, December 2016, https://www.theatlantic.com/magazine/archive/2016/12/chinas-great-leap-backward/505817/.

[‡] David Shambaugh, "Under Xi Jinping, a Return in China to the Dangers of an All-Powerful Leader," *South China Morning Post*, March 1, 2018, https://beta.scmp.com/comment/insight-opinion/article/2135208/under-xi-jinping-return-china-dangers-all-powerful-leader.

it clear that these were expectations of America's was Kurt Campbell. In an article he coauthored with Ely Ratner in the March/April 2018 issue of *Foreign Affairs*, he wrote: "Ever since [rapprochement began under Nixon], the assumption that deepening commercial, diplomatic, and cultural ties would transform China's internal development and external behavior has been a bedrock of U.S. strategy. Even those in U.S. policy circles who were skeptical of China's intentions still shared the underlying belief that U.S. power and hegemony could readily mold China to the United States' liking."*

Why did many thoughtful Americans find it reasonable to assume that close engagement between America and China would lead to America influencing China's political evolution (rather than vice versa)? The simple but honest answer is that Americans confidently believe that democracies stand on the right side of history and communist systems stand on the wrong side. This conviction was strongly reinforced after the spectacular collapse of the Communist Party of the Soviet Union. Hillary Clinton expressed this conviction most clearly when she said that by persisting with Communist Party rule, the Chinese "are trying to stop history, which is a fool's errand. They cannot do it. But they're going to hold it off as long as possible."†

It's revealing that Hillary Clinton used the word *history*. Historians are accustomed to take a long view of human events. With this perspective, it is clear to see that the American republic has enjoyed a history of less than two hundred and fifty years since its founding in 1776. By contrast, the Chinese state has had a long continuous history, whose beginnings can be traced to the first reunification of China by Emperor Qin Shi Huang in 221 BCE. China's political culture and traditions go back almost ten times as long as America's political history. Future historians

---

* Kurt M. Campbell and Ely Ratner, "The China Reckoning: How Beijing Defied American Expectations," *Foreign Affairs*, March/April 2018.

† Edward N. Luttwak, *The Rise of China vs. the Logic of Strategy* (Cambridge, MA: Belknap Press, 2012), 233.

will undoubtedly be puzzled by the strong conviction of American policy-makers that a smaller and younger republic could decisively influence the political evolution of a state that was four times larger in population and with a history that was almost ten times longer.

The Chinese see their history through their own lenses. Over the course of the past twenty-two hundred years, China has been divided and broken up more often than it has been united and cohesive. Each time, central political control from the capital breaks down, disorder results, and the Chinese people suffer a host of deprivations, from starvation and famine to civil war and rampant violence. In Chinese political culture, the biggest fear is of chaos. The Chinese have a word for it: luàn (乱). Given these many long periods of suffering from chaos—including one as recent as the century of humiliation from the Opium War of 1842 to the creation of the People's Republic of China in 1949—when the Chinese people are given a choice between strong central control and the chaos of political competition, they have a re-flexive tendency to choose strong central control.

This long history and political culture may well explain Xi Jinping's decision to remove term limits. The conventional Western view is that he did so to reap personal rewards by becoming dictator for life. Yet, his decision may have been motivated by the view that China faced a real danger of slipping back into chaos. Two major challenges emerged that could have undermined the strong central control of the CCP. The first was the emergence of factions in the CCP led by Bo Xilai and Zhou Yongkang, two powerful members of the CCP. The second was the explosion of corruption. The rampant capitalism unleashed by Deng Xiaoping after the Four Modernizations policy in 1978 had led to massive economic growth as well as the accumulation of large personal fortunes. The temptation to use these huge fortunes to influence public policies was perfectly natural. If these twin threats of factionalism and corruption had not been effectively killed, the CCP could well have lost its legitimacy and political control. Against the backdrop of these major political challenges and the longer sweep of Chinese history, it was perfectly natural for Xi to reassert strong central control to keep China together.

George Magnus described Xi's moves: "When Xi Jinping came to power, though, he knew that the Party had to reboot and restrengthen and China had to change. Consequently, the Party has become more powerful and controlling, and China is now pulling its weight in the world as never before. By 2021, the Party will have ruled China for as long as the Soviet Communist Party ruled the former Soviet Union, and Xi's mission is to keep the Chinese Communist Party away from the liberalisation and openness that are deemed to have driven its Soviet counterpart into oblivion."[*]

It is virtually impossible to convince any Western reader that in the current national and global context, the continuation of strong CCP rule under Xi Jinping could be good for China and for the world. In the Western mind, any undemocratic political system that deprives citizens the ability to choose or remove a leader is by definition evil. This is why no major Western pundit or political figure could have challenged the political avalanche of criticism that descended upon Xi when he removed the term limits on his presidency. Yet, if contemporary Western thinkers had sought advice or guidance from previous generations of Western thinkers, they would have found good advice they could have used. One such piece of advice was provided by Max Weber. In one of his famous essays, he wrote that "it is *not* true that good can only follow from good and evil only from evil, but that often the opposite is true. Anyone who says this is, indeed, a political infant."[†]

---

* George Magnus, *Red Flags: Why Xi's China Is in Jeopardy* (New Haven, CT: Yale University Press, 2018), from introduction, digital edition.

† Max Weber, "Politics as a Vocation," in trans. and ed. H. H. Gerth and C. Wright Mills, *From Max Weber: Essays in Sociology* (New York: Oxford University Press, 1946), 77–128. Originally a speech given at Munich University, 1918. See also a discussion of Weber's essay in Kishore Mahbubani, *20 Years of Can Asians Think?* (Singapore: Marshall Cavendish, 2018), 137–138.

It can be argued that strong central control of China by the Chinese Communist Party under Xi Jinping is producing at least three "global public goods" that the world is indeed benefiting from. And if Max Weber were alive today, he would be astonished to see the absence of strong Western voices observing and documenting how the West (and the rest of the world) is benefiting from the stable and rational rule of China by the CCP.

The first global public good that the CCP is delivering is to rein in a strong nationalist dragon that is clearly alive and well within the Chinese body politic. There are many reasons for nationalism in China. Most Chinese are aware that China was badly trampled upon and humiliated during the century of humiliation after the Opium War. China's recovery today has buoyed their national pride.

Many in the West were shocked when in 2001 the Taliban destroyed the precious antique Buddhist statues in Bamiyan, which had survived fourteen centuries. Yet, those shocked Westerners, outraged by the Taliban's behavior in 2001, failed to remember or mention that barely a hundred and fifty years earlier British and French troops had behaved just like the Taliban in Beijing in 1860. Here is one account of what happened in that episode.

> As the primary residence of five Qing emperors, Yuanmingyuan contained hundreds of palaces, temples, libraries, theaters, pavilions, chapels, gazebos and galleries filled with priceless artworks, antiquities and personal possessions. To ensure an equitable distribution of this imperial property, the commanders agreed to appoint "prize agents" to divvy it up. There followed an orgy of indiscriminate plunder in which anything that could not be carted off was destroyed.
>
> Then, on Oct. 18, British forces were ordered by Lord Elgin—son of the Lord Elgin who removed the marble friezes from Greece's Parthenon—to inflict a final blow, with fire, as revenge for the deaths of British and Indian prisoners in Chinese captivity.

Because Yuanmingyuan was so vast—roughly five times the size of Beijing's Forbidden City and eight times that of Vatican City—it took an entire infantry division of nearly 4,500 men, including four British regiments and the 15th Punjabis, to set it aflame. Gilded beams crashed, porcelain roofs buckled, ash filled the lakes and embers snowed down on Beijing, where clouds of dense smoke eclipsed the sun. Upon hearing the news, the ailing 30-year-old Xianfeng emperor vomited blood; less than a year later he was dead.[*]

If China were to make a sudden transformation into a democracy, the political voices that would dominate the political landscape would not be the calm and soothing voices of democratic leaders like John F. Kennedy or Barack Obama but the angry nationalist voices, like those of Donald Trump or Teddy Roosevelt. In terms of its emergence as a great world power, China in 2020 is probably where America was as it emerged as a great world power at the end of the nineteenth century, when Teddy Roosevelt served as the secretary of the US Navy. This is why Graham Allison of Harvard has wisely warned his fellow Americans against wishing that the Chinese "would be like us."

Over the past decade or so, many American policymakers and commentators have complained vigorously about China's aggressive behavior in the South China Sea. Many of these complaints are justified. Yet, Americans should pause and ask themselves what Teddy Roosevelt would have done if he was running China's policy on the South China Sea. There's no question that he would have found it unacceptable that China, the greatest power in the region, controlled fewer rocks and reefs in the South China Sea, relative to the other claimants (see statistics cited on pages 102–103).

And what would Teddy Roosevelt have done in such a situation? He would have seized all the features in the Paracels and Spratlys for

* Sheila Melvin, "China Remembers a Vast Crime," *New York Times*, October 21, 2010, https://www.nytimes.com/2010/10/22/arts/22iht-MELVIN.html.

China. This is something that China can do effortlessly today. However, it has carefully refrained from doing so, reflecting the desire of the CCP not to upset the international order.

There is no question that if China suddenly becomes a democracy, it would emerge with a leader as interventionist and imperialistic as Teddy Roosevelt, not with a leader as restrained and noninterventionist as Xi Jinping. And why does Xi Jinping have the capacity to restrain the strong Chinese nationalist dragon prowling the Chinese body politic? He has the capacity because the CCP has developed into a politically effective vehicle for governing China. In theory, the Chinese Communist Party is the same as the Communist Party of the Soviet Union. In practice, it is the opposite. The Chinese Communist Party is not run by doddering old apparatchiks. Instead, it has become a meritocratic governance system, which chooses only the best and brightest to be promoted to the highest levels. The CCP is not perfect. No human institution is. It has made mistakes, like allowing corruption to increase significantly in the first decade of the twenty-first century. Yet, it is also a fact that relative to its peers around the world, the Chinese governing class generates more good governance (in terms of improving the well-being of its citizens) than virtually any other government today. Since the Chinese Communist Party is constantly vilified in the Western media, very few people in the West are aware that the members of this Communist Party have delivered the best governance China has ever enjoyed in its entire history.

There is one simple question that all China-watchers should ask themselves: when a team of American negotiators sit down to negotiate an issue with a team of Chinese negotiators, which team is likely to have individuals with a better quality of mind? In the past, perhaps from the 1960s to 1990s, the answer would have been the Americans. Today, it would probably be the Chinese because of the government's capacity to attract the best to serve in the party. When I was on sabbatical in Columbia University, my research assistant was an extremely bright young master's degree student from China. She spoke to me about her dreams. When she had graduated from her high school, she wanted to be the one top student from her school so that she would be the one chosen student to join the CCP. Sadly (in her words), she failed. Fortunately, she did well in the university and finally managed to join the CCP. Having dealt with Chinese officials since I began my diplomatic career in 1971, almost fifty years ago, I have been astonished how the quality of mind of Chinese diplomats has improved, decade by decade. Sadly, for different reasons, the trajectory of the American diplomatic service is in the opposite direction.

This strong and competent Chinese Communist Party is therefore delivering a global public good by ensuring that China behaves as a rational and stable actor on the world stage and not as an angry nationalist actor disrupting the regional and global order. To appreciate why this is important, American officials should spend some time probing the leaders and officials of China's neighbors to ask if they would be happier if the CCP were to be removed from power. Since I live in the neighborhood, I can say with some confidence that most of China's neighbors would prefer to see China led by calm and rational leaders, like Xi Jinping, and not by a Chinese version of Donald Trump or Teddy Roosevelt.

The second global public good that the CCP under Xi Jinping is delivering is to be a rational actor in responding to pressing global challenges. The biggest challenge that humanity faces as a whole is climate change. China has replaced America as the largest emitter of current *flows* of greenhouse gases, although if the *stock* is taken into consideration America is still the number one overall contributor to climate change. The world was relieved when Barack Obama and Xi Jinping reached a global agreement in Paris in December 2015 and shocked when Donald Trump decided to pull the United States out of the Paris Agreement. At that point, with America refusing to accept any responsibilities to deal with the threat of global warming, China could well have done the same. And it would have been perfectly justified to do so.

A democratically elected Chinese government would have been under great political pressure to do what Trump did: withdraw from the agreement and remove all constraints from China's rapid economic development. Instead, a nondemocratic CCP could do long-term calculations on what would be good for China and the world. On this basis, China decided to stick with the Paris Agreement. China has often been criticized for its poor environmental record. Many of these complaints are justified. In the 1980s and 1990s, little attention was paid to the environment as China raced ahead with its economic development. Yet, when China woke up to the harm that had been done to its environment, the CCP had the power and authority to change. Hence, China has emerged as the first country in the world to proclaim the goal of developing an "ecological civilization." Christine Loh, an adjunct professor at the Hong Kong University of Science and Technology's Institute of the Environment and Division of Environment and Sustainability, describes it as follows:

> The concept envisions better planning and carrying out future development within China's ecological capacity and rectifying degradation. It prioritizes pollution reduction, efficient use of natural resources, food security, climate change mitigation and adaptation, to address development-related problems. [. . .] On a theoretical level—always important for the party—ecological civilization needed to be put on a par with economic, political, cultural and social progress, which was done at the 18th Party Congress in 2012. [. . .] With the new ideology in place, the government implemented many major reforms that included issuing compensation guidelines for environmental damage, stronger environmental law enforcement, expanding clean energy pro-

duction and use, creating national parks, nominating senior officials
to protect rivers, restricting industrial projects and promoting green
financing to raise funds for China's transition.*

The third global public good that China has delivered is to emerge
as a "status quo" power rather than as a "revolutionary" power. This goes
against the logic of recent history. The two greatest global powers to
emerge in the twentieth century were the United States and the Soviet
Union. In both cases, despite their different ideological orientations,
they flexed their "imperialist" muscles as soon as they emerged. Douglas Brinkley, for example, has written of a Teddy Roosevelt steadfast in
his belief that the "strongest and swiftest among the [human] species"
ought "to rule the human kingdom . . . [which] meant, in his mind, the
Americans."† Similarly, when the Soviet Union became powerful under
Stalin, the Communist Party used its international arms Cominform
(established 1947) and Comecon (established 1949) to coordinate the
activities of and to financially support the communist parties of different states under Soviet leadership, in opposition to the Truman Doctrine and Marshall Plan. The Communist Party of the Soviet Union
had no hesitation sponsoring revolutionary or subversive activities in
other countries. Here are some examples:

> In the 1960s and 70s, the Soviet Union sponsored waves of political
> violence against the West. The Red Brigades in Italy and the German
> Red Army Faction both terrorized Europe through bank robberies,
> kidnapping, and acts of sabotage. The Soviets wanted to use these

---

* Christine Loh, "Green Policies in Focus as China's Rise to an Ecological Civilisation
Continues Apace," *South China Morning Post*, October 11, 2017, https://www.scmp.com
/comment/insight-opinion/article/2114748/green-policies-focus-chinas-rise-ecological
-civilisation.
† Douglas Brinkley, *The Wilderness Warrior: Theodore Roosevelt and the Crusade for America* (New York: Harper Perennial), 252.

left-wing terror groups to destabilize Italy and Germany to break up NATO. [. . .] Soviet equipment, funding, training and guidance flowed across the globe, either directly from the KGB or through the agencies of key allies, like the Rumanian Securitate, the Cuban General Intelligence Directorate. [. . .] Palestinian groups were enthusiastic participants in Soviet terror largesse. General Alexander Sakharovsky, head of the KGB's First Chief Directorate, famously said in 1971, "Airplane hijacking is my own invention," referring to the Palestinian Liberation Organization's hijackings. In the 1950s and 60s there was, on average, five hijackings a year; in 1969, Palestinian terrorists hijacked 82 aircraft.*

The more powerful the Soviet Union became, the more it intervened in the *internal* affairs of other countries.

Quite amazingly, China is doing the opposite. The more powerful China has become, the less it has intervened in the affairs of other states. From the creation of the People's Republic of China in 1949 to the death of Mao Zedong in 1976, China, like the Soviet Union, supported fellow communist parties, especially in Southeast Asia. The communist parties of Burma, Indonesia, Malaya, the Philippines, and Thailand were supported by the CCP. This support came to a gradual halt after Lee Kuan Yew, then prime minister of Singapore, told Deng Xiaoping in 1978: "Because China was exporting revolution to Southeast Asia, my Asean neighbours wanted Singapore to rally with them not against the Soviet Union but against China."† Since then, the Chinese Communist Party, unlike the Communist Party of the Soviet Union, has stopped supporting its fraternal parties. Ironically, China also has

---

* Nick Lockwood, "How the Soviet Union Transformed Terrorism," *The Atlantic*, December 23, 2011, https://www.theatlantic.com/international/archive/2011/12/how-the-soviet-union-transformed-terrorism/250433/.

† Lee Kuan Yew, *From Third World to First: The Singapore Story; 1965–2000* (New York: HarperCollins, 2000), 665.

difficult relations with the two other communist parties still in power in Asia, in Vietnam and North Korea.

This does not mean that China has not flexed its muscles. It has. This is normal behavior for great powers. Hence, when it feels that its national interests have been damaged, it will react. When the Nobel Peace Prize Committee conferred the Nobel Prize to a Chinese dissident Liu Xiaobo, Norway was put into "cold storage" by China. China significantly reduced its trade with Norway and refused to have any high-level diplomatic exchanges.[*] Similarly, when the conservative government of South Korea under President Park Geun-hye allowed the United States to install the Terminal High Altitude Area Defense (THAAD) in 2016, the Chinese government retaliated by imposing unofficial sanctions on South Korea. It blocked Chinese travel agents from selling tour packages to South Korea. As a result, "arrivals from China nearly halved in the first seven months of this year, dropping to 2.5 million from 4.7 million in the same period in 2016." Meanwhile, state media encouraged boycotts of Hyundai, such that "in the second quarter, [its] China sales plunged 64% compared with a year earlier." Lotte, the conglomerate that ceded land to the South Korean government to build the THAAD missile defense system, was particularly badly hit: "Lotte's duty free business in South Korea has suffered from the plunge in Chinese tourists. Dozens of its retail stores inside China have been closed down by officials. [. . .] The company said sales at its supermarket business in China nosedived 95% in the second quarter."[†] However, in each case, China was responding directly to what it perceived to be an attack on China's national interests. It was not a gratuitous intervention in the affairs of another state.

---

[*] Richard Milne, "Norway Sees Liu Xiaobo's Nobel Prize Hurt Salmon Exports to China," *Financial Times* (London), August 15, 2013, https://www.ft.com/content/ab456776-05b0-11e3-8ed5-00144feab7de.

[†] Jethro Mullen, "China Can Squeeze Its Neighbors When It Wants. Ask South Korea," CNN Business, August 30, 2017, https://money.cnn.com/2017/08/30/news/economy/china-hyundai-south-korea-thaad/index.html.

More recently, there have been allegations that China is using its scholars, students, and even overseas Chinese to meddle in the affairs of other states. The strongest allegations in this area were made by a group of American scholars in a report entitled *Chinese Influence & American Interests*. Its main claim was that "the Chinese Communist party-state leverages a broad range of party, state, and non-state actors to advance its influence-seeking objectives, and in recent years it has significantly accelerated both its investment and the intensity of these efforts." These objectives include "promot[ing] views sympathetic to the Chinese Government, policies, society, and culture; suppress[ing] alternative views; and co-opt[ing] key American players to support China's foreign policy goals and economic interests." Further, "because of the pervasiveness of the party-state, many nominally independent actors—including Chinese civil society, academia, corporations, and even religious institutions—are also ultimately beholden to the government and are frequently pressured into service to advance state interests."* While the Chinese government representatives have occasionally intervened in some events that led to criticisms of China, there have been too few examples to suggest that there is a systematic effort by the Chinese government to intervene in other countries' affairs. Consider, for example, the case of Chinese, University of Maryland commencement speaker Yang Shuping, who delivered a paean to America's "democracy and freedom." Shuping's speech began with the following: "People often ask me: Why did you come to the University of Maryland? I always answer: Fresh air. [. . .] I would soon feel another kind of fresh air for which I will be forever grateful. The fresh air of free speech. Democracy and free speech should not be taken for granted. Democracy and freedom are the fresh air that is worth fighting for." Hours later, the video went viral

* Working Group on Chinese Influence Activities in the United States, *Chinese Influence & American Interests: Promoting Constructive Vigilance* (Stanford, CA: Hoover Institution Press, 2018), https://www.hoover.org/sites/default/files/research/docs/chineseinfluence_americaninterests_fullreport_web.pdf.

in China, "attracting 50 million views and provoking hundreds of thousands of critical comments by Chinese netizens the following day."* She also attracted much criticism from the university's Chinese Student and Scholar Association (CSSA). Yang later posted an apology on Weibo, writing: "The speech was only to share my own experience abroad and did not have any intention of denying or belittling my country and hometown. I deeply apologise and sincerely hope everyone can understand, have learned my lesson for the future. . . . I deeply love my country and my home town, I feel extremely proud of my country's prosperous development and I hope in the future to use my time abroad to promote Chinese culture, contributing positively for my country."†

Such incidents are clearly unfortunate. The Chinese government representatives overreacted to the remarks of one student overseas. However, such overreaction does not indicate that the Chinese government is interfering in the internal affairs of America. There is no credible evidence that China has done this. There is no question that the Chinese government engages in espionage overseas. All major powers do this. There is nothing exceptional in China's behavior in this area. In short, China has been behaving as a normal state defending its normal strategic interests. One major criticism of the report *Chinese Influence & American Interests* is that it failed to make a distinction between "normal" espionage activities and an "abnormal" systematic attempt to undermine the social and political fabric of other societies. There is no evidence that China is attempting to do the latter. Susan Shirk, a former deputy assistant secretary of state during the Clinton administration

---

* Simon Denyer and Congcong Zhang, "A Chinese Student Praised the 'Fresh Air of Free Speech' at a U.S. College, Then Came the Backlash," *Washington Post*, May 23, 2017, https://www.washingtonpost.com/news/worldviews/wp/2017/05/23/a-chinese -student-praised-the-fresh-air-of-free-speech-at-a-u-s-college-then-came-the-backlash /?noredirect=on&utm_term=.e9211670aa19.

† Julia Hollingsworth, "Chinese Student Who Praised US Fresh Air and Freedom Apologises after Backlash in China," *South China Morning Post*, May 23, 2017, https:// www.scmp.com/news/china/society/article/2095319/chinese-student-who-praised -us-freedoms-apologizes-after-backlash.

and a professor at the School of Global Policy and Strategy at the University of California, San Diego, wrote in a dissenting opinion included in the report itself:

> Although I have no problem with the factual research that has gone into specific sections of the report, I respectfully dissent from what I see as the report's overall inflated assessment of the current threat of Chinese influence seeking on the United States. The report discusses a very broad range of Chinese activities, only some of which constitute coercive, covert, or corrupt interference in American society and none of which actually undermines our democratic political institutions. Not distinguishing the legitimate from the illegitimate activities detracts from the credibility of the report. The cumulative effect of this expansive inventory that blurs together legitimate with illegitimate activities is to overstate the threat that China today poses to the American way of life. Especially during this moment in American political history, overstating the threat of subversion from China risks causing overreactions reminiscent of the Cold War with the Soviet Union, including an anti-Chinese version of the Red Scare that would put all ethnic Chinese under a cloud of suspicion. Right now, I believe the harm we could cause our society by our own overreactions actually is greater than that caused by Chinese influence seeking. That is why I feel I must dissent from the overall threat assessment of the report.*

Indeed, relative to its size and influence, China is probably the least interventionist power of all the great powers. Of the five permanent members of the UN Security Council, China is the only one that has not fought in any foreign wars, away from its borders, since World War II. America, Russia, the UK, and France have done so. As this book has documented in several areas, the primary goal of China's rulers is

---

* Working Group, *Chinese Influence & American Interests.*

to preserve peace and harmony among 1.4 billion people in China, not try to influence the lives of the 6 billion people who live outside China. This is the fundamental reason why China is behaving like a status quo, rather than as a revolutionary, power. In so doing, it is delivering a global public good to the international system.

As a great power, China has also shown great strategic restraint in dealing with protests on its doorstep. Take Hong Kong as an example. It has been rocked with demonstrations and civil strife since the Hong Kong chief executive, Carrie Lam, unwisely tried to legislate an extradition agreement with both Taiwan and China on March 29, 2019. And the demonstrations continued even after she formally withdrew the bill on September 4, 2019. After the British returned Hong Kong to China in 1997, Hong Kong is now legally part of China's sovereign territory. Many analysts predicted that China would intervene militarily to suppress the demonstrations in Hong Kong. It could well do so. However, as of the time of the writing of this book, in October 2019, it had not done so.

Indeed, China's restraint is remarkable, especially when its behavior is compared with other great powers. India faced a problem with a troublesome Portuguese colony, Goa, on its doorstep in 1961. Both the then American president John F. Kennedy and British prime minister Harold Macmillan counseled the Indian prime minister Jawaharlal Nehru to exercise restraint and not invade Goa. Nehru ignored their pleas and in a lightning strike took over Goa in thirty-six hours on December 19, 1961. Similarly, President Ronald Reagan faced a troublesome little country, Grenada, on America's doorstep after a leftist revolution overthrew Prime Minister Eric Gairy in 1979 and replaced him with Maurice Bishop. Grenada was not a threat to America; it was only an irritant. It was against international law to invade Grenada. Ignoring all these constraints, America invaded and occupied Grenada on October 25, 1983. Hence, as great powers go, China has behaved with remarkable restraint on Hong Kong.

So why are the Hong Kong people demonstrating? The narrative in the Western media is that they want to establish an independent democracy in Hong Kong. Certainly, some of the leading voices in the demonstrations are making this claim. For example, Joshua Wong has said that "some brand me as a separatist. But just let me make it clear: Hong Kong is asking for election system reform. We just hope to elect our own government. We just hope to elect the chief executive of Hong Kong. . . . Before 1997, Beijing promised to let the Hong Kong people enjoy the right of free election . . . so we will continue our fight until the day we enjoy democracy."* The desire to exercise greater autonomy from mainland China is one factor behind the demonstrations.

Yet, history also teaches us that when the masses, especially the working classes, demonstrate, they are primarily driven by socioeconomic grievances, not ideals. This is sadly true in Hong Kong. Even though the Hong Kong economy has done well in recent decades, the bottom 50 percent in Hong Kong (unlike the bottom 50 percent in China) have seen no improvement in their living standards. Instead, they have worsened, with the bottom 50 percent struggling to access basic housing.

Both Hong Kong and Singapore are at similar stages of development. They have often learned a lot from each other. Here is one shocking difference. In Singapore, US$1 million could buy four apartments (each with a thousand square feet) of public housing. In Hong Kong, a similar amount would buy 250 square feet, sixteen times less space. Many working-class Hong Kongers live in rabbit holes. Two academics, Yin Weiwen and Zhang Youlang, have produced a careful study that documents that "housing prices positively contribute to the salience of localist identity in Hong Kong."† Many seasoned observers of Hong

---

* Agence France-Presse, "Hong Kong's Joshua Wong Denies He's a Separatist," Rappler, September 12, 2019, https://www.rappler.com/world/regions/asia-pacific/239920-hong-kong-joshua-wong-denies-separatist.

† Yin Weiwen and Zhang Youlang, "It's the Economy: Explaining Hong Kong's Identity Change after 1997," China: An International Journal 17, no. 3 (August 2019): 112–128.

Kong have documented that the root cause of unhappiness among poor Hong Kongers is their lack of access to housing.

China has made one strategic mistake with Hong Kong. In 1997, the first chief executive of Hong Kong, C. H. Tung, proposed a "target of achieving a home ownership rate of 70% in ten years . . . [and] pledged that the Administration would increase overall housing supply to at least 85 000 flats a year, and reduce the average waiting time for public rental housing to three years."* Tung was trying to replicate the successful Singapore experience in Hong Kong. Sadly, since this housing program could have lowered the price of land and property owned by a few real estate tycoons in Hong Kong, these tycoons used their influence in Beijing to overrule the housing plans of Tung. These tycoons seduced Beijing, convincing the Chinese government that they knew best what would keep Hong Kong stable. It turned out to be a false promise. Instead, if Beijing had heeded Tung instead, and 1.7 million units of public housing had been built over twenty years, there would probably have been fewer or no public demonstrations in Hong Kong. Even though the popular Western narrative is that the struggle in Hong Kong is between freedom fighters and the oppressive government in Beijing, the real conflict is between the homeless working classes and a few real estate tycoons. Fortunately, it is not too late. Beijing could use its influence and resources to persuade the Hong Kong government to begin a massive public housing program. And it could also advise the few Hong Kong tycoons to withdraw their opposition to this program.

Yet, all these stories of strategic restraint and descriptions of the global public goods delivered by the CCP raise an obvious question of moral philosophy. Is it fair to subject the Chinese people to the one-party rule of the CCP so that the world can enjoy the benefits of rational global public policies? Americans have also benefited from China's

* Housing Bureau, Policy Programme: The 1997 Policy Address, https://www.policyaddress.gov.hk/pa97/english/phb.htm.

rational global policies. One could therefore ask: Why should Chinese citizens be denied American freedoms when Americans are beneficiaries of their lack of rights? Is that fair?

All such questions are based on the assumption that the American population is thriving and doing well and the Chinese population is not. The facts suggest otherwise. In the last thirty years, as documented in this volume, America is the only developed society where the average income of the bottom 50 percent of the population has gone down over the past thirty years. In the same period, the Chinese people have experienced the greatest improvement in their standard of living ever seen in Chinese history. The obvious American retort to such a statement would be to say that the Chinese still don't enjoy the political rights that Americans do. This is true. Yet, it is also true that the Chinese people cherish social harmony and social well-being more than individual rights. Any assessment of how the Chinese are doing must be done against the long and rich history of the Chinese people.

In China's long history, the people have enjoyed benign periods of dynastic rule (for example, under the Tang dynasty in 618–907 CE) and periods of chaos and disunity. How does the seventy-year record of Chinese Communist Party rule compare? In the first thirty years of CCP rule, from 1949 to 1979, the Chinese people did experience some improvements in living conditions (for example, in health and education), but they also suffered terribly in the Great Leap Forward (1958–1962) and the Cultural Revolution (1966–1976). In the forty-year period of 1979–2019, the Chinese experienced a far greater improvement in their living conditions than any dynasty had ever delivered to the Chinese at any point in its twenty-two-hundred-year history. In short, the political dynasty that has done the most for the Chinese people has been the CCP "political dynasty" of 1979 to 2019. It is useful to note here that good Chinese dynasties last two or three centuries. The track record of the CCP so far indicates that it could last a long time, especially since the CCP political dynasty is the first dynasty in Chinese history to rescue the bottom 50 percent of China's population from poverty. For thousands of years, the vast majority of Chinese people had to struggle to survive. When famine came, millions died, as in the Chinese Famine of 1907 (twenty-five million), the Northern Chinese Famine of 1876–1879 (thirteen million), and, most egregiously, the Great Chinese Famine of 1959–1961. Future historians, with a long view, will marvel at how much the CCP dynasty has accomplished.

Given the absence of political freedoms in China—the Chinese people clearly don't have the freedom to organize political parties, speak in a free media, and vote for their leaders—the assumption in the West is that the Chinese people must feel oppressed. However, the Chinese people don't compare their condition with that of other societies. Instead, they compare their lot with what they experienced in the past. And all they can see is that they have experienced the largest explosion of personal freedoms ever experienced in their history. When I first went to China in 1980, the Chinese people couldn't choose where to live, what to wear, where to study, or what jobs to take. No Chinese tourists traveled overseas. Today, the Chinese people can choose where to live, what to wear, where to study (including overseas), and what jobs to take. And each year, 134 million Chinese people choose to travel abroad, including to Western democracies in North America and Europe and its democratic Asian neighbors like Japan and South Korea. Even more amazingly, 134 million Chinese people freely choose to return home from their vacations.

If China was indeed a dark, oppressive Chinese gulag state, those 134 million Chinese people would not have chosen to return home. They would have sought refugee status. It is therefore paradoxical that the period in Chinese history when the Chinese people experienced the greatest improvement of personal freedoms is the period that the Western imagination perceives to be a relatively dark period in Chinese history. The billionaire philanthropist George Soros in 2019 conveyed a dark portrait of China. He described Xi Jinping as "the most dangerous

154 – HAS CHINA WON?

opponent of those who believe in the concept of open society." He added: "Since Xi has declared his hostility to open society, the Chinese people remain our main source of hope."* There is something very paradoxical about this last statement. If he had asked the broad masses of Chinese people what they thought, they would mention that Xi remains their "main source of hope." One clear and undeniable fact about China that most Americans are unaware of is that the Chinese people trust their government. This is confirmed by independent international surveys. The 2018 Edelman Trust Barometer report, which surveyed trust levels in several different countries, found that in terms of the domestic population's trust in their government, China ranked top, while America ranked fifteenth. China's score (84) was also more than double that of America's (33) (see Chart 5).

Soros is right about one essential political fact. There is political oppression in China. Any government that is based on an authoritarian model has no choice but to suppress political dissent. Chinese emperors had to do so for millennia. Yet, if repression were the sole goal and instrument of Chinese government rule, it would not and could not last. A wise Chinese government in the twenty-first century knows that it has to balance three partially contradictory goals to ensure a healthy Chinese society. The three goals are growth, stability, and personal freedom.

Economic growth is vital for two critical reasons: to improve the livelihood of the broad masses of the Chinese people and to make China a strong country again. Both goals have been achieved in a truly spectacular fashion. In 1981, shortly after Deng Xiaoping launched his economic reform programs in 1978, over 50 percent of the Chinese people lived in extreme poverty.† Today, less than 5 percent do so.‡

---

* "Remarks Delivered at the World Economics Forum," World Economics Forum (Davos), January 24, 2019.

† Martin Ravallion and Shaohua Chen, "China's (Uneven) Progress Against Poverty," *Journal of Development Economics* 82 (2007): 1–42, http://siteresources.worldbank.org /PGLP/Resources/ShaohuaPaper.pdf.

‡ World Bank, "China," Poverty & Equity Data Portal, http://povertydata.worldbank .org/poverty/country/CHN.

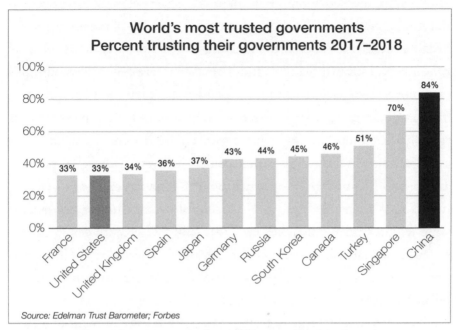

CHART 5. Edelman Trust Barometer (2018)* (Designed by Patti Issacs)

Even seasoned observers like Professor Wang Gungwu have remarked of the rise of China's economy that "few people expected that to happen so quickly."[†] Economic growth has made China a strong country. In 2000, America's economy was eight times larger than that of China. By 2018, it was only 1.5 times larger. Within a decade or two, China's economy will become larger than America's. Economic growth is a critical goal.

Yet economic growth, especially in the free-market system China has now chosen, can be politically disruptive. It can create new political classes with the means to challenge the one-party rule of the CCP. As

---

* Niall McCarthy, "The Countries That Trust Their Government Most and Least," *Forbes*, January 22, 2018, https://www.forbes.com/sites/niallmccarthy/2018/01/22/the -countries-that-trust-their-government-most-and-least-infographic/#6fef5fd1777a.

† Wang Gungwu, *China Reconnects: Joining a Deep-Rooted Past to a New World Order* (Singapore: World Scientific, 2019), 16.

America has learned, money talks in politics: every Republican presidential candidate since Richard Nixon has been a multimillionaire before he became president; billionaires like Donald Trump, Ross Perot, Michael Bloomberg, Howard Schultz, and Tom Steyer are politically ambitious and active. George Soros and the Koch brothers have not run for office but fund political campaigns extensively. European history has taught us that the feudal culture was most effectively destroyed when capitalism produced new middle classes that could challenge established political authority. The middle-class population of China has exploded. According to a McKinsey report: "Just 4 percent of urban Chinese households were within [the middle class] in 2000—but 68 percent were in 2012."[*] In 2015, the British newspaper the *Telegraph* reported that China was now home to the world's largest middle class.[†] In America, the number of billionaires has exploded, and the middle class is in decline.

Western political theory teaches us that the development of a large middle class leads to demands for greater political participation. If a government ignores their demands, there could be a revolution on the streets, and the government would be overthrown. So now that China has the world's largest middle class, why has it not revolted against the authoritarian nondemocratic rule of the CCP? The conventional Western answer is that repression has prevented this from happening. Certainly, repression is a factor. Many revolts are nipped in the bud. Yet, every Chinese government has known for millennia that if the vast majority of the Chinese people choose to revolt, no amount of repression can hold them down. This is why in traditional Chinese political theory, when a broad-based revolt breaks out, the Chinese emperor is deemed

---

* Dominic Barton, Yougang Chen, and Amy Jin, "Mapping China's Middle Class," *McKinsey Quarterly*, June 2013, https://www.mckinsey.com/industries/retail/our-insights/mapping-chinas-middle-class.

† Agency, "China's Middle Class Overtakes US as Largest in the World," *Telegraph* (London), October 14, 2015, https://www.telegraph.co.uk/finance/china-business/11929794/Chinas-middle-class-overtakes-US-as-largest-in-the-world.html.

to have lost "the mandate of heaven." The international relations scholar Luke Glanville explains this concept as follows:

> For over five hundred years, between roughly 770 and 221 BC, Ancient China comprised a system of independent states. During these years, Confucian scholars, in particular Mencius, developed a political philosophy grounded in the moral virtue of benevolence. Drawing on the ideas of Confucius and the earlier Chinese concept of the Mandate of Heaven, Mencius claimed that the ruler of a state was established by Heaven for the benefit of the people. The ruler possessed the Heavenly Mandate to rule only so long as he retained the support of the people, for it was through the "heart" of the people that Heaven made its will known. The people, in turn, could rightfully hold their rulers to account. They had the right to banish a bad ruler and even to kill a tyrant.[*]

So repression is not the sole reason why the Chinese middle classes are basically calm. Most of them accept an implicit social contract between the Chinese people and the Chinese government. As long as the Chinese government continues to deliver economic growth (with improvements in living conditions, including better environmental living conditions) and social and political stability, the Chinese people will accept the rule of the CCP. If one assumes that the broad masses of the Chinese people are sober and rational in their calculations, as they probably are, it would be perfectly natural for them to prefer to see the continuation of CCP rule in China as it has delivered a far greater improvement to the livelihoods of the Chinese people than any previous dynasty has. China does not allow many polls. Yet, it allows some polls. All these polls show that the Chinese people are among the most satisfied and most optimistic people in the world. According to a 2015

---

[*] Luke Glanville, "Retaining the Mandate of Heaven: Sovereign Accountability in Ancient China," *Millennium* 39, no. 2 (December 2010): 323–343.

Pew survey, 88 percent of Chinese believe that when their children grow up, they will be better off financially than their parents, compared to a median of 51 percent among other emerging countries and 32 percent in the United States.[*] If the Chinese people were truly suffering from "repression," would the polls show such confidence?

There is also a functional reason why the Chinese government cannot rely only on repression to keep China politically stable. At the end of the day, a society can only thrive when people feel that they have sufficient freedom to chase their own personal dreams. Chinese rulers have known for millennia that a wise emperor does not sit heavily on his own people. This is why Ronald Reagan had to turn to Chinese political wisdom to describe wise and beneficent rule. He quoted Lao Tzu as saying, "Govern a great nation as you would cook a small fish; do not overdo it."[†]

To understand how, in relative terms, China is a less repressive society than the Soviet Union was, one need only compare Chinese Communist Party rule with Soviet Communist Party rule in the treatment of their own citizens. The Soviet Union didn't allow any Russians to travel overseas for fear that they would return home with ideas that could threaten Soviet Communist Party rule. China allows 134 million to travel overseas freely. The Soviet Union also tightly controlled the number of foreign tourists into its country: "Foreign tourism in the USSR was nearly nonexistent during the reign of Stalin. The first stage in the development of international tourism began during the Khrushchev reform period in the late 1950s and early 1960s, when [. . .] the USSR needed hard currency and hoped to gain politically by show-

---

* Bruce Stokes, "Global Publics: Economic Conditions Are Bad," Pew Research Center, July 23, 2015, http://www.pewglobal.org/2015/07/23/global-publics-economic-conditions-are-bad/.

† Ronald Reagan, "Transcript of Reagan's State of the Union Message to Nation," *New York Times*, January 26, 1988, https://www.nytimes.com/1988/01/26/us/transcript-of-reagan-s-state-of-the-union-message-to-nation.html.

ing some carefully selected attractions to foreigners. At the same time, however, most of the country remained closed to international visitors [...]." After the 1975 Helsinki Accords, "the number of foreign tourists increased from less than 500,000 in 1956 to over 5 million in 1981, to more than 6 million in 1988." However, most of the foreign tourists came from Soviet bloc countries: "in 1972 they constituted 62% of foreign tourists and in 1988, 67%."[*] In short, few foreign tourists went to the Soviet Union. By contrast, China has allowed an explosion of foreign tourists to take place. In 2018, 141 million tourists visited China.[†]

The Soviet Union would never have allowed the minds of its best and brightest young people to be corrupted by the unchecked academic freedom of American universities. China has sent millions of its best and brightest. There were 351,000 Chinese students in the United States in just one year, 2016–2017. In 2016, "544,500 Chinese studied abroad, more than triple the 179,800 that sought out education overseas in 2008."[‡]

The relative freedom that the Chinese people enjoy compared to the Soviet Union also means that visitors to China do not encounter a police state. With the exception of cities like Urumqi and Kashgar, which I have visited, one barely sees policemen in the streets. The social order in China, which is relatively high, is a result of the Chinese people voluntarily accepting the rules and norms of their society. A striking comparison can be made between the relative sense of well-being of the bottom half of the Chinese population with the bottom half of the American population. In terms of per capita income, the bottom half in

---

[*] V. Arefyev and Z. Mieczkowski, "International Tourism in the Soviet Union in the Era of Glasnost and Perestroyka," *Journal of Travel Research* 29, no. 4 (April 1991): 2–6.

[†] "China's Inbound Tourism Remains Steady in 2018," State Council, People's Republic of China, February 6, 2019, http://english.gov.cn/archive/statistics/2019/02/06/content_281476510410482.htm.

[‡] "More Chinese Students Study Abroad," *China Daily*, March 30, 2018, http://www.chinadaily.com.cn/a/201803/30/WS5abe02d6a3105cdcf65156e2.html.

America is better off. However, in terms of social progress, the average income of the bottom half of the Chinese people is rising much faster, albeit from a lower starting point. By contrast, the average income of the bottom half of the American people went down from 1980 to 2010, as documented by my colleague in the National University of Singapore, Professor Danny Quah.*

John Rawls, the political philosopher, wrote in *A Theory of Justice* that the most just society is one that one would choose to be born into if one didn't know whether one would be born among the most or least advantaged in society. A rational choice would be to pick the society where the least advantaged are better off. Rawls wrote:

> Now it seems impossible to avoid a certain arbitrariness in actually identifying the least favored group. One possibility is to choose a particular social position, say that of the unskilled worker, and then to count as the least favored all those with approximately the income and wealth of those in this position, or less. Another criterion is one in terms of relative income and wealth with no reference to social positions. For example, all persons with less than half of the median may be regarded as the least advantaged segment. This criterion depends only on the lower half of the distribution and has the merit of focusing attention on the social distance between those who have the least and the average citizen. Either of these criteria would appear to cover those most disfavored by the various contingencies and provide a basis for determining at what level a reasonable social minimum might be set and from which, in conjunction with other measures, society could proceed to fulfill the difference principle.†

---

* Danny Quah, "The US Is, Indeed, the Exceptional Nation: Income Dynamics in the Bottom 50%," Lee Kuan Yew School of Public Policy, January 2019, http://www .dannyquah.com/Quilled/Output/2019.01-Danny.Quah-Income-Dynamics-in-the -Bottom-50.pdf.

† John Rawls, *A Theory of Justice*, rev. ed. (Cambridge, MA: Belknap Press, 1999), 81.

By these criteria, would a rational person choose to be born among the least advantaged of China or America? In theory, the answer would be America since it is wealthier. In reality, it could well be China, as the least advantaged in China have a far greater chance to improve their living conditions than their counterparts in America. John Rawls also emphasized that one should not just look at economic conditions. Liberty should also be factored in as a key consideration. If Rawls only had in mind political liberty, then one would again choose to be born in America. However, if one factored in personal liberty, one might well choose China since the chance of being incarcerated in America (if one is born in the bottom 10 percent, especially among the black population) is at least five times higher than China. America sends 0.655 percent (or 2.12 million) into jails. By contrast, China sends 0.118 percent (or 1.65 million) into jails. A 2019 study tried to understand which ethnic group in America had the greatest percentage of individuals with family members in jail or prison. The average figure for all Americans was 45 percent. The figure for whites was 42 percent, Hispanics 48 percent, and blacks 63 percent.[*]

America's judicial system is clearly far more independent and, in many functional ways, superior to China's judicial system. Yet, I had a very interesting conversation with an American who held a senior position with an American NGO. For over ten years, he had worked with Chinese judges in China. He left China with two main impressions. First, under the veneer of uniformity and conformity, the Chinese judges had a rich plurality of views, which they expressed in their private conversations. Second, the Chinese judges were concerned with treating all classes equally. Once an American legal consultant, in an effort to be helpful, told a Chinese judge that China should consider abolishing the death penalty for all crimes except murder. The Chinese judge wisely

---

[*] Peter K. Enns et al., "What Percentage of Americans Have Ever Had a Family Member Incarcerated?: Evidence from the Family History of Incarceration Survey (FamHIS)," *Socius: Sociological Research for a Dynamic World* 5 (January 2019).

replied that the implementation of this rule would result in China's judicial system becoming like the American judicial system, with only poor people, not rich people, being sent to the gallows.

In short, by various standards of social justice, China's society may not be doing badly, helped by the fact that as people become better off, they have greater vested interest in voluntarily maintaining a good social order. There is one aspect of the Chinese mind that the Western mind finds difficult to relate to: the Chinese like order. And they like measures that lead to greater order. This attitude accounts for the sharp difference in Western and Chinese reactions to a new measure introduced by the Chinese government to bring about social order: the social credit scheme. Bing Song of the Berggruen Institute has described the social credit system as follows:

> In a 2014 document, the Chinese government outlined its vision for such a system and noted that it involved four distinct segments: a government trust system, a commercial credit system, a social trust system and a judicial trust system. What drives this gargantuan project is an effort to build a culture of trust in Chinese society.[*]

George Soros captured well the negative Western reaction to the social credit system when he said, "The social credit system, if it becomes operational, would give Xi total control over the people." The only application Soros could see for China was an Orwellian vision, in which the state could have total control over the lives of the Chinese people. Vice President Mike Pence has also stated this explicitly in his October 2018 speech at the Hudson Institute: "China's rulers aim to implement an Orwellian system premised on controlling virtually every facet of human life."

---

[*] Bing Song, "The West May Be Wrong About China's Social Credit System," *Washington Post*, November 29, 2018, https://www.washingtonpost.com/news/theworldpost/wp /2018/11/29/social-credit/?noredirect=on&utm_term=.69d772fd4953.

George Orwell described such a society in *Nineteen Eighty-Four* as follows: "There was of course no way of knowing whether you were being watched at any given moment. How often, or on what system, the Thought Police plugged in on any individual wire was guesswork. It was even conceivable that they watched everybody all the time. But at any rate they could plug in your wire whenever they wanted to. You had to live—did live, from habit that became instinct—in the assumption that every sound you made was overheard, and, except in darkness, every movement scrutinized."

Yet, when even the Western media reported the reactions of ordinary Chinese people to the introduction of the social credit system, they observed that most people welcomed it as it would mean that they would know whom they could trust in their social and economic interactions. The *New York Times* reported: "Judging public Chinese reaction can be difficult in a country where the news media is controlled by the government. Still, so far the average Chinese citizen appears to show little concern. Erratic enforcement of laws against everything from speeding to assault means the long arm of China's authoritarian government can feel remote from everyday life. As a result, many cheer on new attempts at law and order."[*]

There is one key reason why Chinese cherish order. They live in close proximity to one another. Someone who has explained this well is Ambassador Chas Freeman. In a speech he gave at the St. Petersburg Conference on World Affairs on February 12, 2019, in Florida, he commented on the demographics of China:

China is slightly larger than the United States—6.3 percent of the world's landmass vs. 6.1 percent for the U.S. But there are 1.4 billion Chinese, with only one-third the arable land and one-fourth the water

---

[*] Paul Mozur, "Inside China's Dystopian Dreams: A.I., Shame and Lots of Cameras," *New York Times*, July 8, 2018, https://www.nytimes.com/2018/07/08/business/china -surveillance-technology.html.

we Americans have. If we had the same ratio of population to agricultural resources that the Chinese do, there would be almost 4 billion Americans—about 600 million of them over sixty-five—most of them probably planning to retire in Florida. [. . .] I suspect that, if there were that many people crammed into the United States, Americans would have a much lower tolerance for social disorder and a different attitude toward family planning than we now do. We'd also be more worried about the prospects for individual security and survival. Sixty years ago, perhaps 30 million Chinese died in a man-made famine known as the "Great Leap Forward." Chinese are acutely aware that they have narrow margins for error. This makes them naturally risk averse and, in most respects, a more predictable actor in foreign affairs than we now are.

The relative comfort of the 1.4 billion people of China with a social and political order that is vastly different from the Western order ought to encourage the West to undertake a deep process of introspection. Is it wise to believe that there is only one road for all societies to travel on if they want to grow and progress? Are we now turning a new corner of human history where alternative models of social and economic development are emerging? It was an Indian political scientist, Pratap Bhanu Mehta, who alerted me to a significant difference between the democratic Indian society and communist Chinese society. He shrewdly observed that India was an open society with a closed mind, whereas China was a closed society with an open mind. The same observation may well apply to American society.

American thinkers and public intellectuals have a particularly closed mind when it comes to grasping and understanding China. When it comes to analyzing political systems, American analysts tend to veer toward a black-and-white view of the world: open or closed society, democratic or totalitarian society, liberal or authoritarian. Yet, even as we move away from an aberrant two-hundred-year period of Western domination of world history, we are also moving away from a black-and-white world. Societies in different parts of the world, including in China and Islamic societies, are going to work toward a different balance between liberty and order, between freedom and control, between discord and harmony.

The Chinese thinkers were also once convinced that the only way to succeed was for China to replicate Western societies. This is why, at the moment of greatest despair for Chinese society, in the 1920s, many Chinese intellectuals said (like the Japanese reformers in the Meiji Restoration) that the only path ahead for China was to copy the West in all dimensions. The Chinese historian Chow Tse-tsung documents: "Lu [Xun] declared that the Chinese should live for themselves instead of for their ancestors. To learn modern science and Western knowledge was more important than to recite the Confucian classics. [. . .] Rather than worship Confucius and Kuan Kung one should worship Darwin and Ibsen. Rather than sacrifice to the God of Pestilence and the Five Classes of Spirits, one should worship Apollo. [. . .] Lu [Xun] was sincere from his realistic and utilitarian point of view; if the new was more useful than the old, he asked, in effect, why should one bother whether it was Chinese or foreign?"* One hundred years later, China no longer lies prostrate. It has stood up and become self-confident. After all the recent travails in both Europe and America, few in China believe that China's destiny in the twenty-first century is to mimic the West. Instead, they believe China should follow its own road. It will be an interesting addition to human history.

John Maynard Keynes once famously observed "When the facts change, I change my mind. What do you do?" The biggest fact of the last thirty years is that many societies of the world that tried Western

---

* Chow Tse-Tsung, *The May Fourth Movement: Intellectual Revolution in Modern China* (Cambridge, MA: Harvard University Press, 1960), 309.

liberal democratic systems have come to realize that it does not fit them. And in some cases, it has led to disasters. One good project for Western liberal thinkers is to do an objective audit of all the so-called color revolutions that the West has sponsored since the end of the Cold War. Color revolutions are often nonviolent civil resistance movements. The word *color* surfaced because some protesters adopted colors or motifs as symbols during their demonstrations. How many have succeeded? How many have failed? Here's a rough analysis.

Clearly, the democratic revolutions that overthrew the pro-Soviet regimes in the former Warsaw Pact countries were successful. Poland, Hungary, the Czech Republic, and Slovakia are thriving. Yet, their successes were exceptional. They succeeded because they already had significant middle-class populations and gained easy entry into the rich European Union, which transferred significant resources to them. By contrast, the former republics of the Soviet Union, including Georgia, Ukraine, and Kyrgyzstan, have struggled to achieve political stability. Melinda Haring of the Foreign Policy Institute has documented that the failure in all these three cases was a result of a common delusion in all three polities that the revolutions were the "apogee of democracy," when, in fact, they were but a means to it. As a result of this delusion, the leading figures were able to hijack the revolutions and regress to autocracy. In Kyrgyzstan, for example, Tulip Revolution leader Kurmanbek Bakiyev "quickly established himself as a political strongman."* Similarly, the revolutions in Egypt and Libya, once loudly cheered on by Western intelligentsia, did not result in better outcomes. Libya remains a broken state. The removal of Gaddafi in Libya led to the splintering of the country and continued civil war and conflict, from which the country has not recovered. Americans grieved

---

* Melinda Haring and Michael Cecire, "Why the Color Revolutions Failed," *Foreign Policy*, March 18, 2013, https://foreignpolicy.com/2013/03/18/why-the-color -revolutions-failed/.

over the American ambassador J. Christopher Stevens, who was killed in Benghazi. The unnecessary loss of his life deserves to be mourned. Yet, many more Libyan lives were lost in the chaos and destruction that followed the removal of Gaddafi. As a country, America has a unique ability to act both ethically, when it comes to supporting color revolutions, and unethically, when it comes to walking away from the consequences of them. In the collective memory of many thoughtful Americans, the ethical dimensions of intervention are remembered but the unethical dimensions of walking away are soon forgotten. In short, most of the democratic revolutions failed to deliver broad-based prosperity and democracy.

Probably the one government that has done the most intensive study of all the recent color revolutions is China. It would have been ir-responsible for the Chinese government not to study them, because any potential adversary of China, including America, would obviously look for ways and means of sparking a color revolution in China if the goal is to destabilize the strong authoritarian rule of the Chinese government. Since most Americans believe that a democracy can do no harm, they believe that it would only be an unmitigated good if a spontaneous color revolution led to the overthrow of the CCP.

This belief sounds both innocent and moral. Precisely because of this perception, it is very dangerous because the Chinese will perceive this belief to be both destructive and immoral. To understand the Chi-nese point of view, Americans should remember how they felt when Osama bin Laden carried out his attack on America on 9/11 and killed nearly three thousand Americans. I was in Manhattan when the attack happened. I personally experienced the bewilderment, grief, anger, and outrage that Americans felt to see so many innocent people killed by Osama bin Laden's attack. The desire to retaliate was strong and palpa-ble. And perfectly understandable. As a result, America lashed back and invaded Afghanistan.

With these memories of 9/11 firmly implanted in their minds, Americans could begin to understand how the Chinese would feel if thousands (if not millions) of Chinese are killed by the chaos launched by a color revolution sponsored by America. This figure of millions might not be an exaggeration; in previous periods of turmoil in Chinese history, millions have died. If millions died, it is not difficult to imagine an explosive and angry reaction from the Chinese people. The Americans who sponsor the color revolution may well believe that their intentions are noble and moral. Yet, if the results are catastrophic, as they have been in the case of most recent color revolutions, an angry and vitriolic Chinese response would be entirely natural.

If America wants to promote a "moral" agenda in their dealings with China, the best way to be moral is to refrain from interfering in the internal affairs of China for there is a real danger of chaos or *luàn* (乱) emerging as a result, with the potential loss of life of millions.

This does not mean that the present Chinese political system will remain frozen in its present form forever. No regime can last in Beijing if it is no longer in tune with the wishes and aspirations of its people. In theory, the government in Beijing could use all the powerful instruments of repression to stay in power forever. However, a government in Beijing that relied only on repression to stay in power could never succeed in its broader goal of "reali[zing] the Chinese Dream of national rejuvenation."*

Yet, the Chinese political system also appears to be resilient, rather than fragile. Why is this so? It is astonishing how so few people in the world are aware of the "big secret" about the governance of China. The main reason why the Chinese political system appears to be resilient is

---

* Xi Jinping, "Secure a Decisive Victory in Building a Moderately Prosperous Society in All Respects and Strive for the Great Success of Socialism with Chinese Characteristics for a New Era," speech delivered at the 19th National Congress of the Communist Party of China, October 18, 2017, http://www.xinhuanet.com/english/download/Xi_Jinping's _report_at_19th_CPC_National_Congress.pdf.

that China has one of the most intelligent governments in the world. The Chinese Communist Party recruits only the best graduates in China. Every society has an IQ pyramid. In many societies, because of corruption or relics of a feudal mentality, the ruling classes are *not* selected on the basis of merit. The Chinese government stands out in the world because it is the most disciplined and rigorous government in selecting only the best minds among its population to serve in its ranks.

At the same time, in contrast to the bureaucracy of the former Soviet Union, which was rigid and inflexible, the Chinese bureaucracy has become responsive and accountable. This is how Yuen Yuen Ang, a political science professor at the University of Michigan, Ann Arbor, describes the reforms that China has undertaken:

> Since opening its markets in 1978, China has in fact pursued significant political reforms—just not in the manner that Western observers expected. Instead of instituting multiparty elections, establishing formal protections for individual rights, or allowing free expression, the CCP has made changes below the surface, reforming its vast bureaucracy to realize many of the benefits of democratization—in particular, accountability, competition, and partial limits on power—without giving up single-party control.
>
> Although these changes may appear dry and apolitical, in fact, they have created a unique hybrid: autocracy with democratic characteristics. In practice, tweaks to rules and incentives within China's public administration have quietly transformed an ossified communist bureaucracy into a highly adaptive capitalist machine.[*]

---

[*] Yuen Yuen Ang, "Autocracy with Chinese Characteristics: Beijing's Behind-the-Scenes Reforms," *Foreign Affairs*, May/June 2018, https://deepblue.lib.umich.edu/bitstream /handle/2027.42/148140/Autocracy%20With%20Chinese%20Characteristics %2C%20posted%20version.pdf?sequence=1&isAllowed=y.

This high quality of mind explains the extraordinary progress that China has made in economic and social development. It also explains the high degree of trust that the Chinese people have in their governing classes. A 2017 study of political trust in Asian societies by Cary Wu and Rima Wilkes found that in China, unlike most other Asian societies, there is not only a high level of trust in the national government but also a relatively higher level of trust in the national government compared to local governments.[*]

Western scholars and commentators resist the idea that the CCP may well be a well-functioning instrument of governance because of a deep residual abhorrence of both communism and authoritarian rule. Given this, it is not surprising that Western scholars rarely discuss the CCP objectively and rationally. One example of flawed analysis of the CCP can be found in Richard McGregor's *The Party*, where he says the following: "The Chinese communist system is, in many ways, rotten, costly, corrupt and often dysfunctional. The financial crisis has added a dangerous dash of hubris to the mix. But the system has also proved to be flexible and protean enough to absorb everything that has been thrown at it, to the surprise and horror of many in the west."[†]

There is an obvious contradiction here. This contradiction is so brazen that it must indicate the author's deep reluctance to acknowledge the facts: he wants to see a rotten system, yet the system has in fact not rotted through at all. He won't acknowledge that China's current leaders have been extremely vigilant for signs of corruption and have sought to root it out, publicly. Is that evidence of a rotten government, or a government determined to eradicate rot? One reason the CCP, despite being communist, is "flexible and protean" is because of

---

[*] Cary Wu and Rima Wilkes, "Local-National Political Trust Patterns: Why China Is an Exception," *International Political Science Review* 39, no. 4 (September 2018): 436–454.

[†] Richard McGregor, *The Party: The Secret World of China's Communist Rulers* (London: Allen Lane, 2010), 273.

the C-word in CCP: Chinese. The educated Chinese mind is remarkably open, supple, and perceptive. Most Chinese leaders, including
modern, Western-educated Chinese leaders, are steeped in the classics
of Chinese thought. These classics in turn open their minds to a lot of
ancient Chinese philosophy—theirs is a thoughtful culture. From this
they understand that the greatest mistake for any Chinese leader would
be to be rigid, ideological, and doctrinaire. Hence, even though many
Chinese leaders reaffirm their commitment to Marx and even Mao,
they also know that these examples must be adapted and implemented
in a flexible way. Ancient Chinese traditions of governance continued
under CCP rule. Martin Jacques cites the historian Wang Gungwu
as arguing that the new Communist state was "a replacement for the
old emperor-state."[*] He also cites Suisheng Zhao, who makes the same
point somewhat differently: "A Chinese nation-state was forged under
the leadership of the Communist Party and the guidance of Marxism.
However, it had far more to do with Chinese nationalism, with the re-
assertion of China's former glory and future modernization, than with
the universal principles of communism."[†]

The three strongest Chinese leaders in the past hundred years have
been Mao Zedong, Deng Xiaoping, and Xi Jinping. The Western view
of these three men emphasizes how different they are: Mao is perceived
as a brutal and destructive ruler, Deng as the wise and patient reformer,
and Xi as the ruthless dictator, returning China to its Maoist roots. Yet,
these one-dimensional portraits fail to capture the extraordinary complexity of these remarkable leaders. Mao may have been brutal, but he
was by far the most philosophical of these three leaders, deeply rooted
in ancient Chinese thinking. Deng could be as ruthless as Mao. Xi is
also acutely aware of ancient Chinese history and culture and turns to it

---

[*] Martin Jacques, *When China Rules the World: The End of the Western World and the Birth
of a New Global Order* (New York: Penguin, 2009), 97.
[†] Ibid.

when he has to make difficult decisions, like how to handle the tempestuous and unpredictable Donald Trump.[*]

The greatest source of misunderstanding of the CCP comes when the West focuses on the word *communist* instead of the word *Chinese*. Although the Chinese have not succeeded in creating a perfect governance system, theirs does reflect thousands of years of Chinese political traditions and wisdom. The overall weight of the Chinese government on the Chinese people is not a heavy one. The CCP does not actively interfere in the daily lives of its citizens. Indeed, the Chinese people have enjoyed more personal freedom under the CCP than any other previous Chinese government. And who is more rigid: the Chinese, who have clearly adapted their systems of government and economy, or an American constitutionalist who believes that the Supreme Court should regard the Constitution of 1776 as an immutable doctrine?

One statistic that many Western commentators use to describe the fragility and vulnerability of the Chinese political system is the 187,000 protests that take place in China each year. Christian Göbel, a researcher at the University of Vienna, has explained how many media reports have arrived at this figure: "In 2011, a study published by Landesa Survey claimed that, according to 'Chinese researchers', in 2010 China saw '187,000 mass incidents [...], 65 percent of them related to land disputes.'[†] Drawing on this figure, a headline in the Atlantic made the misleading claim that '500 protests [occurred] every day.' Despite the fact that little is known about how the unnamed 'Chinese researchers' cited in the Landesa survey arrived at this figure, most publications, including that of the author, refer to it. However, these figures contribute

---

* Ali Vitali, "Trump Dines with China Leader: 'We Have Developed a Friendship,'" NBC News, April 6, 2017, https://www.nbcnews.com/politics/white-house/trump-dines-china-leader-we-have-developed-friendship-n743626.

† Yu Gao, "China: One Fire May Be Out, but Tensions over Rural Land Rights Are Still Smoldering," Landesa: Rural Development Institute, February 6, 2012, https://www.landesa.org/china-fire-out-tensions-rural-land-rights-smoldering/.

little to a better understanding of social unrest in China. Instead, they conjure up the powerful image of a China in serious turmoil."*

Göbel, through his study of 74,452 protests that occurred in China between 2013 and 2016, concludes that "protests in China are widespread but tend to occur seasonally and involve less than 30 participants. Most protests are recorded in the days before Chinese New Year, when factories close their accounts and migrant workers return home. Financial compensation, not substantive rights are at the heart of most protests, and repression is especially likely where small, homogeneous groups of people are involved, examples in case being farmers, hawkers, and the victims of medical mistakes."†

Clearly, any protests have to be taken seriously by the central government in Beijing. Yet, it is also clear that these protests are not seen as a major threat because most of these protests are over local issues. They are not protests against the central government. Indeed, the goal of the protests is to attract the attention of the central government, whom they often perceive as their savior and benefactor against corrupt local officials.

I had the opportunity to visit Moscow in 1976, when the Soviet Communist Party seemed to be strong and invincible. There was no question that in Moscow the people were frightened and intimidated by their government. It was a harsh top-down society. When I took the train from Moscow to Leningrad one evening, I found the toilet locked at night. After waiting for a while outside the toilet, I came to realize that the door had been deliberately barred. I went to search for the train conductor. Eventually, I found a large and gruff Russian woman who scowled at me. And why was the toilet door locked? Because in the communist Soviet Union, the spirit of the law was that everything was forbidden unless it is specifically allowed. There was no law that toilet doors on trains had to be kept open; hence, they were kept closed.

---

* Christian Göbel, "Social Unrest in China: A Bird's Eye Perspective," October 20, 2017, https://christiangoebel.net/social-unrest-in-china-a-birds-eye-perspective.
† Ibid.

Anyone who has visited the old communist Soviet Union and the new communist China will know that they are worlds apart in terms of personal freedoms. The old Soviet Union never had any entrepreneurs because there was no economic freedom there. By contrast, China has developed millions of entrepreneurs. Thousands of start-ups are launched in China each year. China has also learned the best practices from other modern cities, like Hong Kong and Singapore, and makes it very easy to launch a new business in Shanghai or Shenzhen, two of the most vibrantly entrepreneurial cities in the world. The 2019 World Bank "Doing Business Report," which monitored the ease of doing business in Beijing and Shanghai, noted that "China carried out a record number of reforms during the past year to improve the business climate for small and medium enterprises, earning the country a spot in this year's top 10 global improvers [. . .]. China implemented the largest number of reforms in the East Asia and Pacific region."

Bert Hofman, the former World Bank Country Director for China, was also quoted as saying: "China has made rapid progress in improving its business climate for domestic small and medium enterprises in the past year. This progress, which now puts China among the top 50 economies in the world, signals the value the government places on nurturing entrepreneurship and private enterprise."* The World Bank report also observed that "since last year, three procedures were removed and consequently it now takes 9 days to start a business, on par with most OECD high income countries. In addition, Beijing is now one of only two cities in the world where the process of starting a business is completely free."† An obvious point needs to be emphasized here. No entrepreneurship

---

* World Bank, "Doing Business Report: China Carries Out Record Business Reforms, Edges into Top 50 Economies," The World Bank press release, October 31, 2018, https://www.worldbank.org/en/news/press-release/2018/10/31/doing-business-report-china-carries-out-record-business-reforms-edges-into-top-50-economies.
† Ibid.

can happen unless people feel that they have the freedom to take risks and make individual decisions.

Yet, even though China has progressively opened up (relative to the old Soviet Union) and allowed an explosion of personal freedoms, its leaders must be aware that current political system, where the Chinese Communist Party (CCP) has absolute control, cannot last forever. As Chinese society evolves and China develops the world's largest and possibly best-educated middle class that also travels around the world regularly, it would be perfectly natural for this group to progressively ask for a greater say in managing their social and political affairs. This demand will come. History also teaches us that it is difficult to make a transition from an authoritarian political system to a more participatory political system.

Curiously, the leaders who are the most aware of the difficulty of making political transitions are Chinese. This was revealed when the notes of a conversation between Wang Qishan and Francis Fukuyama, one of the most influential political theorists of our time, were released inadvertently. The fact that such a meeting took place is extraordinary. No previous Soviet leader would have dared to meet an American political theorist to discuss political transitions. Chinese leaders are aware of the huge challenge they face in trying to manage this transition away from a fully authoritarian system. They are researching, thinking, and preparing to change, at a time they feel is right.

As Wang Qishan admitted to Fukuyama, the most dangerous period for any society is the period of transition. He provided a few examples: "The revolution of France and the reform of British capitalists, which one is better between a reform and a revolution? In different historical contexts there are different conclusions. The French thought that the Revolution has ultimately solved the problem; The British said that the social cost of a reform is low. On different models, there was also a great debate after the Imperialism had ended in China:

Should we establish a Constitutional Monarchy or a Republic?"* Wang added:

> Another Chinese character should be mentioned when we are talking about this new beginning: We have 1.3 billion people. Together with our long history—This is the context where we get started again, where we explore [our way] in the light of great historical meaning. We are fully aware of the suggestion from you about China's reform, however, the extent of this very reform should be carefully considered. We fairly know the difference: The population of all developed countries only makes up 1.1 billion whereas China has 1.3 to 1.4 billion citizens. I repeatedly discuss about this difference with my American friends. The change of China is huge: Economically, it is extraordinary that 1.3 billion people have lift themselves out of poverty; but in the field of culture and education, we still have a long way to go, and this issue has a great impact on our political and economic development. Once I told to Mr. Henry Kissinger in this room: "Once China is developing in a certain direction, it is impossible to push 1.3 billion people walking on the side of [a] cliff; every one of these 1.3 billion people is important for our achievement." [Note: the meaning of this phrase is unclear in the English translation. What Wang Qishan probably meant to say is that 1.3 billion Chinese people could not be pushed toward a direction they did not wish to go to.] When implementing policies in China, we still have to be very cautious.†

Awareness of a challenge does not mean that one can manage the challenge well. And not all transitions are the same. East Asian democratic systems are different from American or European democratic

---

* Qizuan Yang, "New Statement from Wang Qishan: We Are Determined, and We Are Careful," April 28, 2015, https://qixuanyang.wordpress.com/chinas-politics/wangqishan/new-statement-from-wang-qishan-we-are-determined-and-we-are-careful-3/.
† Ibid.

systems. In the Western political context, it is almost inconceivable for the same political party to remain in power for several decades, yet staying in power for long periods has been the norm in East Asia. The Liberal Democratic Party (LDP) of Japan, even though it lost power briefly from 1993 to 1994 and 2009 to 2012, has effectively run Japan for over five decades. Similarly, the People's Action Party (PAP) of Singapore has been in office from 1959 to today, for over sixty years. Clearly, the cultures of East Asian societies are more comfortable with political continuity and political stability. Change is not welcomed for its own sake.

So why should America promote American-style democracy in China? Democracy is an absolutely desirable good. It should always be supported. Yet, even the recent history of America shows that the United States doesn't always support democracy. America has always had a vital national interest in having a stable regime in Saudi Arabia and in Egypt. Hence, when America had to choose between promoting its ideals or its interests, it chose to set democracy aside. This may have been wise; it was certainly not idealistic. Similarly, for much of the Cold War, when China was considered a vital partner against the Soviet Union, America did not try to export democracy there. As Harvard professor Alastair Iain Johnston argues:

> Human rights in China, let alone democratization, has never been a prominent element in the practice of U.S. engagement policy, and little external pressure has been applied. Engagement can hardly be blamed for not achieving an outcome that it never took all that seriously or never expected to progress very far.*

Ambassador Chas Freeman has also explicitly stated:

---

* Alastair Iain Johnston, "The Failures of the 'Failure of Engagement' with China," *Washington Quarterly* 2, no. 2 (2019): 99–114, https://www.tandfonline.com/doi/abs/10.108 0/0163660X.2019.1626688.

Those Americans who criticized U.S. policies of engagement with Beijing as slighting efforts to democratize China and westernize its human rights and economic practices now cite the failure of engagement to meet their expectations as proof of policy failure. But the success of policies can only be measured in terms of their objectives. However much Americans may have hoped or expected that China would Americanize itself, U.S. policy was almost entirely aimed at changing China's external behavior rather than its constitutional order.[*]

So why does America promote the idea of democracy in China? Americans believe that democracies are essentially better than autocracies because they provide freedom to individuals. This freedom in turn enables individuals to thrive and flourish, using all their natural talents to do the fullest. This will result in a society becoming more prosperous and stronger. There is a lot of merit to this belief. Hence, if China does the same, the theory goes that China would emerge as a much more productive society, and its economy would grow even faster. Indeed, if this political experiment works and the average Chinese citizen becomes half as productive as the average American citizen, China would then have an economy that will be twice as large as America's economy and the potential to become four times as large.

But does it really serve US national interests to have a Chinese economy that is twice or four times as large as its own? One key goal of the current American security establishment is to maintain American primacy for as long as possible. So it would then clearly be against America's national interests to promote democracy in China if democracy was such a growth engine. Since America's security establishment is full of thoughtful and intelligent people, they might argue that the

---

[*] Chas W. Freeman Jr., "Sino-American Interactions, Past and Future," paper prepared for January 2019 conference at Carter Center, Atlanta, Georgia, https://chasfreeman.net /sino-american-interactions-past-and-future%ef%bb%bf/.

country should immediately stop exporting democracy to China for fear that it would create an even bigger rival.

Yet, the American security establishment continues to promote the export of democracy to China. Why? Because in practice, democracy promotion can have the opposite effect of what the theory suggests. It can destabilize and weaken societies, instead of strengthening them.

Successful democratic revolutions have included Portugal and Spain as well as some of the former Eastern European states—and the common factor in all these cases is that they had well-developed societies, with a strong middle-class and established civic cultures. Equally important was their neighborhood. All their immediate neighbors were strong, well-established democracies they could learn from. They could also join the European Union, which provided strong support for institution building. In short, several critical factors had to be in place to make a successful transition to stable and prosperous democratic rule.

In most of the other cases, where the critical factors were not in place, the transition to democracy proved to be disastrous. Yugoslavia fell apart. About one hundred thousand died in conflict. Similarly, even as the Soviet Union collapsed, the main component state, Russia, suffered a great deal as its economy imploded and its people suffered. Several former Soviet states, including Georgia and Ukraine, experienced conflict.

Against this recent historical backdrop, it would be reasonable for many Chinese leaders to believe that when America promotes democracy in China, it is not trying to strengthen China. It is trying to bring about a more disunited, divided China, a China beset by chaos. If that was China's fate, America could continue to remain the number one unchallenged power for another century or more.

Such a Machiavellian goal may seem far-fetched. Yet, it would be a perfectly reasonable move for a great power if it believes that its primacy is being challenged. Chinese leaders have no doubt that this is the real goal of those Americans trying to promote democracy in China.

As a result, they believe that they have no choice but to take all necessary measures to ensure that any Machiavellian scheme to weaken, destabilize, and divide China does not work. There is a very high degree of consensus among the ruling elites of China on this point. After Xi Jinping removed the term limits on his presidency, he continued to remain popular in China. The long history of China has taught the Chinese people a vital lesson: when the country has weak leaders, it falls apart.

Having been a lifelong student of Western philosophy, I'm acutely aware that Western philosophers have debated the best form of government for thousands of years. Many in the West have no doubt that the best form of government is democracy. Yet, the founder of Western philosophy, Plato, warned us, as Edward Luce reminded us, that "democracy was the rule of the mob—literally *demos* (mob) and *kratos* (rule)." Andrew Sullivan believes that the election of Trump has proven Plato to be prophetic. This is also why Plato said the best form of rule was by a philosopher king.

There is a very strong potential that Xi Jinping could provide to China the beneficent kind of rule provided by a philosopher king. He has experienced great personal hardship in his early life. He struggled to rise in the Communist Party. He has studied the world carefully. He is thoughtful and measured in his public comments. He does not do wild tweets. Few rulers in our world today are as qualified as he is. If he can deliver both political stability and economic growth to China for the next decade or two, he could well go down in Chinese history as the ruler who finally liberated China from centuries of poverty and made it into a modern well-developed economy, on par with the best economies in the West. The removal of term limits, for which he was roundly criticized, may turn out to be one of the biggest blessings that China has had. And it may be one critical reason why China wins the contest against America.

Yet, even if Xi were able to deliver decades of stability and prosperity to the Chinese, he would also know, as an acute student of history, that even a good ruler of China can be followed by decline and deterioration. Emperor Qianlong, who reigned from 1735 to 1796, for sixty-one long years, was probably China's last good emperor. Yet, within a few decades of his passing, China experienced its century of humiliation.

Xi's main challenge will be to ensure that China continues to remain stable and prosperous after he leaves. History teaches us that this will not be easy. Unless Xi starts assembling a strong team of potential successors, as well as strengthen the institutional frameworks that will enable a smooth succession after he retires, all his good work could be eroded. The contest between America and China will not be short term. It will be a marathon race. To ensure that China wins this marathon race, Xi will have to put in place sound succession mechanisms. If he succeeds in doing so, the odds will shift in favor of China. If not, America could win.

CHAPTER 7

THE ASSUMPTION OF VIRTUE

T HE SINGLE BIGGEST OBSTACLE TO IMPROVING RELATIONS between America and China is a powerful but invisible mental construct that has been deeply embedded in American minds: the assumption of virtue.

It is difficult to describe the precise scope and impact of this assumption on American attitudes and behavior, yet there is also no doubt that this assumption of virtue provides the bedrock of how Americans perceive themselves and their role in the world. Several American scholars have described why Americans believe themselves to be exceptional. Stephen Walt noted that "over the last two centuries, prominent Americans have described the United States as an 'empire of liberty,' a 'shining city on a hill,' the 'last best hope of Earth,' the 'leader of the free world,' and the 'indispensable nation.'"[*]

---

[*] Stephen M. Walt, "The Myth of American Exceptionalism," *Foreign Policy*, October 11, 2011, https://foreignpolicy.com/2011/10/11/the-myth-of-american-exceptionalism/.

He also explains why many Americans believe that America is the best country in the world: "Most statements of 'American exceptionalism' presume that America's values, political system, and history are unique and worthy of universal admiration. They also imply that the United States is both destined and entitled to play a distinct and positive role on the world stage." He then goes on to make a claim that most Americans would reject: "The only thing wrong with this self-congratulatory portrait of America's global role is that it is mostly a myth." Instead of trying to summarize his cogent arguments, I have attached his brief but brilliant essay as an appendix to this book so that Americans can read how a fellow American persuasively argues his case that "the idea that the United States is uniquely virtuous may be comforting to Americans. Too bad it is not true."

The assumption of virtue does not just rest on the claim that America has been a benign actor on the world stage (a claim that Stephen Walt debunks). It also relies on the idea that the quality of life that the United States provides its citizens is the best in the world. In short, America is the greatest society in the world in improving the lives of its citizens.

This belief rests on a strong historical foundation. From colonial times, white Americans had a higher standard of living than their contemporaries in Europe. More recently, there was a period, probably from the end of World War II to roughly about 1980, when the broad mass of the American people, including the bottom 50 percent, experienced a significant improvement in their standard of living. Those were happy times. Growing up in Singapore in the 1960s, I used to watch with envy the TV sitcoms from America, including *My Three Sons* and *I Love Lucy*, which showed an American middle class enjoying an idyllic life, living in separate homes with two-car garages surrounded by spacious lawns. There was clearly a period when the whole world envied America's record in social and economic development.

Income in thousand euros	1980	1990	2000	2010	2015
US	7.8	7.3	6.6	6.8	n/a
EU	8.3	8.2	8.1	9.9	10.3
China	0.8	1.2	1.3	2.6	3.9
Asia excluding Middle East	1.1	1.5	1.7	2.3	2.8
World	1.7	2.0	2.1	2.7	3.0

CHART 6. Average Income of an Individual in the Bottom 50 Percent of the Nation or Region[*]

That period, however, is over. Now, the more thoughtful observers of America around the world (and there are many of them) see that something has gone seriously wrong in American society. Many of the key indicators are turning negative. Quite shockingly, America is the only major developed society where the average income of the bottom 50 percent has stagnated over a thirty-year period, 1980–2010, as documented by Professor Danny Quah of the National University of Singapore. In a short but brilliant paper, he documents some remarkable facts about the socioeconomic condition of American society. First, from 1980, "over the subsequent three decades the US bottom half had its average income decline. This occurred in no other major bloc or economy in the world. Nowhere else did the poor systematically become poorer."[†] Chart 6, which compares the average income of an individual in the bottom 50 percent of the United States, EU, China, and all of Asia, documents clearly how the bottom 50 percent of the American population has suffered a decline in income in a way that no other major region has suffered. Given this extraordinary track record, it is useful to ponder why so few Americans are aware that, as Danny Quah points out, America is truly an "exceptional" nation in this area.

---

* Quah, "The US Is, Indeed, the Exceptional Nation."
† Ibid.

Sadly, this stagnation of income has also resulted in a lot of human pain and suffering, as documented by two Princeton University economists, Anne Case and Angus Deaton. The white working classes of America used to carry the American dream of getting a better life in their hearts and souls. Today, as Case says, there is a "sea of despair" among them. She and Deaton conclude: "Ultimately, we see our story as about the collapse of the white, high-school-educated working class after its heyday in the early 1970s, and the pathologi/es that accompany that decline."* The detailed study of Case and Deaton documents how poor economic prospects "compounds over time through family dysfunction, social isolation, addiction, obesity and other pathologies."†

What would one of America's greatest moral and political philosophers of recent times, John Rawls, think of America's economic and social trajectory? He formulated a test on how societies should measure their success in delivering social justice: "the higher expectations of those better situated are just *if and only if* they work as part of a scheme which improves the expectations of the least advantaged members of society."‡ In short, if America wanted to judge whether it is the world's greatest society on the basis of Rawls's advice, it would study the data to see how its "least advantaged members of society" are doing.

If Rawls were alive today, he would be shocked to see how badly off the least advantaged Americans have become. In his book *Oligarchy*, American political scientist Jeffrey Winters provides a stunning illustration of just how dire US inequality has become: the average wealth of the richest one hundred American households relative to that of the

---

* Joel Achenbach and Dan Keating, "New Research Identifies a 'Sea of Despair' Among White Working-Class Americans," *Washington Post*, March 23, 2017, https://www.washingtonpost.com/national/health-science/new-research-identifies-a-sea-of-despair-among-white-working-class-americans/2017/03/22/c777ab6e-0da6-11e7-9b0d-d27c98455440_story.html?utm_term=.f16ccaa3e0c5.
† Ibid.
‡ John Rawls, *A Theory of Justice* (Cambridge, MA: Belknap Press, 1971), 75.

Ratio of average income in the top 1% to average income in the bottom 50%	1980	2015
US	41	138 (2010)
EU	24	32
China	12	47
Asia excluding Middle East	38	66
World	100	108

CHART 7 The Ratio of Average Income in the Top 1 Percent to That in the Bottom 50 Percent*

bottom 90 percent approximates the wealth disparity between a Roman senator and a slave at the height of the Roman Empire.[†] This massive surge in inequality has taken place in recent decades. Danny Quah has also provided valuable data comparing the inequality in America with other major regions. Please see Chart 7.

As Quah observes, "in the US this ratio of rich person to poor person was 41 in 1980. It then more than tripled, to 138, in the thirty years following. Looking down the rows of [the table], we see that, indeed, inequality has increased everywhere in the world. By this measure, that in China has quadrupled in the last 30 years; in Asia, almost doubled. However, nowhere has inequality risen to the extent it has in the US."[‡]

America's Founding Fathers were intent on creating a society that was the opposite of the feudalism that migrants had left behind in Europe. It is therefore shocking to read contemporary American writers describing how American society is now similar to feudal Europe. This is how Joel Kotkin describes the main divides in America today: "The current conflict fundamentally reprises the end of the French feudal era, where the Third Estate, made up of the commoners, challenged

---

* Quah, "The US Is, Indeed, the Exceptional Nation."
† Jeffrey A. Winters, Oligarchy (New York: Cambridge University Press, 2011).
‡ Ibid.

the hegemony of the First Estate and Second, made up of the church and aristocracy." He adds: "Today's neo-feudalism recalls the social order that existed before the democratic revolutions of the 17th and 18th Century, with our two ascendant estates filling the roles of the former dominant classes."[*]

Other influential Americans have also documented the major social deterioration in America. Ray Dalio runs the largest, most successful hedge fund in the world, which has succeeded through rigorous empirical research. Dalio has now applied this research to understanding poverty and inequality in America. On his LinkedIn page, Dalio spells out the dramatic decline in the living standards of the majority of Americans and points out that "most people in the bottom 60% are poor" and cites "a recent Federal Reserve study [that showed that] 40% of all Americans would struggle to raise $400 in the event of an emergency."[†] Worse, Dalio notes that "they are increasingly getting stuck being poor . . . the odds of someone in the bottom quintile moving up to the middle quintile or higher in a 10-year period . . . declined from about 23% in 1990 to only 14% as of 2011." The data on social deterioration in America is undeniable. It undercuts the claims that America is a society where hard work brings rewards. For most people, the rewards have dried up. The platitude "virtue is its own reward" turns out to be grimly and limitingly true.

Why has America performed so badly? There are two ways to explain the data. The first is that this period is a temporary situation, similar to the temporary socioeconomic aberration of the Great Depression

---

* Joel Kotkin, "American Renewal: The Real Conflict Is Not Racial or Sexual, It's Between the Ascendant Rich Elites and the Rest of Us," Daily Caller, September 11, 2019, https://dailycaller.com/2019/09/11/middle-working-class-neo-estates-liberal/.

† Ray Dalio, "Why and How Capitalism Needs to Be Reformed (Part 1)," LinkedIn, April 4, 2019, https://www.linkedin.com/pulse/why-how-capitalism-needs-reformed-ray-dalio/. See also Board of Governors of the Federal Reserve System, *Report on the Economic Well-Being of U.S. Household in 2017*, May 2018, https://www.federalreserve.gov/publications/files/2017-report-economic-well-being-us-households-201805.pdf, quoted in Dalio.

of 1929 to 1939. America quickly recovered from it to have several more decades of prosperity. The same could happen this time. America could be expected to recover fully, especially if one believes that its democratic political system is built to be self-correcting. American democracy should guarantee that the interests of the majority of the population are always protected.

The second explanation is that it demonstrates that a fundamental change has taken place in America's political arrangements, without the American people noticing it. Every two to four years Americans go to the polls to elect their congressmen, senators, governors, and state legislative assembly representatives. And yet, under the surface guise of a functioning democracy, with all the rituals of voting, America has become a society run by a moneyed aristocracy that uses its money to make major political and social decisions. As a result, this class has been able to enact the greatest transfer of wealth that has ever taken place in American society.

Rawls explained: "The liberties protected by the principle of participation lose much of their value whenever those who have greater private means are permitted to use their advantages to control the course of public debate." Almost fifty years ago, he warned that if those with "greater private means" are allowed to control the course of public debate, American democracy would be subverted.*

This is exactly what happened when the US Supreme Court overturned, in a landmark ruling in *Citizens United v. Federal Election Commission (FEC) (2010)* and in other decisions, many of the legislative restraints on the use of money to influence the political process. A report by the Center for Public Integrity reported that: "The Citizens United ruling, released in January 2010, tossed out the corporate and union ban on making independent expenditures and financing electioneering communications. It gave corporations and unions the green light to spend

---

* Rawls, *A Theory of Justice*, 225.

unlimited sums on ads and other political tools, calling for the election or defeat of individual candidates."[*] The impact of this and other Supreme Court decisions was monumental. Effectively, they may be transforming the American political system. Martin Wolf says that "the Supreme Court's perverse 2010 'Citizens United' decision held that companies are persons and money is speech. That has proved a big step on the journey of the US towards becoming a plutocracy."[†] American legal scholar Laurence Tribe described well the folly of the Citizens United decision in particular: the Supreme Court "has reached out to decide issues not squarely before it while implausibly downplaying, and at times all but denying, the baleful corruption of American politics by means short of criminal bribery—by means that are lamentable precisely because they are lawful."[‡] As a result of this line of court decisions, the major substantive public policy decisions made by US legislators are no longer the result of one person one vote because of how the votes are funded.

Two Princeton University professors have documented how ordinary American citizens have lost their political power and influence. Martin Gilens and Benjamin Page studied the relative influence that the views of average Americans and mass-based interest groups have on policy outcomes versus the views of the economic elite in 1,779 cases. They found that

> economic elites and organized groups representing business interests
> have substantial independent impacts on U.S. government policy,
> while average citizens and mass-based interest groups have little or

---

[*] John Dunbar, "The 'Citizens United' Decision and Why It Matters," The Center for Public Integrity, October 18, 2012, https://publicintegrity.org/federal-politics/the -citizens-united-decision-and-why-it-matters/.

[†] Martin Wolf, "Why the US Economy Isn't as Competitive or Free as You Think," Financial Times, November 14, 2019, https://www.ft.com/content/97be3f2c-00b1-11ea -b7bc-f3fa4e77dd47.

[‡] Laurence H. Tribe, "Dividing 'Citizens United': The Case v. the Controversy," SSRN, March 9, 2015, https://papers.ssrn.com/sol3/papers.cfm?abstract_id=2575865.

no independent influence. [. . .] When the preferences of economic elites and the stands of organized interest groups are controlled for, the preferences of the average American appear to have only a minuscule, near-zero, statistically non-significant impact upon public policy. [. . .] Furthermore, the preferences of economic elites (as measured by our proxy, the preferences of "affluent" citizens) have far more independent impact upon policy change than the preferences of average citizens do. [. . .] In the United States, our findings indicate, the majority does *not* rule—at least not in the causal sense of actually determining policy outcomes.

They reach the following alarming conclusion:

Americans do enjoy many features central to democratic governance, such as regular elections, freedom of speech and association, and a widespread (if still contested) franchise. But we believe that if policymaking is dominated by powerful business organizations and a small number of affluent Americans, then America's claims to being a democratic society are seriously threatened.[*]

In the past, the broad middle classes of America had a strong say in determining the fundamental direction of American society. Today, they no longer do. The decisions of the US Congress are not determined by the voters; they are determined by the funders. As a result, America is becoming functionally less and less of a democracy, where all citizens have an equal voice. Instead, it looks more and more like a plutocracy, where a few rich people are disproportionately powerful.

---

[*] Martin Gilens and Benjamin I. Page, "Testing Theories of American Politics: Elites, Interest Groups, and Average Citizens," *Perspectives on Politics* 12, no. 3 (September 2014): 564–581, https://scholar.princeton.edu/sites/default/files/mgilens/files/gilens_and _page_2014_-testing_theories_of_american_politics.doc.pdf.

A 2018 study by scholars Alexander Hertel-Fernandez, Theda Skocpol, and Jason Sclar, of the School of International and Public Affairs, Columbia University, further argued that

> since the mid-2000s, newly formed conservative and progressive donor consortia—above all the Koch seminars [founded by brothers Charles and David Koch] and the DA [Democracy Alliance]—have magnified the impact of wealthy donors by raising and channeling ever more money not just into elections but also into full *arrays of cooperating political organizations*. . . . The Koch seminars . . . allowed donations to be channeled into building a virtual third political party organized around AFP [Americans for Prosperity], an overarching political network able not only to electorally support the Republican Party but also to push and pull its candidates and office holders in preferred ultra-free-market policy directions. . . . To the degree that wealthy donor consortia have succeeded in building organizational infrastructures, they have shifted the resources available for developing policy proposals, pressing demands on lawmakers, and mobilizing ordinary Americans into politics. . . . When plutocratic collectives impose new agendas on political organizations seeking to attract financial resources, the funders reshape routines, goals, and centers of power in U.S. politics well beyond the budgetary impact of particular grants.[*]

---

[*] Alexander Hertel-Fernandez, Theda Skocpol, and Jason Sclar, "When Political Mega-Donors Join Forces: How the Koch Network and the Democracy Alliance Influence Organized U.S. Politics on the Right and Left," *Studies in American Political Development* 32, no. 2 (2018): 127–165, doi:10.1017/S0898588X18000081; also available at https://scholar.harvard.edu/files/ahertel/files/donorconsortia-named.pdf. See also page 2 of the PDF: "On the right, the *Koch seminars* directed by Charles and David Koch and their close associates were launched in 2003 as twice-yearly gatherings of very wealthy conservatives aiming to push the Republican Party and U.S. government toward libertarian and ultra-free-market politics. . . . the *Democracy Alliance*—called the 'DA' for short—was launched in 2005 to bring together more than a hundred left-leaning wealthy liberals to meet twice a year and channel contributions to advocacy and constituency organizations operating on the left edge of the Democratic Party."

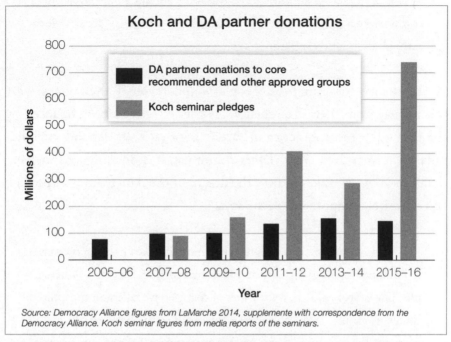

Koch and DA partner donations

CHART 8. Democracy Alliance Figures and Koch and DA Partner Donations (Designed by Patti Issacs)

Chart 8 from their study illustrates the hundreds of millions of dollars that wealthy donors have raised annually within the donor consortia to finance their political interests.

The authors thus conclude:

Our analysis of the Koch and DA consortia highlights that a great deal of big-money influence flows through mechanisms other than individual or business donations to the electoral and lobbying operations ... To understand how the wealthy are reshaping U.S. politics, we need to look not just at their election and lobbying expenditures but also at their concerted investments in many kinds of political organizations operating across a variety of fields and functions. Only in this way can we account for the stark inequalities in government responsiveness documented by researchers such as Martin Gilens, Larry Bartels, and Benjamin Page.*

In theory, the American people would revolt if their votes were taken away from them. Yet, their votes have effectively been hijacked by the rich—but most Americans haven't noticed it yet. Anand Giridharadas, a former *New York Times* columnist, has documented in great detail in *Winners Take All* how the dream of the American middle class has effectively evaporated. As he says:

A successful society is a progress machine. It takes in the raw material of innovations and produces broad human advancement. America's machine is broken. When the fruits of change have fallen on the United States in recent decades, the very fortunate have basketed almost all of them. For instance, the average pretax income of the top tenth of Americans has doubled since 1980, that of the top 1 percent has more than tripled, and that of the top 0.001 percent has risen more than sevenfold—even as the average pretax income of the bottom half of Americans has stayed almost precisely the same. These familiar figures amount to three and a half decades' worth of wondrous, head-spinning change with zero impact on the average pay of 117 million Americans.†

Giridharadas claims that the American people are beginning to "feel" that the system is unfair:

Thus many millions of Americans, on the left and right, feel one thing in common: that the game is rigged against people like them. [. . .]

---

* Hertel-Fernandez, Skocpol, and Sclar, "When Political Mega-Donors Join Forces," 76 (of the PDF).
† Anand Giridharadas, "Prologue," in *Winners Take All: The Elite Charade of Changing the World* (New York: Alfred A. Knopf, 2018).

There is a spreading recognition, on both sides of the ideological divide, that the system is broken, that the system has to change.*

American scholars on political systems are fond of quoting Lord Acton's famous quip: "Power corrupts. Absolute power corrupts absolutely." After quoting him, they probably whisper under their breaths, "Thank God, we are a democracy with separation of powers. This couldn't happen to us." All those scholars should consider this variation on Lord Acton instead: "Money corrupts. Absolute money corrupts absolutely."

The corrupting effect of money on political processes should be more prominently highlighted in American political discourse. In most societies, when individuals or corporations use money to influence public policy decisions, it is called out as corruption. Even people in third world countries that suffer from widespread corruption know it is illegal, though they often do not have the means to oppose it. But in America, it is not considered corruption to use money to influence public policy decisions because the Supreme Court legalized it.

It is a huge irony that Congress passed the Foreign Corrupt Practices Act in 1977, which specifically prohibits the "authorization of the payment of money or anything of value to any person, while knowing that all or a portion of such money or thing of value will be offered, given or promised, directly or indirectly, to a foreign official to influence the foreign official in his or her official capacity, induce the foreign official to do or omit to do an act in violation of his or her lawful duty, or to secure any improper advantage in order to assist in obtaining or retaining business for or with, or directing business to, any person."† Effectively, this means that if an American corporation uses money to influence an Egyptian or Indonesian legislator, he will be punished under American

---

* Ibid.

† "Foreign Corrupt Practices Act," US Department of Justice, https://www.justice.gov /criminal-fraud/foreign-corrupt-practices-act.

law. However, if the same American corporation uses money (through campaign and super PAC contributions) to influence American legislators, it is part of the democratic process.

Here, Rawls warned that if "those who have greater private means are permitted to use their advantages to control the course of public debate," this would be the corrupting result:

> Eventually, these inequalities will enable those better situated to exercise a larger influence over the development of legislation. In due time they are likely to acquire a preponderant weight in settling social questions, at least in regard to those matters upon which they normally agree, which is to say in regard to those things that support their favored circumstances.[*]

This is precisely what has happened over the past few decades: the affluent have gained "preponderant weight . . . in regard of those things that support their favored circumstances." There has been a relative transfer of wealth and political power from the vast majority of America's population to a privileged superminority.

In a society where there is real equality of opportunity, where there is a level playing field for all young people to compete in and to grow and thrive, we should not have seen such a dramatic divergence between the incomes of the top 1 percent and the bottom 50 percent, as documented in Chart 7 by Danny Quah. "Equal" opportunities have been effectively disappearing. The data document this. As New York University's Michael Hout notes: "American men and women born since 1980—the millennials—have been less upwardly mobile than previous generations of Americans."[†] And why

---

[*] Rawls, *A Theory of Justice*, 225.

[†] Michael Hout, "Social Mobility," *Pathways: A Magazine on Poverty, Inequality, and Social Policy; State of the Union, Millennial Dilemma*, Special Issue 2019, 29–32, https://inequality .stanford.edu/sites/default/files/Pathways_SOTU_2019.pdf.

is this so? The complete answer is complex, but one simple observation is that though many ladders have been available for people at the bottom to reach the top—good schools, access to good health care, crime-free neighborhoods, two-parent families—all these ladders have deteriorated, as documented by Case and Deaton earlier in this chapter. Americans have only begun to notice and ask why this is happening.

Remarkably, the myth that America is a society of equal opportunity has not been shattered. Despite strong evidence to the contrary, Americans' belief in equal opportunity remains strong. This belief also explains why few Americans resent billionaires. If I believe that I could also make it, why should I resent the one who has made it? Successful people show that the doors are open for my advancement. The many billionaires of the past three decades—from Bill Gates to Larry Page, from Mark Zuckerberg to Jeff Bezos—keep alive the American dream that opportunity exists for everybody.

America has effectively become a class-stratified society where the prospects of someone from the bottom 10 percent reaching the top 10 percent are extremely low, indeed lower than many advanced societies in the rest of the world. Recent data reported in *The Economist* shows that "an American born to a household in the bottom 20% of earnings, for instance, only has a 7.8% chance of reaching the top 20% when they grow up."* Data provided in a study published in the *American Economic Review*, reproduced in Chart 9, shows the differences among actual and perceived intergenerational mobility in several different countries.†

---

* "Americans Overestimate Social Mobility in Their Country," *The Economist*, February 14, 2018, https://www.economist.com/graphic-detail/2018/02/14/americans-overestimate -social-mobility-in-their-country.

† Alberto Alesina, Stefanie Stantcheva, and Edoardo Teso, "Intergenerational Mobility and Preferences for Redistribution," *American Economic Review* 108, no. 2 (2018): 521– 554, https://pubs.aeaweb.org/doi/pdfplus/10.1257/aer.20162015.

	US		UK		France		Italy		Sweden		US versus EU	
	Actual	Perceived	Actual	Perceived	Actual	Perceived	Actual	Perceived	Actual	Perceived	Perceived US	Perceived EU
	(1)	(2)	(3)	(4)	(5)	(6)	(7)	(8)	(9)	(10)	(11)	(12)
Q1 to Q5	7.8	11.7 (0.00)	11.4	10.0 (0.00)	11.2	9.1 (0.00)	10.4	10.1 (0.48)	11.1	9.2 (0.00)	11.7	9.6 (0.00)
Q1 to Q4	12.7	12.0 (0.00)	12.9	10.6 (0.00)	12.8	10.5 (0.00)	15.6	11.2 (0.00)	17.3	11.2 (0.00)	12.0	10.9 (0.00)
Q1 to Q3	18.7	22.3 (0.00)	19.9	19.4 (0.13)	23.0	21.5 (0.00)	21.0	21.9 (0.03)	21.0	24.5 (0.00)	22.3	21.6 (0.06)
Q1 to Q2	27.7	21.8 (0.00)	25.1	22.2 (0.00)	23.8	23.6 (0.55)	25.8	23.1 (0.00)	23.8	23.1 (0.09)	21.8	23.0 (0.00)
Q1 to Q1	33.1	32.2 (0.07)	30.6	37.8 (0.00)	29.2	35.3 (0.00)	27.3	33.6 (0.00)	26.7	32.0 (0.00)	32.2	34.9 (0.00)
Observations		2,170		1,290		1,297		1,242		881	2,170	4,710
p-value from joint test		0.00		0.00		0.00		0.00		0.00	0.00	0.00

NOTES: The first five rows of the table report the average perceived probabilities (in even columns) and actual probabilities (in odd columns) that a child born to parents in the bottom quintile of the income distribution will be in quintiles 5, 4, 3, 2, and 1 respectively, when adult. Columns 11 and 12 show the perceived probabilities for the United States and the four European countries. P-values for tests of equality of the average perceived probability to the actual probability, or of the average perceived probability in the United States to the one in Europe, are in parentheses. The last row shows the p-value from the joint test that the average perceived probabilities are jointly different from the actual probabilities, and, in column 12, that the average perceptions in the United States are jointly different from those in Europe.

CHART 9. Perceived and Actual Transition Probabilities Across Countries

The most significant statistic in Chart 9 is the top left-hand figure: 11.7 percent of people at the bottom believe they can make it to the top; 7.8 percent actually do so. This is also the lowest percentage among all the countries compared in the chart. The pattern at the bottom of the same column is the opposite.

If one asks thoughtful and well-informed Americans which country, America or China, provides a better opportunity for a child from the bottom 10 percent to reach the top 10 percent, 99 percent would reply, without a shadow of a doubt, that, of course, America provides a better opportunity. Yet, the data show that there is greater social mobility in China than in America. In November 2018, the *New York Times* reported:

> Like the United States, China still has a yawning gap between the rich and the poor—and the poorest Chinese are far poorer, with nearly 500 million people, or about 40 percent of the population, living on less than $5.50 a day, according to the World Bank. But by some measures Chinese society has about the same level of inequality as the United States.

Significantly, Chart 10 shows that China has more social mobility than America does. The *New York Times* report the chart is originally from adds:

> Xu Liya, 49, once tilled wheat fields in Zhejiang, a rural province along China's east coast. Her family ate meat only once a week, and each night she crammed into a bedroom with seven relatives. Then she attended university on a scholarship and started a clothing store. Now she owns two cars and an apartment valued at more than $300,000. Her daughter attends college in Beijing. "Poverty and corruption have hurt average people in China for too long," she said.

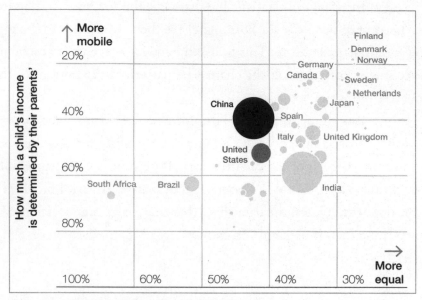

CHART 10. Social Mobility (Designed by Patti Issacs)

"While today's society isn't perfect, poor people have the resources to compete with rich people, too."[*]

Chart 11 from the World Inequality Database also documents that in the field of social equity, China is doing better than America.[†] While the total accumulated growth of the top 10 percent in China from 1980 to 2015 was 1232 percent, compared to 124 percent for America, the total growth of the top 10 percent in America was 41 times larger than the bottom 50 percent. By contrast, the total growth in China was only 4 times larger.

When an abundance of data contradicts the myth of America being a land of equal opportunity, why does it endure? One answer is that this

---

[*] Javier C. Hernández and Quoctrung Bui, "The American Dream Is Alive. In China," *New York Times*, November 18, 2018, https://www.nytimes.com/interactive/2018/11/18/world/asia/china-social-mobility.html.

[†] "Top 1% Net Personal Wealth Share," World Inequality Database, https://wid.world/world/#shweal_p99p100_z/US;CN/last/eu/k/p/yearly/s/false/14.1905/60/curve/false/country.

Income growth and inequality in China and the United States, 1980–2015				
	China		US	
Income group	Average annual growth rate	Total cumulated growth	Average annual growth rate	Total cumulated growth
Full population	6.4%	776%	1.4%	63%
Bottom 50%	4.6%	386%	0.1%	3%
Middle 40%	6.2%	733%	1.9%	44%
Top 10%	7.7%	1232%	2.3%	124%
Top 1%	8.8%	1800%	3.3%	208%
Top 0.1%	9.5%	2271%	4.2%	325%
Top 0.01%	10.2%	2921%	5.0%	460%
Top 0.001%	10.8%	3524%	5.9%	646%

CHART 11. Differential Levels of Social Mobility (Designed by Patti Issacs)

myth is an essential part of the American identity. The American spirit would be much poorer if it were taken away. Equally important, the myth of equal opportunity is tied to the myth that America has been an exceptionally successful society because it imposes the fewest restrictions on the freedom of the individual. *Freedom* is a hallowed word in American discourse. Because Americans enjoy exceptional political and economic freedoms, they believe they can achieve a comfortable middle-class standard of living without legislating income equality. America worships freedom.

But America also worships reason. Most Americans believe that America is fundamentally a rational society. All ideas are exposed to the sunlight of public debate (now, often online). Compared to many other societies, few limits are placed on rational discourse. As a result, many Americans believe that American society has no sacred cows.

Why, then, don't more Americans question the use of money to influence elections? The answer is that they, like the majority of the Supreme Court, see any curb on the use of money as a curb on the freedom to participate in elections. Since any curbs on freedom of speech are unacceptable in American society, any curbs on using money in election campaigns are also unacceptable.

Yes, there are exceptions. Bernie Sanders and Elizabeth Warren support restrictions on campaign finance and have been elected to the Senate. Similarly, more recently, an avowedly socialist candidate like Alexandria Ocasio-Cortez has been elected to the House of Representatives. However, the only effective impact of these exceptions is that they help to strengthen the myth that it is the broad majority of the American people who are freely choosing their representatives. By protecting and strengthening this myth, they provide legitimacy to the laws made by the US House of Representatives and the US Senate, many of which serve the interests of the moneyed aristocracy or well-funded special interest groups, not the majority population. For example, a majority of the American people have long supported some measure of gun control.* As the American journalist Elizabeth Drew lamented in the aftermath of the consecutive shootings in El Paso, Texas, and Dayton, Ohio, on the first weekend of August 2019:

> On the face of it, adopting meaningful gun-control legislation after such a horrendous tragedy should not have been a problem. Polls showed that ninety-two percent of the public supported closing loopholes in the requirement for background checks—which at present don't include examinations of individuals purchasing firearms at gun shows, privately from another individual, or online—and that 62% supported a ban on high-capacity magazines. It was hard to ignore the emotional appeal of the shattered parents who'd come to Wash-

---

* Ninety-two percent of Americans, for example, support universal background checks: "Universal Background Checks," Giffords Law Center, https://lawcenter.giffords.org/gun-laws/policy-areas/background-checks/universal-background-checks/.

ington to plead their case. Yet, even in the wake of Sandy Hook, the US Senate voted down two measures to tighten gun-control laws.[*]

The US Congress is incapable of voting for gun controls because any members of Congress who vote for gun control will find that their opponents in the next election will be funded massively by the pro-gun lobby.

Similarly, a vast majority of Americans are in favor of higher taxes for those with ultrahigh annual incomes. A survey by CNBC found that

> fully 60% of millionaires support [Senator Elizabeth] Warren's plan for taxing the wealth of those who have more than $50 million in assets. [. . .] Polls show that a majority of Americans also back a wealth tax. But the support from millionaires, some of whom would presumably pay the tax, shows that some millionaires are willing to accept higher taxes amidst growing concern over inequality and soaring fortunes of the rich. While 88% of Democrats support the wealth tax, 62% of independents support it along with 36% of Republicans. Even the upper tier of millionaires, those worth more than $5 million, support a wealth tax, with two-thirds in favor.[†]

Yet, it is almost impossible for members of Congress to vote for higher taxes as they would be targeted by special interest lobbies. Even more insidiously, most ordinary Americans do not know that they effectively pay higher taxes than the ultrawealthy because the ultrawealthy

---

[*] Elizabeth Drew, "What's Behind America's Mass Shootings?," Project Syndicate, August 13, 2019, https://www.project-syndicate.org/commentary/america-gun-control-mass -shootings-by-elizabeth-drew-2019-08.

[†] Robert Frank, "Most Millionaires Support a Tax on Wealth above $50 Million," CNBC Survey Says," CNBC, June 12, 2019, https://www.cnbc.com/2019/06/12/most -millionaires-support-tax-on-wealth-above-50-million-cnbc-survey.html.

are able to employ innocuous-sounding tax provisions that effectively lower their tax rate. One such example is the tax treatment of carried interest. As the *New York Times* reported in 2017:

> For decades, the carried interest provision has enabled wealthy private equity managers, hedge fund managers and real estate investors to pay the lower capital gains rate (20 percent, not counting the Obama health care surcharge of 3.8 percent) on their income rather than the rate on ordinary income (a maximum of 39.6 percent). . . . the primary argument against the carried interest loophole . . . [is] that the "carry"—the percentage of an investment's gains that the manager takes as compensation—should be treated as a payment for services and taxed like regular income, and not be viewed as a return on invested capital, in which the manager has put assets at risk.[*]

In this way the interests of the new moneyed aristocracy trump the interests of the majority of the population.

There is a paradox in this American worship of freedom. In theory, the profound difference between the American political system and the Chinese political system is that the American people are free to change their political system while the Chinese people are not free to do so. In reality, at this point in their history, the American people have as little freedom as the Chinese people to fundamentally change or alter their political system to ensure that it benefits the majority. However, since the American people nurture the illusion that they can change their political system, they are inclined to support it. This makes the American political system more stable than the Chinese political system, since the American people have no fundamental desire to change a system that they believe they control.

---

[*] James B. Stewart, "A Tax Loophole for the Rich That Just Won't Die," *New York Times*, November 9, 2017, https://www.nytimes.com/2017/11/09/business/carried-interest-tax-loophole.html.

Here it helps that the Americans are among the most patriotic people in the world. They genuinely and with great affection salute their flag and sing their national anthem with great gusto. They are dedicated to the US Constitution and the political system legitimized by it. With the tremendous emotional devotion Americans have to the political ideals and practices of the republic, it is difficult for an outside observer, however well intentioned, to call them into question.

The fact is that the American social contract has come to rest on one ideological pillar, freedom, instead of the traditional two pillars of democracies, freedom and equality. In functional terms, the American political system is moving from being a democracy to becoming a plutocracy, betraying the ideals of its Founding Fathers.

Imagine what America's Founding Fathers would say about America's current social contract. First, they would note that America's social progress should be judged against the principles enunciated by the great European political philosophers, whose ideas had inspired them in writing the Declaration of Independence and the Constitution. Thomas Jefferson, for example, used the writings of Montesquieu as his lodestar:

> He considers political virtue or the Armor Patriae as the energetic principle of a democratic republic; moderation, that of an aristocratic republic; honor, that of a limited monarchy; and fear, that of a despotism; and shews that every government should provide that its energetic principle should be the object of the education of its youth. . . . That its laws also should be relative to the same principle. In a democracy, equality and frugality should be promoted by the laws, as they nurse the Armor Patriae.*

* Matthew P. Bergman, "Montesquieu's Theory of Government and the Framing of the American Constitution," *Pepperdine Law Review* 18, no. 1 (December 15, 1990): 1–42, https://digitalcommons.pepperdine.edu/cgi/viewcontent.cgi?article=1659&context=plr.

If he were alive today, Jefferson would find it difficult to find either equality or frugality in contemporary America. John Adams, in a letter to a friend, lamented "the lack of republican virtue in the nation, . . . fear[ing] that the colonialists had become so corrupted by the principle of monarchy that they would be unable to manifest the requisite frugality and virtue to sustain a republican form of government."*

Rawls explicitly carried forward the ideas of social justice propounded by Locke, Rousseau, Montesquieu, and Kant. On the basis of their works, Rawls formulated two principles of justice, namely:

> First: each person is to have an equal right to the most extensive scheme of equal basic liberties compatible with a similar scheme of liberties for others.
>
> Second: social and economic inequalities are to be arranged so that they are both (a) reasonably expected to be to everyone's advantage, and (b) attached to positions and offices open to all.†

The second principle, which emphasizes that inequality can only be justified if it is "reasonably expected to be to everyone's advantage," is vital. Rawls goes on to emphasize the following point: "All social values—liberty and opportunity, income and wealth, and the social bases of self-respect—are to be distributed equally unless an unequal distribution of any, or all, of these values is to everyone's advantage."‡

I have no doubt that Rawls would be distressed by the inequality in contemporary America and how this inequality has distorted the political system to favor the rich, not the least advantaged. Locke, Rousseau, and Kant all emphasized the importance of both freedom and equality because they had lived through the distortions caused by the dominance of a hereditary aristocracy in Europe. The Founding Fathers of America

---

* Ibid.
† Rawls, *A Theory of Justice*, 53.
‡ Ibid., 54.

had inherited from these philosophers a deep antipathy to the concept of aristocracy. Yet, if a member of the eighteenth-century European aristocracy were to arrive in modern America, he or she would truly envy the hereditary privileges that the moneyed aristocracy have created for themselves. Journalist Edward Luce has cited this statistic to drive home this point: "Studies show that an eighth grade (14-year-old) child from a lower income bracket who achieves maths results in the top quarter is less likely to graduate than a kid in the upper income bracket scored in the bottom quarter. This is the reverse of how meritocracy should work."*

The reverse of meritocracy is aristocracy. In a meritocracy, if you are given a decent start in life, your destiny is determined by your performance in life; in an aristocracy, your destiny is determined at birth. Even though the American system has effectively created a new moneyed aristocracy, many Americans cannot see it. Attackers of this system are often labeled "socialists"—implying that they don't subscribe to the ideals of America's Founding Fathers, when in fact it is the system itself that has failed those ideals. New thoughtful elites are emerging around the world, many of whom have been educated in the best traditions of leading Western universities, and many of them are beginning to see equally well both the strengths and the weaknesses of the current American social contract. They are inspired by America's entrepreneurial energy, but few of them want to replicate the contemporary American social contract on their soil. When they want a sociopolitical model, they may look instead to the Nordic countries, whose systems value both freedom and equality and not just freedom alone. Equally important, they are puzzled by the "assumption of virtue" that American policymakers and

---

* Edward Luce, "Amy Chua and the Big Little Lies of US Meritocracy," *Financial Times* (London), June 13, 2019, https://www.ft.com/content/7b00c3a2-8daa-11e9-a1c1 -51bf8f989972. https://1gyhoq479ufd3yna29x7ubjn-wpengine.netdna-ssl.com/wp-content /uploads/FR-Born_to_win-schooled_to_lose.pdf, quoted in https://www.ft.com/content /7b00c3a2-8daa-11e9-a1c1-51bf8f989972.

pundits bring to the table when discussing America's social and political system today. There is much to admire; yet, there are also serious flaws.

Many Americans would retort that the American political system is certainly better than that of China's. It is far easier to reform a democratic system than to reform a Communist state. Look at what happened to the Soviet Union when the Communist Party gave up its monopoly on power. This, then, is the challenge that lies ahead for China: as China develops over time into the world's largest middle-class society, its political system will have to adjust and give a greater political voice to its people. China has studied the painful implosion at the end of the Soviet era in Russia carefully and is not likely to allow a replication of the Russian experience in China.

Yet, even though it is true that it will be far more difficult to reform the Chinese political system, it is equally true that under its political system, as of today, the quality of life of the majority of its people is improving more than that of Americans under their far more open system. In many key indicators of social well-being, the conditions of the majority of Americans are regressing, not progressing. Although many Americans are becoming troubled by these data, they remain optimistic about their future prospects because they believe that their political system is self-curing. If there is a big problem, the open and flexible processes of democracy will find the right solution.

Certainly, in the past, the American political system has made radical fixes to solve deep structural problems. The huge success stories of political reform include the eradication of slavery (although this took a major civil war to accomplish), the Civil Rights legislation of the 1960s, which finally protected African Americans' right to vote, and the economic and political reforms of the Progressive Era (1890–1920). Similarly, on the economic front, when Congress enacted the disastrous Smoot-Hawley Tariff Act, aggravating the Great Depression, the US political system was also able to self-correct. Legislation passed in the New Deal uplifted the lives of many Americans, and Congress in later years shunned extreme protectionism. In short, those who believe that the American political system is inherently self-correcting have a lot of evidence to back up their belief.

The big question facing the American body politic is whether it faces a minor ailment that can be easily fixed through normal political processes or a life-threatening condition that requires massive surgery and painful treatment (which will inflict pain on some key American political constituencies). As of now, even though Americans are becoming increasingly troubled by economic and social conditions, there is no widely shared desire to undertake massive surgery of the political system. Nor is there any major American political figure advocating it. But that may be what the system needs.

More and more Americans are becoming aware that the American political and economic system may require significant reforms. Jean Fan makes an important observation: "In the U.S., we face an ongoing crisis of governance. We need to understand our own failures, and we need to grapple with unexpected demonstrations of success—even if they come from non-liberal societies. China's success challenges our implicit ideology and deep-seated assumptions about governance. It needs to be studied—not just to bring about better coordination, but because in its accomplishments, we may find important truths needed to bring about American revitalization."[*]

The relative strengths and weaknesses of the American and Chinese political systems are central to the main question of this book. If the contest between America and China is a contest between a healthy and flexible democracy and a rigid and inflexible communist party system, then America will prevail. However, if the contest is one between a rigid and inflexible plutocracy and a supple and flexible meritocratic political system, China will win.

---

[*] Jean Fan, "The American Dream Is Alive in China," *Palladium Magazine*, October 11, 2019, https://palladiummag.com/2019/10/11/the-american-dream-is-alive-in-china/.

CHAPTER 8

HOW WILL OTHER COUNTRIES CHOOSE?

THERE ARE 193 COUNTRIES IN THE WORLD. TWO OF THEM ARE America and China. It would be a safe bet to say that the remaining 191 countries are beginning to prepare actively for the roller-coaster global environment that has been and will continue to be generated by the growing geopolitical contest between America and China. A few brave leaders have begun to speak openly about the dangers posed to other countries. While visiting China, German chancellor Angela Merkel said in September 2019 that "we hope that there will be a solution in the trade dispute with the United States since it affects everybody."* Similarly, speaking at the opening of the prestigious Shangri-La Dialogue on May 31, 2019, the prime minister of Singapore, Lee Hsien Loong, bravely said that initiatives by the United States and China, like the Belt and Road Initiative (BRI) and Indo-Pacific co-operation, "should

---

* "German Chancellor Angela Merkel Hopes US-China Trade War Will Be Over Soon," *Straits Times* (Singapore), September 7, 2019, https://www.straitstimes.com/asia/east -asia/merkel-hopes-us-china-trade-war-will-be-over-soon.

strengthen existing cooperation arrangements centered on ASEAN . . . not undermine them, create rival blocs, deepen fault lines or force countries to take sides. They should help bring countries together, rather than split them apart."*

Chancellor Merkel and Prime Minister Lee were probably speaking for many countries when they warned that America and China were damaging the interests of other countries with their unending trade war. However, the silence of other leaders does not mean that they will sit idly by and not defend their interests; many are working actively to defend and enhance their long-term interests. In theory, when America, under Trump, began to walk away from free trade agreements (FTAs), this move could have sounded the death knell for FTAs. Instead, the opposite has happened. Even though America unwisely walked away from the Trans-Pacific Partnership (TPP), the other eleven members continued to implement it under a new name, the Comprehensive and Progressive Agreement for Trans-Pacific Partnership (CPTPP). The EU and Mercosur also announced an in-principle agreement to proceed with an FTA in June 2019. Equally significantly, the African countries also proceeded with their African Continental Free Trade Agreement (AfCFTA) on May 30, 2019.† Even more significantly, the largest trade agreement (in terms of population numbers involved and share of global GDP) will probably be completed in 2020. It will involve the ten ASEAN countries and Australia, China, Japan, New Zealand, and South Korea. India may join later. This trade agreement, the Regional Comprehensive Economic Partnership (RCEP), will certainly lead to closer economic integration among Asian countries. It will include China. This shows the lack of wisdom of Trump's advisers who are rec-

---

* Lee Hsien Loong, keynote address, International Institute for Strategic Studies, Shangri-La Dialogue, Shangri-La Hotel, Singapore, May 31, 2019, https://www.pmo .gov.sg/Newsroom/PM-Lee-Hsien-Loong-at-the-IISS-Shangri-La-Dialogue-2019.
† Agreement Establishing the African Continental Free Trade Area, African Union, 2019, https://au.int/en/treaties/agreement-establishing-african-continental-free-trade-area.

ommending a "decoupling" of the American and Chinese economies. If these advisers succeed with decoupling, the result will be an America decoupled not just from China but also from the massive growth prospects of the fifteen RCEP economies.

In short, it would be unwise for either Beijing or Washington to assume that other countries would automatically line up to support them. Instead, each of them will carefully defend their own long-term interests. Since it is impossible to cover the reactions of 191 countries in one brief chapter, I discuss the reactions of a few key players who will be directly or indirectly affected, namely Australia, the European Union (EU), Japan, India, ASEAN, and Russia.

In the coming, inevitable geopolitical contest between America and China, each will be tempted to use its sturdy geopolitical muscles to cajole, bribe, pressure, and arm-twist other countries to join its side. This is normal superpower behavior.

Except the world has moved on since the Cold War. America's relative economic power and cultural influence has diminished since its heyday. China's relative economic power is far greater than that of the former Soviet Union. The most important ratio is that between the relative combined weight of America and China and that of the rest of the world. Many countries and regions have become big enough to walk away from both America and China. Most countries have also become shrewder at weighing and acting on their own geopolitical interests. Chan Heng Chee, who served as Singapore's ambassador to Washington from 1996 to 2012, observed that many Asian countries "are carefully defining their own positions, pushing back against pressure to choose sides between the US and China."[*] Hence, both America and China will have to get used to dealing with other countries that have become more confident and less compliant over time.

---

[*] Chan Heng Chee, "Resisting the Polarising Pull of US-China Rivalry," *Straits Times* (Singapore), June 18, 2019, https://www.straitstimes.com/opinion/resisting-the-polarising-pull-of-us-china-rivalry.

The country that will have to make the most difficult geopolitical choice will be Australia. In terms of defense and culture, it is tied almost completely to America. Indeed, President George W. Bush proudly described Australia as the deputy sheriff of America in 2003, a phrase that not all Australians liked but one that stuck in the popular imagination. During the Cold War, even though Australia was far away from the Soviet Union and had no reason to confront it, the country enthusiastically supported the global US containment policy and never hesitated to send troops to fight in America-led causes, including the bloody Vietnam War, in which 521 Australian soldiers lost their lives.[*] As a result, the respect and affection for Australia in the Washington, DC, establishment is profound and real. Australia gained a lot by being America's most loyal ally during the Cold War.

Today, Australia would probably lose a lot and gain little by joining America's side against China. Its economy is far more tied to China than to America. In 2018, its total trade with China was AU$174 billion,[†] while its trade with America was AU$44 billion. If Australia were to heed the extreme American voices calling for US allies to decouple themselves from the Chinese economy, it would virtually commit national economic suicide. A former Australian ambassador to China, Geoff Raby, said: "Our interests are not identical to the U.S. That doesn't mean we can't have a close, warm relationship with the United

---

[*] "From the time of the arrival of the first members of the Team in 1962 almost 60,000 Australians, including ground troops and air force and navy personnel, served in Vietnam; 521 died as a result of the war and over 3,000 were wounded. The war was the cause of the greatest social and political dissent in Australia since the conscription referendums of the First World War. Many draft resisters, conscientious objectors, and protesters were fined or jailed, while soldiers met a hostile reception on their return home": "Vietnam War 1962–75," Australian War Memorial, https://www.awm.gov.au/articles/event/vietnam.

[†] Statistics Section, Office of Economic Analysis, Investment and Economic Division, *Composition of Trade Australia 2017–18*, Department of Foreign Affairs and Trade, January 2019, https://dfat.gov.au/about-us/publications/Documents/cot-2017-18.pdf.

States. But we cannot join the U.S. in a policy premised on China being a strategic competitor."*

However, for Australia, it will not just be a matter of economics. There is an essential identity question that Australia will have to grapple with in the twenty-first century and beyond. As Western power slowly but steadily recedes from Asia, Australia could be left stranded, together with New Zealand, as the sole Western entities in Asia.† As Western power recedes globally, Australia's predominantly Western population could feel very isolated and lonely in Asia.

In the twenty-first century, Australia can only have a secure and confident long-term future if it integrates itself, politically and culturally, with its immediate neighborhood and its key neighbor is ASEAN. ASEAN, the second-most successful regional organization in the world after the European Union, has emerged as a geopolitical gift to Australia (and New Zealand) as it provided these two Western countries a valuable buffer from the growing power and influence of China in the region.‡

With Australia dealing with the extremely difficult, almost existential, challenges of adapting to an Asian century, an American call to Australia to once again become a loyal "deputy sheriff" would be disastrous. This is why many leading Australian voices have warned their fellow Australians against blindly following American interests and policies. The scholar Hugh White wrote: "it seems we're still clinging to the idea that America will remain the dominant power in Asia, that it will be there to shield us from China, and that China can somehow

---

* Neil Irwin, "Red Wines a Sign of the Times in Australia's Ties with US and China," *Straits Times* (Singapore), May 14, 2019, https://www.straitstimes.com/opinion/red -wines-a-sign-of-the-times-in-australias-ties-with-us-and-china.
† Kishore Mahbubani, "Australia's Destiny in the Asian Century (Part 1 of 2)," *Jakarta Post*, September 7, 2012, http://mahbubani.net/articles%20by%20dean/Australia %20destiny%20in%20the%20Asian%20Century_The%20Jakarta%20Post-joined.pdf.
‡ Kishore Mahbubani and Jeffery Sng, *The ASEAN Miracle: A Catalyst for Peace* (Singapore: National University of Singapore Press, 2017).

be convinced happily to accept this. So our government has once again failed to come to terms with the full implications of the profound shifts that are transforming our international setting. It is a triumph for wishful thinking over serious policy."* Similarly, it would be equally fatal for China to try to force Australia to take its side as Australian culture is far too deeply pro-Western for Australia to be comfortable joining the Chinese camp.

The wisest approach for both Beijing and Washington, DC, to take is to allow Australia to play the role of a neutral and helpful intermediary between them. Sadly, such wisdom is lacking in both capitals. Even Barack Obama, one of America's least belligerent and most thoughtful presidents, arm-twisted the Australian government *not* to join the Asia Infrastructure Investment Bank (AIIB), when most of Australia's neighbors did so, including all ten ASEAN member states. Future American presidents are likely to be less considerate than Barack Obama. Australia can expect to receive a lot of arm-twisting in the future. It should stop being passive in its foreign policy and take a proactive approach of persuading both Beijing and Washington, DC, why they should give Australia more space as an independent and neutral actor in the forthcoming geopolitical contest.

Given Europe's geographic distance from China, America's policymakers would be outraged if the core members of the European Union didn't follow America's bidding in the geopolitical contest against China. When Robert Zoellick was deputy secretary of state in the second Bush Administration from 2005 to 2006, he warned the Europeans that they would face drastic consequences if they were to lift their arms embargo, preventing arms sales from European companies to China. He used graphic language to make his point, suggesting that

---

* Hugh White, "America or China? Australia Is Fooling Itself That It Doesn't Have to Choose," *Guardian* (Manchester, UK), November 26, 2017, https://www.theguardian.com/australia-news/2017/nov/27/america-or-china-were-fooling-ourselves-that-we-dont-have-to-choose.

the EU would be painting bull's-eyes on the backs of US soldiers if they sold arms to China.*

It is striking that a moderate and centrist figure like Robert Zoellick would use such strong language, especially since Zoellick had once wisely promoted the idea of China emerging as a "responsible stakeholder" in the global system:

> We now need to encourage China to become a responsible stakeholder in the international system. As a responsible stakeholder, China would be more than just a member—it would work with us to sustain the international system that has enabled its success. Cooperation as stakeholders will not mean the absence of differences—we will have disputes that we need to manage. But that management can take place within a larger framework where the parties recognize a shared interest in sustaining political, economic, and security systems that provide common benefits.[†]

If a thoughtful voice like Robert Zoellick calls on Europe to be careful about its relations with China, it should not surprise the Europeans that most members of the American establishment would expect European Union members to fall in line in the coming geopolitical contest against China. In fact, this has already happened. When several EU members announced that they would consider using Huawei equipment to build their 5G telecommunication networks, the Trump administration reacted strongly and harshly. The American ambassador to the EU, Gordon Sondland, said in February 2019: "There are no compelling reasons that I can see to do business with the Chinese, so long

---

* Michael E. O'Hanlon, "The Risk of War over Taiwan Is Real," Brookings Institution, May 1, 2005. https://www.brookings.edu/opinions/the-risk-of-war-over-taiwan-is-real/.
† Robert B. Zoellick, "Whither China: From Membership to Responsibility?," US Department of State, September 21, 2005, https://2001-2009.state.gov/s/d/former/zoellick/rem/53682.htm.

as they have the structure in place to reach in and manipulate or spy on their customers. Those who are charging ahead blindly and embracing the Chinese technology without regard to these concerns may find themselves in a disadvantage in dealing with us."[*] Similarly, the US secretary of state Mike Pompeo said:

> If a country adopts this [Huawei] and puts it in some of their critical information systems, we won't be able to share information with them, we won't be able to work alongside them. In some cases there's risk—we won't even be able to co-locate American resources, an American embassy, an American military outpost. . . . We can't forget these systems were designed . . . alongside the Chinese PLA, their military in China. They are creating a real risk for these countries and their systems, the security of their people.[†]

In contrast to the views of Sondland and Pompeo, Bill Gates has decried the "paranoid" view fuelling the current high-tech rivalry between the US and China. He said that trying to stop Beijing from developing innovative technologies is "beyond realistic." "Huawei, like all goods and services, should be subject to an objective test," Mr. Gates said at the New York Times DealBook Conference. "The rule that everything that comes from China is bad . . . that is one crazy approach to trying to take advantage of innovation."[‡]

Yet, it would also be unwise for Washington, DC, to exert such pressures because Europe, like Australia, has its own existential geo-

---

[*] Nikos Chrysoloras and Richard Bravo, "Huawei Deals for Tech Will Have Consequences, U.S. Warns EU," Bloomberg, February 7, 2019, https://www.bloomberg.com /news/articles/2019-02-07/huawei-deals-for-tech-will-have-consequences-u-s-warns-eu.

[†] Keegan Elmer, "Huawei or US: Mike Pompeo Issues Warning to Allies That Partner with Chinese Firm," South China Morning Post, February 22, 2019, https://www .scmp.com/news/china/diplomacy/article/2187275/huawei-or-us-mike-pompeo -issues-warning-allies-partner-chinese.

[‡] Marrian Zhou, "Bill Gates: Paranoia on China Is a 'Crazy Approach' to Innovation," Nikkei Asian Review, November 8, 2019.

graphic challenges to deal with. Europe happily signed up as a willing and loyal ally of America in the Cold War because Europe was immediately and directly threatened by Soviet tanks and missiles stationed at its borders. There was a high degree of trust and strategic cooperation between American and European policymakers, underpinned by close cultural links. It helped a lot that America, Australia, and Europe traced their roots to a common Judeo-Christian heritage and Greco-Roman cultural underpinnings. Cultural affinity matters.

Yet, cultural affinity cannot overcome geopolitical realities. Many American thinkers don't understand the importance of geographic realities because America has been blessed with the best geography in the world. Americans are blessed with a large and productive continent, separated from the populous masses in Eurasia and Africa by two vast oceans, and they have only had to worry about the military threats posed by Canada and Mexico. Given such an environment, Americans don't understand the real meaning of the word *geopolitics*, a combination of geography and politics, of which geography may be the more important.

Europe is cursed with an unlucky geography. In the twenty-first century, Europe will not be threatened by Russian tanks and missiles. The prospect of a direct war with Russia is practically zero, although proxy wars may take place in territories like the former Yugoslavia and Ukraine. However, the prospect of Europe being overwhelmed by millions of migrants coming in from Africa in little boats is very real. There is one demographic statistic that spells out clearly the number one *geopolitical* threat the European Union will face. In 1950, the EU's combined population (379 million)[*] was nearly double that of Africa's (229 million). Today, Africa's population (1.2 billion in 2015)[†] is double that

---

[*] EEA, "Population Trends 1950–2100. Globally and Within Europe," European Environment Agency, https://www.eea.europa.eu/data-and-maps/indicators/total-population-outlook-from-unstat-3/assessment-1.

[†] UN, "World Population Prospects 2019," United Nations, DESA/Population Division, https://population.un.org/wpp/Download/Standard/Population/.

of the EU countries (513 million in 2018).[*] By 2100, Africa's population is projected to be almost ten times larger, 4.5 billion[†] versus 493 million.[‡]

In the years 2015 to 2017, there was a surge in migrants from both Africa and the Middle East arriving in Europe. The impact on European politics was tumultuous. After politics dominated by moderate centrist parties (from both the left and right) for decades, Europe saw a surge of support for extreme populist parties, with some of them even joining governments in countries like Austria, Hungary, Poland, Italy, and Estonia. The real tragedy was that the German chancellor Angela Merkel, probably the best European leader of her time, announced she would not seek another term of office, in part because of the domestic repercussions of her decision to allow a million Syrian immigrants into Germany in 2015. Merkel made a morally courageous (and indeed economically sensible) decision but a politically unpopular one. If economic and political conditions in the African continent don't improve in the twenty-first century, Europe can expect tens, if not hundreds, of millions of Africans to knock on its doors seeking a better life in Europe. It doesn't take a genius to figure out that this surge of migrants will drastically change the social and political texture of European societies and provoke resentment in the European body politic unaccustomed to such massive demographic change. Indeed, at the January 2019 meeting of the World Economic Forum, I was shocked to hear a moderate and sensible European whisper to me: "Kishore, there is only one solution to African migration. We will let them drown in the Mediterranean."

---

[*] Eurostat, "Population and Population Change Statistics," Statistics Explained, https://ec.europa.eu/eurostat/statistics-explained/index.php/Population_and_population_change_statistics.

[†] United Nations, DESA/Population Division, World Population Prospects 2019, https://population.un.org/wpp/Graphs/Probabilistic/POP/TOT/.

[‡] Eurostat, "Population on 1st January by Age, Sex and Type of Projection" (chart), https://appsso.eurostat.ec.europa.eu/nui/show.do?dataset=proj_18np&lang=en.

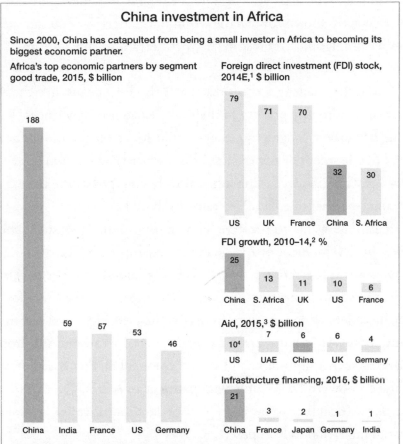

China investment in Africa

Since 2000, China has catapulted from being a small investor in Africa to becoming its biggest economic partner.

Africa's top economic partners by segment good trade, 2015, $ billion

Foreign direct investment (FDI) stock, 2014E,[1] $ billion

US 79 · UK 71 · France 70 · China 32 · S. Africa 30

China 188 · India 59 · France 57 · US 53 · Germany 46

FDI growth, 2010–14,[2] %

China 25 · S. Africa 13 · UK 11 · US 10 · France 6

Aid, 2015,[3] $ billion

US 10[4] · UAE 7 · China 6 · UK 6 · Germany 4

Infrastructure financing, 2015, $ billion

China 21 · France 3 · Japan 2 · Germany 1 · India 1

[1]Estimated according to compound annual growth rate from 2009 to 2012.
[2]For countries other than China, we made projections using historical data.
[3]Office of Development Assistance and other official flows, 2015 for Organisation for Economic Co-operation and Development (OECD) countries, 2012 for China.
[4]According to United States Agency for International Development data, US foreign aid to Africa was $11.9 billion in FY 2015 and $7.4 billion in FY 2016. The discrepancy with OECD data shown is likely due to the fact that US fiscal years start in October, whereas OECD data is for calendar years.

Source: Bilateral trade database, International Trade Centre trade map, 2015; Bilateral FDI database, UN Conference on Trade and Development, 2012; Foreign Aid Explorer, USAID; Ministry of Commerce, People's Republic of China, 2015; "Infrastructure Financing Trends in Africa–2015," The Infrastructure Consortium for Africa, 2015.

CHART 12. China Investment in Africa (Designed by Patti Issacs)

Such moral callousness goes against the liberal and open spirit Europe has previously shown toward the world in the postwar era. Indeed, the number of migrant lives lost in the Mediterranean spiked from 424 in 2014 to 2,042 in 2015.[*]

Given the challenges this presents, if the Europeans, like the Australians, want to give priority to their own existential challenges (which result from their geography), they should focus on the economic and social development of Africa. The best partner to work with to develop Africa is China. Indeed, China has already emerged as the largest new economic partner of Africa.[†] Please see Chart 12.

If Europe wants to preserve its own long-term interests, it should make the development of Africa, in partnership with China, an immediate priority. The country that attracts the largest number of African leaders to summit meetings is China. The most sensible thing for European leaders to do is to join, en masse, the next high-level meeting of Chinese and African leaders in Beijing. A massive turnout of European leaders at such a summit would send a powerful market signal. It could catalyze a powerful wave of new investment in Africa. Over time, with a strong African economy, there will be less incentive for widespread African migration to Europe.

There is only one obstacle to Europe doing this sensible thing: America will object. Just look at American officials' attempts to dissuade other countries from participating in China's BRI (a major source of Chinese investment into the African continent). "When China comes calling, it's not always to the good of your citizens," Secretary of State Mike Pompeo cautioned in a press conference after meeting the president of Panama in October 2018, adding that the

---

[*] "Migrants: Tracking Deaths along Migration Routes," Missing Migrants Project, https://missingmigrants.iom.int/region/mediterranean.
[†] Aubrey Hruby, "Dispelling the Dominant Myths of China in Africa," Atlantic Council, https://www.weforum.org/agenda/2018/09/three-myths-about-chinas-investment-in-africa-and-why-they-need-to-be-dispelled/.

United States objects "when state-owned enterprises show up in a way that is clearly not transparent, clearly not market-driven, and is designed not to benefit the people of Panama but rather to benefit the Chinese government."[*] American pressure on its European allies will certainly increase if the European nations decide to work together with China on investing in Africa's future.

However, it is truly unwise for America to ask Europeans to ignore their own long-term existential challenges in their dealings with China. The emergence of China does not pose a threat to Europe. Indeed, it could help to enhance Europe's long-term security if China promotes Africa's development. America could, of course, try to match China in developing Africa. However, the amount of funds America has offered to deploy is amazingly small. China has offered to spend over a trillion dollars to promote infrastructure investments under its BRI. America cannot match such a sum.

The country that has had the most troubled relationship with China in the last century or so has been Japan. For half a century or so, Japan inflicted humiliation after humiliation upon China. In 1895, it convincingly defeated China in the Sino-Japanese War. The conditions Japan imposed on China after this defeat were onerous, including the Japanese annexation of Taiwan. (This is one reason why China is working hard toward reunification with Taiwan. It wants to remove the last vestige of that century of humiliation.) The Japanese military occupation of China from 1937 to 1945 was even more brutal. By even conservative estimates, fourteen million Chinese lost their lives in this military occupation,[†] including up to three hundred thousand (by Chinese

---

* Owen Churchill, "Mike Pompeo Warns Panama and Other Nations About Accepting China's 'Belt and Road' Loans," *South China Morning Post*, October 20, 2018, https://www.scmp.com/news/china/diplomacy/article/2169449/mike-pompeo-warns-panama-and-other-nations-about-accepting.

† Rana Mitter, *Forgotten Ally: China's World War II, 1937–1945* (New York: Houghton Mifflin Harcourt, 2013).

estimates) in a few days in the famous Nanjing Massacre.* Americans who are sometimes puzzled by the Chinese obsession with Japanese behavior should ask themselves if they could have forgiven Japan if they had suffered a similar number of casualties.

A lot of Chinese nationalist anger toward Japan, which emerges from time to time, is therefore real. Yet there is no doubt that some of it is also manufactured. This is demonstrated by the fact that China has shown a capacity to ignore this painful chapter in Sino-Japanese relations when it suited Chinese interests to do so. This is how Ambassador Bilahari Kausikan describes the selective use of history in China:

> Consider, for example, this statement: "As you have formally apologised for the debts you incurred in the past, it is not reasonable to ask you for payments of those debts. You cannot be asked to apologise every day, can you? It is not good for a nation to feel constantly guilty. . . .
>
> This is not some right-wing Japanese politician trying to justify Japan's wartime record. It is a statement by Chairman Mao himself to a delegation of the Japanese Diet only a decade after the end of World War Two. And when Mao Zedong met former Japanese Prime Minister Kakuei Tanaka in 1972, he brushed aside Tanaka's attempts to apologise, saying that he was grateful to Japan because without the war the CCP would not [have] been able to seize power.†

When Richard Nixon decided to visit Beijing in 1972 and began the process of normalizing relations, there was a real political shock in

---

* Kate Merkel-Hess and Jeffrey N. Wasserstrom, "Nanjing by the Numbers," *Financial Times* (London), February 9, 2010, https://foreignpolicy.com/2010/02/09/nanjing -by-the-numbers/.
† Bilahari Kausikan, "Dealing with an Ambiguous World, Lecture II: US-China Relations: Groping Towards a New Modus Vivendi," IPS-Nathan Lectures, Stephen Riady Centre, Singapore, February 25, 2016, https://lkyspp.nus.edu.sg/docs/default -source/ips/mr-bilahari-kausikan-s-speech04800a7b46bc6210a3aaff0100138661 .pdf?sfvrsn=47c3680a_0.

Japan. The Japanese even have a term for it: Nixon *shoku*. Even though Japan was a close treaty ally of America, the Nixon administration did not keep Japan informed when it began its secret rapprochement with China. Sadly, the Japanese never really learned the real lesson of this whole exercise: when great powers like China and America come together, the interests of even major middle powers like Japan can be sacrificed. Surprisingly, despite having demonstrated that Japanese interests are dispensable, most American policymakers still expect Japan to be a totally loyal American ally, under any circumstances.

Fortunately, it is currently in China's national interest to see Japan remain an American ally. If America walks away now from its commitment to defend Japan under the Treaty of Mutual Cooperation and Security of 1951 (revised in 1960), which clearly states in Article V that "each Party recognizes that an armed attack against either Party in the territories under the administration of Japan would be dangerous to its own peace and safety and declares that it would act to meet the common danger in accordance with its constitutional provisions and processes,"* Japan would have no choice but to strengthen its capability to defend itself. Japan could be forced to acquire nuclear weapons. This is exactly what Henry Kissinger told Premier Zhou Enlai on July 9, 1971:

> Our defense relationship with Japan keeps Japan from pursuing aggressive policies. If Japan builds its own military machine, which it will do if it feels forsaken by us, and if it builds nuclear weapons, as it could easily do, then I feel the fears which you have expressed could become real indeed.

Indeed, of all the non-nuclear powers in the world, the one power that could develop and deploy nuclear weapons in the shortest possible

---

* "Japan-U.S. Security Treaty," Treaty of Mutual Cooperation and Security Between Japan and the United States of America, Ministry of Foreign Affairs of Japan, https://www.mofa.go.jp/region/n-america/us/q&a/ref/1.html.

time would be Japan. In a few months, if not a few weeks, the Japanese could bring together their supply of plutonium and uranium, their technical knowledge, and their expertise in rocketry and develop a formidable array of nuclear weapons. Indeed, Japan has the capacity to develop the second-best nuclear capacity after America. Both America and China would then have to develop a credible defense capacity against Japan, which is in the interest of neither.

Yet, even while the alliance remains, it would be unwise for the Japanese not to develop an independent, reasonably friendly relationship with China. There is one overriding reason to do so. In the next two or three decades, it is highly likely that America will retain a strong military, economic, and political presence in East Asia. It has the capability and, as of now, the desire to remain in East Asia. Yet, by 2050, when the Chinese economy could effectively be twice as large as the American economy, it is conceivable that America could give up its forward deployment in East Asia. America could withdraw from the Western Pacific Ocean and retreat back into its hemisphere and live seven thousand miles away from China.

Japan cannot retreat. It will always have to live a few hundred miles away from China. The first recognition of Japan (referred to as Wa [倭] by the Chinese) in Chinese dynastic histories can be traced to the first century BCE.* For most of the next two thousand years, with the exception of a few brief wars, China and Japan have lived at peace with each other. It is perfectly conceivable for China and Japan to live in peace for the next two thousand years. As Ezra Vogel has observed:

Is there hope that China and Japan can develop good relations in the long run? Yes. As former premier Zhou Enlai said years ago, and as

---

* Wm. Theodore de Bary, Donald Keene, George Tanabe, and Paul Varley, eds., *Sources of Japanese Tradition: From Earliest Times to 1600*, vol. 1 (New York: Columbia University Press, 2001), https://www.gwern.net/docs/japanese/2001-debary-sourcesofjapanese tradition.pdf.

national leader Deng Xiaoping repeated later, China and Japan have had some two thousand years of relations, and the really troubled relations involved only half a century, from 1894 to 1945. Well over a millennium ago, during China's Sui and Tang dynasties (contemporary with the Nara and Heian periods in Japan), the Japanese acquired their basic culture—including written language, Buddhism, Confucianism, architecture, governmental organization, city planning, and art—from China.*

The cultural relationship between China and Japan is fascinating. In theory, China represents the mother civilization. A lot of Japanese culture is derived from Chinese culture: Japan's script, religious tendencies, aesthetic, form of art, ceramics and pottery, Confucian philosophy, and divination and geomancy.† Moreover, "the Taika reform (starting in year 645) borrowed directly from the Tang Dynasty's bureaucratic and political structure, and tax and economic systems."‡ When the Japanese prime minister Kakuei Tanaka met Mao Zedong in 1972, he told Mao: "In the Tang period, Japan had a very famous monk named Kūkai, also known as the Kōbō-Daishi. During the Tang dynasty, he went to China to study Buddhism and he founded what is known as the Shingon school of Buddhism in Japan. I am a believer of this school, but am not too well versed in his teachings."§ Indeed, the deep cultural relationship between China and Japan has been documented in many scholarly works. One publication has observed the following:

---

* Ezra Vogel, "Can China and Japan Ever Get Along?" in *The China Questions: Critical Insights into a Rising Power*, ed. Jennifer Rudolph and Michael Szonyi (Cambridge, MA: Harvard University Press, 2018), 114–115.

† de Bary, Keene, Tanabe, and Varley, eds., *Sources of Japanese Tradition*.

‡ Ibid.

§ "Excerpt of Mao Zedong's Conversation with Japanese Prime Minister Kakuei Tanaka," trans. Caixia Lu, History and Public Policy Program Digital Archive, Wilson Center, Washington, DC, September 21, 1972, https://digitalarchive.wilsoncenter.org /document/118567.pdf?v=71cad3a9f99def657fdfb83057f844c2.

Zen found a home in the state-recognized Buddhist establishment in the form of the Five Mountain (Gozan) temple networks of Kamakura and Kyoto. [. . .] At the top tier were the large urban monasteries in Kyoto that performed tantric rites for the benefit of the state, sponsored foreign trade with China, managed the military government's estates, and, most of all, promoted the latest styles of Chinese culture. Five Mountain temples became centers of learning for the study of Neo-Confucian metaphysics, Chinese poetry, painting, calligraphy, and material arts such as printing, architecture, garden design, and ceramics. The role of Five Mountain Zen temples in introducing new styles of Chinese arts into medieval Japan has helped foster an indelible association between Zen and medieval forms of artistic expression.[*]

As a result, the deep cultural affinity between the Chinese and Japanese is real. The relationship is also complex. In theory, the Japanese have learned from the superior Chinese civilization. In practice, the Japanese have brought many Chinese art forms to a higher level. David Pilling wrote in a *Foreign Policy* article on the distinctiveness of Japanese culture:

Shintaro Ishihara, the former governor of Tokyo whose 2012 plan to buy and develop the contested Senkaku/Diaoyu islands in the East China Sea triggered the current Sino-Japanese standoff, once told me proudly that Japanese poetry was unique. The novelist Andre Malraux, he said, had personally told him that the Japanese were "the only people who can grasp eternity in a single moment." Ishihara, blinking in his owlish way, went on, "The haiku is the shortest poetic style in the world. This was not created by the Chinese but by the Japanese."[†]

---

[*] de Bary, Keene, Tanabe, and Varley, eds., *Sources of Japanese Tradition.*
[†] David Pilling, "Why Is Japan So . . . Different?," *Foreign Policy*, March 17, 2014, https://foreignpolicy.com/2014/03/17/why-is-japan-so-different/.

This explains the extraordinary number of Chinese who choose to travel to Japan nowadays. Many of us have gotten used to TV scenes of hundreds, if not thousands, of Chinese demonstrating against the Japanese. What we do not see on TV screens are the millions, if not soon hundreds of millions, of Chinese who choose to visit Japan and enjoy the beauty of many Japanese cultural products. Indeed, it is conceivable that the Chinese may actually see in Japanese culture the future potential of Chinese culture to further excel in many areas.

This culturally symbiotic relationship between China and Japan provides hope that they can overcome the painful chapter of the first half of the twentieth century and return to the more traditional millennial relationship of calm and harmony. In geopolitical terms, if this were to happen over time, many American geopolitical thinkers may see this as a "loss" for America. But it would not be.

It is almost certain, even as China opens up and integrates itself with the rest of the world, that it will not become a political or social replica of a Western liberal-democratic society. The cultural gap between China and the West is too great for the Chinese to feel comfortable in replicating Western social and political forms. However, the cultural gap between China and Japan is not as wide. In theory, Japan has become a member of the Western club, especially after it joined the OECD and the Group of Seven economies. In practice, Japan remains a culturally and socially conservative society. The "soul" of Japan has not been Westernized. As a result, there has often been a cultural discomfort between America and Japan, as described by Richard McGregor:

George Kennan, the renowned strategist, called Japan's partnership with the United States "an unnatural intimacy," born of conflict and agony between two very different countries, which, over time, developed into a close relationship of its own. This intimacy, if that is what in fact it is, has been hard won. A remarkable number of senior American officials, from Henry Kissinger to James Baker to Robert

Zoellick, have not hidden their dislike for dealing with Tokyo. Brent Scowcroft, a hard-nosed veteran of America's national security establishment, interacted with all manner of recalcitrant and brutal governments and leaders in his years at the top in the White House. Yet in his authorized biography, Scowcroft called Japan "probably the most difficult country" the United States had to deal with: "I don't think we understood the Japanese and I don't think the Japanese understood us."*

Even though Japan has replicated the electoral methods of Western democracies, it has had very different outcomes, effectively remaining a one-party state for over five decades. If China ever moves toward a democratic model, the outcome is likely to be much closer to Japan than to America.

A closer symbolic relationship between China and Japan could over time influence the political evolution of China. Japan has remained politically stable, socially conservative, and culturally authentic, while adopting the trappings of Western electoral methods. It is conceivable that over time the Chinese could be influenced to importing various aspects of the Japanese model. However, it has to happen through a symbiotic process, not as a result of external pressures.

The most natural way to create a more open society in China is not to lecture or pressure China but to encourage millions of Chinese to visit Japan. Fortunately, this is already happening. However, the number of visits could increase dramatically if the political relations between China and Japan became less negative. America should therefore encourage more high-level exchanges between China and Japan. For example, Naruhito, the new emperor of Japan, was installed in May 2019. One of the first overseas visits that the new emperor should consider

---

* Richard McGregor, *Asia's Reckoning: China, Japan, and the Fate of U.S. Power in the Pacific Century* (Viking: New York, 2017).

making should be to China. This would be a powerful signal and lead to hundreds of millions of Chinese visiting Japan.

If exposure to Japanese democracy could persuade thoughtful Chinese to consider the virtues of democracy, exposure to Indian democracy would have exactly the opposite effect. Whereas Japanese democracy is reassuringly calm and stable (reflecting the Japanese emphasis on harmony in interpersonal relations and its Confucian heritage), Indian democracy is loud and rambunctious, reflecting the spirit of the argumentative Indian. I know this spirit well as I was born an argumentative Indian.

I was also personally present in India when a senior and significant Chinese visitor spoke against the ostensible virtues of India democracy. Indeed, he was amazingly undiplomatic. In 2006, Bo Xilai, before he was brought down by scandal, was then the commerce minister of China. Most Chinese leaders speak diplomatically overseas. He didn't. He was brutal and blunt in his criticism of democracy. This is how the *New York Times* reported his remarks:

> The next day, the Chinese commerce minister, Bo Xilai, came as close as senior Chinese figures do to fighting back, describing democracy as a "means," not an "end." [. . .] "I'm not of the view that we should classify countries as democratic countries and nondemocratic countries," Bo said through an interpreter, to vigorous applause from many in the Chinese delegation of 200 bureaucrats and businesspeople. "If you simply understand or interpret democracy as allowing people to go on protest in the streets, then I think it's not always necessarily a good thing." Without citing India or the majority of Mumbai's population that lives in slums or the shanties ringing the conference venue, Bo referred to "some developing countries" that cram their poor into "clusterings of shantytowns" where life is too bleak for freedom to mean anything. "Some people in those places cannot even have a shower for years on end. And these people—most of them have no access to

education," he said. "So how can you imagine that these people are in a position to talk about democracy when they are simply illiterate?"*

I was personally present in the room when he said all this. What I remember especially vividly is how strongly and powerfully the Chinese delegation clapped when he spoke. They applauded his courage in telling off the predominantly Indian and American audience in the room and disputing their claim on the virtues of democracy. I had never before or since seen a senior Chinese figure being so publicly disputatious. This may also explain why Bo failed in his quest to become the paramount leader of China. If he had succeeded, he would have behaved as unpredictably and capriciously as Donald Trump. Fortunately, China is not ready for a Trump-like leader.

Yet, despite the significant dissimilarities between Indian and Chinese cultures, they remain fellow Asian cultures. Some of their roots are the same. For example, the religion of Buddhism, which originated in India, has had a major impact on Chinese culture and the Chinese soul. This is how one scholarly work describes the impact of Buddhism on China:

The coming of Buddhism to China was an event with far-reaching results in the development of Chinese thought and culture and of Buddhism itself. After a long and difficult period of assimilation, this new teaching managed to establish itself as a major system of thought, contributing greatly to the enrichment of Chinese philosophy, and also as a major system of religious practice which had an enduring influence on Chinese popular religion. Indeed, it came to be spoken of along with the native traditions, Confucianism and Taoism, as one

---

* Anand Giridharadas, "News Analysis: China and India's Big Debate on Democracy," *New York Times*, March 22, 2006, https://www.nytimes.com/2006/03/22/world/asia /news-analysis-china-and-indias-big-debate-on-democracy.html.

of the Three Teachings or Three Religions, thus achieving a status of virtual equality with these beliefs.*

As Buddhism originated in India, my Hindu mother used to take me as a child to both Hindu and Buddhist temples as she felt culturally comfortable in both, even though in Singapore most of the Buddhist monks were Chinese rather than Indian. These common cultural roots between China and India will certainly play a role in their future relationship.

This is why it would be a mistake for any American policymaker or pundit to believe that India could one day become (like Japan or the UK) a reliable compliant ally to be used against China. There are some loud and influential Indian voices advocating that India should become an ally of America against China. C. Raja Mohan wrote in *Foreign Policy* in 2010:

> As the power of a rising China today radiates across the subcontinent, the Indian Ocean, and the western Pacific, balancing Beijing has become an urgent matter—especially given the relative decline of the United States. In the past, India balanced Beijing through a de facto alliance with the Soviet Union. Today, it needs a strategic partnership with the United States to ensure that China's rise will continue to be peaceful.†

Raja Mohan is right on one critical point. Given the rapidly changing geopolitical environment, the time has come for India to do a major reboot of its global strategic policies. It can no longer proceed on autopilot and assume that the hallowed policies of the past can guide India in this new era. To be fair, India, under Prime Minister Narendra Modi,

---

* Wm. Theodore de Bary and Irene Bloom, *Sources of Chinese Tradition: From Earliest Times to 1600*, vol 1. (New York: Columbia University Press, 1960), 266.

† C. Raja Mohan, "India's Strategic Future," *Foreign Policy*, November 4, 2010, https://foreignpolicy.com/2010/11/04/indias-strategic-future-2/.

has already begun doing this. Clearly, he is aware that in this new geopolitical environment he can maximize India's geopolitical advantages by maintaining good relations with both President Donald Trump and President Xi Jinping. Modi has begun doing this. On September 22, 2019, Modi spoke at an enthusiastic gathering of overseas Indians in Texas, in the presence of Trump, and he even implicitly endorsed Trump by calling him "my friend, a friend of India, a great American president."[*] Barely a few weeks later on October 11–12, Modi hosted Xi Jinping to a two-day visit at the ancient temple site of Mamallapuram. Modi and Xi spent two days together having intense conversations. Tarun Das, a former chief executive of the Confederation of Indian Industry, has observed that Modi and Xi will have had five informal summits by 2022. He believes that "five informal summits, in spite of multiple challenges all-around, should build a growing level of trust. This is a reasonable expectation for 2022."[†]

Yet, even though Modi has enhanced his personal bonds with Xi, he has not been able to persuade his own government to be as pragmatic. If astute and strategic minds were advising Modi, with the strategic acumen of the likes of Lee Kuan Yew and Henry Kissinger, his government could be pursuing more pragmatic policies toward China. When principles trump pragmatism in geopolitics, valuable opportunities are lost. Even though the participation by India in China's BRI could bring rich economic dividends to India by boosting India's infrastructure capabilities, India has, as a matter of principle, refused to participate in the BRI because in the China-Pakistan Economic Corridor, China and Pakistan will build a road through Pakistan-occupied Kashmir, a region claimed by India in its border dispute with Pakistan.

---

[*] "Trump Pushes Unity with India at 'Howdy, Modi!' Event in Houston," CBS News, September 22, 2019, https://www.cbsnews.com/news/howdy-modi-trump-rally-pushes-unity-prime-minister-narendra-modi-houston-texas-today-2019-09-22/.

[†] Tarun Das, "India and China in 2022," *Business Standard*, November 1, 2019, 9.

On the matter of principle, India is absolutely right. However, wiser geostrategic thinkers have always balanced principles with pragmatism in making long-term strategic decisions. China has demonstrated this best in the handling of the Taiwan issue (which is even more politically sensitive to China than Kashmir is to India). India knows realistically that when a final settlement is made concerning Kashmir, it will not get back this Pakistan-occupied region. The de facto line of control in Kashmir will eventually become the de jure line of control, as two leaders (Pervez Musharraf and Atal Bihari Vajpayee) almost agreed in 2001. By contrast, China has not given up its claims to Taiwan and will never do so.

But despite China's greater sensitivity concerning Taiwan, it could allow pragmatism to trump principles. When China established diplomatic relations with America in January 1979, America dropped its diplomatic recognition of the government in Taipei and switched it to Beijing. Since Jimmy Carter was perceived to have dropped a long-standing ally in Taiwan, the US Congress reacted by passing the Taiwan Relations Act with the intention of defending the government in Taiwan, which China regarded as renegade. Since this was a violation of the spirit, if not of the letter, of the diplomatic agreement signed between America and China, China could have, as a matter of principle, suspended all its economic dealings with America.

Instead, China did some careful long-term pragmatic calculations. Having come to realize how backward the Chinese economy had become, the Chinese leaders led by Deng Xiaoping decided to "swallow the bitter pill of humiliation" (a well-known Chinese phrase) and use the massive American economy to boost its own economic growth. Forty years later, we know how wise and shrewd this pragmatic Chinese decision was. The Taiwan Relations Act was passed in 1979. In that year, in PPP terms, the Chinese economy was only about 10 percent that of America's. By 2014, China's economy had become larger. This shows the value of being pragmatic over being principled in international relations.

Today, India's economy, in PPP terms, is about 40 percent that of China's. By spurning participation in the BRI, India is sacrificing a valuable opportunity to grow its economy rapidly. However, its refusal to participate in the BRI is not the only strategic disadvantage India has imposed on itself. In late 2019, it also announced that it would not join RCEP even though India had been negotiating actively for several years to join this agreement.

To be fair, Prime Minister Narendra Modi was personally keen to join RCEP. He could see clearly the long-term economic and strategic benefits India would get from joining RCEP. Unfortunately, he could not do so because of opposition from his own political allies in the Rashtriya Swayamsevak Sangh and the opposition Congress Party. The sad part of this Indian decision to opt out of RCEP is that India is shooting itself in the foot. India will eventually become a great power. However, if it wants to fast-track its emergence as a great power, it has to do what China did with its economy: apply externally induced shock therapy to shake out the uncompetitive elements of the Chinese economy and develop new competitive dimensions. This was the goal of Zhu Rongji when he negotiated China's entry into the WTO in 2001. This shock therapy worked. In 2000, China's economy was eight times smaller than America's economy in nominal market terms. In 2016, it was only 1.5 times smaller. Applying external shock therapies does make economies grow faster.

By foregoing several opportunities to grow its economy faster, India is only putting itself in a disadvantageous position in the larger geopolitical game. India's commerce minister Piyush Goyal has announced that instead of joining RCEP, India will expedite its free trade agreement with the EU. He may have forgotten that given India's relative economic weaknesses, the EU tried to impose some humiliating conditions on India. In previous rounds of negotiations, the EU tried to insert in this EU-India agreement some standard human rights clauses that had been put in all EU cooperation agreements. These standard clauses called on India to respect some fundamental human rights. A 2013 report stated that some Member States have pushed for certain provisions in the FTA that have been poorly received by India and resulted in stalled talks. For example, the Netherlands pressed for the inclusion of a human rights clause. [. . .] India's position throughout the negotiations has been that human rights conditions as well as environmental standards or non-proliferation clauses should not be included or connected to the FTA. According to Rajendra Jain, a prominent Indian author, the EU needs to change its attitude and seek to cooperate with the emerging economies rather than demanding compliance with its values.*

No country had ever resisted these standard EU clauses. The first country to do so was India. Negotiations were suspended in 2013.

The Europeans were puzzled. If every other country had accepted these standard human rights conditions, why should India object? Privately and secretly, whispering under their breath, the European diplomats probably said to themselves: How dare these Indians object? We are being financially generous to them in aid and assistance and the Indians have the audacity to turn down the expression of European values in a Europe-India cooperation agreement. Few Europeans realized how insulted the Indians were. Shashi Tharoor wrote in a 2012 column:

> Indians have an allergy to being lectured to, and one of the great failings in the EU-India partnership has been the tendency of Europe to preach to India on matters we consider ourselves quite competent to handle on our own. As a democracy for over six decades (somewhat longer than several member states of the EU), India sees human rights as a vital domestic issue. There is not a single human rights problem about India that has been exposed by Amnesty International

---

* Jan Wouters et al., "Some Critical Issues in EU-India Free Trade Agreement Negotiations," Working Paper No. 102, Leuven Centre for Global Governance Studies, February 2013, https://ghum.kuleuven.be/ggs/publications/working_papers/2013/102 woutersgoddeerisnatensCiortuz.

or Human Rights Watch or any European institution, which has not been revealed first by Indian citizens, journalists and NGOs and handled within the democratic Indian political space. So for the EU to try to write in human rights provisions into a free trade agreement, as if they were automobile emissions standards, gets Indian backs up. Trade should not be held hostage to internal European politics about human rights declarations; the substance of human rights is far more important than the language or the form.*

Any Indian official who accepted such conditions would have been excoriated by his fellow Indians for allowing five hundred million Europeans to lecture over a billion Indians on what was good for them. Indian democracy was as robust as European democracies. The Indian human rights record is not perfect. But neither is the European record.

It is not shocking that the EU should try to impose its views on India. Its economy in nominal market terms is about seven times larger than that of India. However, it is truly shocking that a small Western country like Australia, with a population of only twenty-five million compared to India's 1.3 billion and with an economy smaller than India's, had the audacity to impose sanctions on India when India carried out a nuclear test in 1998. An Australian government report records the following:

On 12 May 1998, within hours of the announcement of the tests, the Australian Minister for Foreign Affairs called in the Indian High Commissioner to convey the Australian Government's "condemnation of the tests in the strongest possible terms." The Australian Government also recalled its High Commissioner from New Delhi

---

* Shashi Thardor, "Reconsider Relations with the European Union," *India Today*, May 18, 2012, https://www.indiatoday.in/opinion/shashi-tharoor/story/european-union -india-ties-india-eu-joint-action-plan-102549-2012-05-18.

for consultations. After India's second series of tests, the Government announced that it had decided: to suspend bilateral defence relations with India, including the withdrawal of Australia's Defence Adviser stationed in New Delhi; to cancel ship and aircraft visits, officer exchanges and other defence-related visits; to withdraw Australian Defence Force personnel currently training in India; to request the immediate departure of three Indian defence personnel currently at defence colleges in Australia; to suspend non-humanitarian aid; and to suspend ministerial and senior official visits.*

Why did Australia think that it could get away with imposing sanctions on India? The simple answer is that India's economy was not muscular enough to frighten Australia. By contrast, no Australian government would dream of imposing similar sanctions on China. This is, therefore, the real damage that India is imposing on itself by taking the principled and slower, rather than the pragmatic and faster, route to economic growth. And as long as India's economic growth continues at a slower rate, it will not enjoy the same respect globally as China.

One hard truth that Indians have to contend with is that America has also had difficulty treating India with respect. In recent years, many Americans have proudly proclaimed that America and India have a friendship built on a strong foundation since both are fellow democracies. This argument cuts little ice among thoughtful Indians since most of them remember well that America stood shoulder to shoulder with communist China and dictatorial Pakistan for several decades during the Cold War and beyond. One of the critical weaknesses of Washington, DC, is that the administrations and their officials change regularly; they have poor memories.

---

* "Chapter Six: Australia's Response to Nuclear Tests in South Asia," Parliament of Australia, https://www.aph.gov.au/Parliamentary_Business/Committees/Senate/Foreign _Affairs_Defence_and_Trade/Completed_inquiries/1999-02/nuclear/report/c06.

Many Americans, like many of their fellow Westerners, have a higher degree of respect for Chinese civilization than they do of Indian civilization. Many Americans will deny it because it is an uncomfortable truth. They will proclaim loudly that they respect India as much as they respect China. But you cannot feign respect: it is best demonstrated not through words but in deeds. Every country in the world demonstrates its respect for another country by the amount of time and attention it gives to that country, and America has devoted far more time and attention to China than it has to India. If America wants to develop a close long-term relationship with India over the long run, it needs to confront the deep roots of its relative lack of respect for India. Is it a result of a perception among Western scholars that Indian civilization is not as impressive as Chinese civilization? Is this a result of the fact that the American media has broadcast a steady stream of stories about poverty in India, so much so that just as Americans naturally associate Africa with poverty, they may also do the same with India? Or were America's condescending cultural attacks a result of romantic fascination with British dramas set in British India, with Indian culture presented as inferior? Unless Americans reflect on the roots of their lack of respect for India, they will fail to develop a strong partnership of equals.

The tragedy of this failure is that such a partnership would bring massive benefits to both countries. As the American century gradually fades away in the coming decades and an Asian century emerges in force, America will need to build bridges to engage the new self-confident Asian societies. Clearly, China cannot provide America a bridge to the new Asia as China will be perceived as the main challenger to America for the coming decades. However, India can, as there are several common links to build upon. The first is the exceptional success of the Indian community in America. America's free enterprise system is, in many ways, the most competitive market in the world for human achievement as the best minds from nations all over the world migrate to America. The pool of migrants in America represents the highest achieving segments of societies around the world. When the best brains of the world compete on a level playing field, which ethnic community does the best? The data show it is the ethnic Indian community in America.

Indians have the highest median household income in America at US$119,858 (2018).* A significant number of signature American companies have been run by ethnic Indians. A partial list includes Google (Sundar Pichar), Microsoft (Satya Nadella), PepsiCo (Indra Nooryi), Adobe (Shantanu Narayen), Nokia (Rajeev Suri), MasterCard (Ajay Banga), and Micron (Sanjay Mehrotra). Similarly, many leading US business schools have had deans from the ethnic Indian community. They include Sunil Kumar (provost of Johns Hopkins University, former dean of University of Chicago Booth School of Business), Madhav Rajan (dean of Chicago Booth School), Nitin Nohria (dean of Harvard Business School), Rangarajan Sundaram (dean of New York University Stern School of Business), and Paul Almeida (dean of Georgetown University McDonough School of Business).

Given the strong presence of ethnic Indians in significant elite positions in America, it is probable that the elite-to-elite connectivity between America and India is higher than that between America and any other country.

Given both the factors of geopolitical convergence of interests (vis-à-vis China) and elite connectivity, relations between America and India have been drifting closer. Three of the four most recent US presidents developed, over time, a certain personal affection for India, namely Bill Clinton, George W. Bush, and Barack Obama. By contrast, their

---

* US Census Bureau, "Selected Population Profile in the United States," American Community Survey, 2018: ACS 1-Year Estimates Selected Population Profiles, TableID: S0201, United States Census Bureau, https://data.census.gov/cedsci/table?q=&hidePreview=false&table=S0201&tid=ACSSPP1Y2018.S0201&t=013%20-%20Asian%20Indian%20alone%20%28400-401%29%3AIncome%20and%20Earnings&lastDisplayedRow=50.

two immediate predecessors, George H. W. Bush and Ronald Reagan, showed little interest or affection for India. Logically speaking, relations between America and India should have hit a new high when Donald Trump was elected because, as a right-wing nationalist leader, Trump is in the same ideological camp as India's Prime Minister Narendra Modi. Indeed, relations went well initially between these two leaders. Modi visited Washington, DC, on June 24–26, 2017. During the visit, Trump and Modi "pledged to deepen defense and security cooperation, building on the United States' recognition of India as a Major Defense Partner."* But Trump has not visited India, and he turned down an invitation to be the chief guest at the Republic Day Parade in 2018, even though other world leaders, like Putin, Sarkozy, Abe, and Obama, have accepted these invitations in the past.†

Moreover, in the second year of the Trump administration, several difficulties surfaced in the Indo-American relationship. Given his concern for jobs for Americans, Trump sharply cut down on H1-B visas. This hurt India the most as it is the largest supplier of talented foreign workers, especially in the field of information technology. For many decades, given India's status as a developing country under WTO standards, India has received preferential tariff treatment for its exports to America under the Generalized System of Preferences (GSP), an American "trade program designed to promote economic growth in the developing world" instituted in 1976,‡ which allowed India to "export

---

* "Joint Statement—United States and India: Prosperity Through Partnership," Media Center, Ministry of External Affairs, Government of India, June 27, 2017, https://mea.gov.in/bilateral-documents.htm?dtl/28560/United_States_and_India _Prosperity_Through_Partnership.

† Nirmala Ganapathy, "Trump Declines to Be Chief Guest on India's Republic Day," *Straits Times* (Singapore), November 1, 2018, https://www.straitstimes.com/asia/south -asia/trump-declines-to-be-chief-guest-on-indias-republic-day.

‡ Information Center, US Customs and Border Protection, https://help.cbp.gov/app /answers/detail/a_id/266/~/generalized-system-of-preferences-%28gsp%29.

nearly 2,000 products to the U.S. duty-free."* On May 31, 2019, the Trump administration decided to unilaterally withdraw these concessions by ending India's status as a developing nation. President Trump declared: "I have determined that India has not assured the United States that India will provide equitable and reasonable access to its markets. Accordingly, it is appropriate to terminate India's designation as a beneficiary developing country effective June 5, 2019."† Since Indian exports to America make up a minuscule portion of American imports (2.1 percent or $54.4 billion in 2018‡), the net impact on the American economy was virtually zero. So why alienate a potential friend or ally for minimal economic gain?

To make matters worse, Trump has also made fun of Modi on several occasions. The *Washington Post* reported in January 2018: "Senior administration officials said that the president has been known to affect an Indian accent and imitate Indian Prime Minister Narendra Modi."§ In January 2019, Trump also mocked Modi for funding a library in Afghanistan:

> Mr. Trump brought up India's aid during a press appearance at a Cabinet meeting as he defended his push for the United States to invest less overseas. While stating that he got along with Mr. Modi, he said the Indian leader was "constantly telling me he built a library in

---

* Justin Sink and Jenny Leonard, "India Roiled as Trump Yanks Its Status as a Developing Nation," Bloomberg, May 31, 2019, https://www.bloomberg.com/news/articles/2019-06-01/trump-ends-india-s-trade-designation-as-a-developing-nation.
† Ibid.
‡ See US Census Bureau, "Top Trading Partners—December 2018," Foreign Trade, United States Census Bureau, https://www.census.gov/foreign-trade/statistics/highlights/top/top1812yr.html; and US Census Bureau, "Trade in Goods with India," Foreign Trade, United States Census Bureau, https://www.census.gov/foreign-trade/balance/c5330.html.
§ Greg Jaffe and Missy Ryan, "Up to 1,000 More US Troops Could Be Headed to Afghanistan This Spring," *Washington Post*, January 21, 2018.

Afghanistan.""You know what that is? That's like five hours of what we spend," Mr. Trump said. "I don't know who's using it in Afghanistan."[*]

Fortunately, Modi didn't take offense. He brushed off the insults. Still, the whole world could see clearly the stark differences between the warm and respectful statements made by Trump about Xi Jinping and the derogatory comments made toward Modi. Since China is emerging as the number one geopolitical competitor of America and India is emerging potentially as the number one geopolitical ally of America, these attitudes make no geopolitical sense, except that they inadvertently imply the reality that Americans have more respect for China than for India.

Eventually, in either 2021 or 2025, we will move into a post-Trump world. When that happens, America can begin to try to work out a consistent long-term policy of deep engagement with India. There should be annual high-level meetings between American presidents and Indian prime ministers. Just as America has set up high-level strategic dialogues with China (involving the treasury secretary and secretary of state) since 2009, it should do the same with India. Even more boldly, America should propose an FTA with India and offer India some unilateral concessions. A deep and bold partnership between America and India would enable India to play a significant role in acting as a bridge between America and the Asian century.

ASEAN (Association of Southeast Asian Nations) could also play a significant bridging role. However, if India suffers from a lack of strategic respect in Washington, DC, ASEAN suffers something even more severe: strategic ignorance. Many senior American policymakers may

---

[*] "Trump Mocks Modi over Funding for Afghan Library," *Straits Times* (Singapore), January 4, 2019, https://www.straitstimes.com/world/trump-mocks-modi-over-funding-for-afghan-library.

have heard the name ASEAN, but they would have great difficulty understanding the significance of ASEAN to American strategic interests.

The best way to explain why ASEAN is a miracle for America is to compare Southeast Asia to Iran. America had two major strategic failures in the 1970s. It withdrew ignominiously from Vietnam in 1975, and it was expelled from Iran in 1979. At the time of these two failures, when Indochina (Cambodia, Laos, and Vietnam) was taken over by communist governments, the region that looked more fragile was Southeast Asia. Some American pundits warned that the original five noncommunist ASEAN (Indonesia, Malaysia, Philippines, Singapore, and Thailand) would end up as "dominoes". Instead, the opposite happened. Within two decades, the three communist governments had joined ASEAN.

Today, ASEAN represents one of the most promising economic regions in the world. ASEAN countries have gone from having economies that were among the poorest in the world to developing the fourth-largest economy in the world by 2030.* While the 70 million people in Iran continue to provide a strategic challenge to America, the 650 million people in Southeast Asia represent a major strategic opportunity for America. The sensible thing for American policymakers would be to pay attention to this strategic opportunity. Instead, American policymakers pay more attention to Iran, and ASEAN continues to suffer from ignorance and neglect in Washington, DC. American officials groan when they have to schedule visits of US presidents and secretaries of state to Southeast Asia. Indeed, many US secretaries of state have canceled or

---

* PwC, "Emerging Trends in Real Estate," PricewaterhouseCoopers, https://www.pwc .com/gx/en/growth-markets-centre/publications/assets/pwc-gmc-the-future-of-asean -time-to-act.pdf; Loong, keynote address; and ASEAN, "Investing in ASEAN, 2013– 2014," https://www.usasean.org/system/files/downloads/Investing-in-ASEAN-2013 -14.pdf.

shortened visits to ASEAN meetings because a new "crisis" has broken out in the Middle East. This behavior is irrational.

Fortunately, it is not too late. ASEAN remains a region of great geopolitical opportunity for America. When the topic of Southeast Asia surfaces, Americans often only remember how painful the Vietnam War was. The memory of the ignominious defeat of 1975 is one that Americans want to forget, and so they overlook forty-five years of success during which the American-supported, noncommunist economies of Southeast Asia (remembered in the American imagination as near-dominoes) actually succeeded and emerged among the most successful countries in the developing world. There is one fact about Southeast Asia in particular that most Americans are unaware of: Southeast Asia is one of the most pro-American regions in the world.

Future historians will no doubt wonder why in the three critical decades after the end of the Cold War, when the Middle East, no longer an arena of US-Soviet competition, lost its importance, and Southeast Asia gained importance as a potential arena of US-China competition, American strategic thinkers and policymakers continued to give so much more attention to the Middle East (draining the spirits and resources of Americans in futile wars) instead of Southeast Asia, an oasis of peace and prosperity. Unknown to most Americans, many of the leaders and elites of Southeast Asia have studied in leading American universities. Some of the most active overseas chapters of the alumni of Ivy League universities can be found in Southeast Asia.

Happily, this reservoir of pro-American sentiment in Southeast Asia is not going to disappear soon. If America can work out a sensible, thoughtful, comprehensive, and long-term strategy for ASEAN, it will find a strong partner.

Today, when most American policymakers and pundits look at Southeast Asia, they view it through the distorting prism of the US-China rivalry. Southeast Asia is close to China geographically; its largest internal waterway is called the South China Sea. Many Americans assume that Southeast Asian states will naturally become political and cultural satellites of China. But despite the geographic proximity, nine of the ten Southeast Asian states have an Indic cultural foundation. The one Southeast Asian state that has a Sinic cultural base is Vietnam, which treasures its independence from China the most since it was occupied by China for almost a thousand years.

Most Americans know little about the history of Southeast Asia. It is fascinating. Of the 650 million people living in ASEAN, there are 266 million Muslims, 146 million Christians, and 149 million Buddhists—both Mahayana and Hinayana Buddhists. In addition, there are millions of Confucians, Taoists, Hindus, and even communists living mostly together in peace in Southeast Asia.

In fact, American neglect of Southeast Asia after the end of the Cold War may have helped the region—an idea that will be immediately contested by American policymakers. However, a sober assessment of the results of the trillions of dollars that America has wasted on futile wars in the Middle East should demonstrate to future American policymakers: less is more.

Neglect also does not mean complete disengagement. Although America withdrew from all military conflicts in Southeast Asia, it remained diplomatically engaged with ASEAN. It's true that American attention was inconsistent and unpredictable. Nonetheless, overall, the American-ASEAN relationship has had a fundamentally positive tone.

In short, the ASEAN region remains one of the most important regions of the world if America is interested in trying out a diplomacy-first strategy to match the growing Chinese influence in the world. While Southeast Asia's geographic proximity to China might give the impression that America is likely to lose a geopolitical contest for hearts and minds in the region, a deeper study of Southeast Asian history and culture will reveal opportunities for American diplomatic engagement.

Over time, however unlikely this seems as I write in 2019, I predict that Russia will emerge as a key ally of America when the level of geopolitical competition between America and China intensifies. The country that has the longest border with China is Russia. The relative economic and political weights of Russia and China have shifted dramatically. In 1979, after Mao's policies in the Great Leap Forward and the Cultural Revolution had seriously weakened China, the economy of the then Soviet Union, led by Russia, was several times larger than that of China.

In 2019, China's economy ($12.2 trillion) is 7.75 times larger than that of Russia's ($1.6 trillion).[*] By 2050, China's economy will become even larger. Even though Russia has a nuclear arsenal that dwarfs that of China and Russia need never fear an outright military invasion from China (as it will never happen), it would still be prudent for Russia to find an ally to balance a neighbor that much larger in size and influence. The most natural ally is America. It makes sense then if, sometime in the next few decades, an alliance develops between America and Russia.

However, for this to happen, American leaders must be able to speak frankly to their Russian counterparts. They must acknowledge some undeniable historical truths, even though they may be painful and uncomfortable. Recently, the most obviously uncomfortable truth is the Russian meddling in the 2016 US presidential election.

Americans have a more substantial truth to confront if they wish to reset their relations with Russia. After the end of the Cold War, American leaders betrayed the explicit and implicit promises that they made to the Russian leaders. America had promised Russia that, after the dismantling of the Warsaw Pact, America would not expand NATO eastward to threaten Russia.

* World Bank, "World Bank Open Data," The World Bank data, https://data.worldbank .org.

What geopolitical calculations played out in American minds as they made this fatal decision to expand NATO? Did they believe that since Russia was weak and struggling in the 1990s (with an imploding economy and a financial crisis that brought great suffering to the Russian people) America could once and for all time eliminate Russia as a potential competitor? Since most Americans are openhearted and generous by nature, it seems hard to believe that America had a sinister plot to permanently eliminate Russia as a geopolitical competitor. Nonetheless, America's disregard for Russia's interests in the 1990s and 2000s looks to have been the result of a concerted plan.

Regardless of whether there was a "conscious" American plan to weaken Russia after the end of the Cold War, it would be useful for Americans and Russians to have a frank discussion face-to-face of their respective perceptions of what happened. All the difficult episodes that bedeviled relations between the two countries should be surfaced: the expansion of NATO, the American sponsorship of color revolutions in Ukraine and Georgia, the invasion of Iraq, the interventions in Libya and Syria.

A frank reassessment by Americans of their policies toward Russia could result in several dividends for US long-term geopolitical thinking. The past cannot be changed; however, if Americans become more aware of the humiliation that US policies inflicted upon the Russians, they can begin to remove some of the key psychological obstacles preventing the early emergence of an effective Russo-American alliance.

As soon as the Cold War ended, Vietnam began the process of adjusting to the new geopolitical environment caused by the collapse of the Soviet Union. Many of Vietnam's erstwhile adversaries also adjusted quickly. For example, the five founding members of ASEAN had been locked in an adversarial relationship with Vietnam throughout the 1980s. Yet, by 1995, Vietnam was admitted as a member of ASEAN. The relatively poor developing member states of ASEAN, with none of the sophistication of the strategic think tank industry of Washington, DC, were able quickly to adjust to the new geopolitical environment by admitting a former adversary to ASEAN. Fortunately, America kept pace with ASEAN, with President Bill Clinton lifting the trade embargo against Vietnam in 1994 and normalizing relations in 1995.[*]

In theory, good geopolitical thinking should be driven by cold, hardheaded evaluations of geopolitical realities. Reason should always trump emotion in geopolitical analysis and behavior. Curiously, in part because of the overwhelming power America has enjoyed over several decades, America has enjoyed the luxury (or paid the price) of allowing emotions, rather than reason, to guide its geopolitical behavior. Such behavior may be acceptable or simply possible for a number one power in the world that is far more powerful than any of its potential competitors. However, when that powerful country becomes number two, it could be fatal for it to allow emotions to trump reason in its geopolitical thinking and behavior.

As America glides toward becoming inevitably the number two power in the world, it will no longer have the luxury of having its geopolitical policies driven by emotion. A deep American effort will be needed to understand how and why its relations with several countries (including Russia) went wrong after the Cold War. This should lead to a better self-understanding by American society of its own geopolitical reflexes and impulses, and self-understanding is one key to geopolitical success.

America is less likely to make serious mistakes in its future geopolitical policies toward China if it develops a good understanding of the positive moves and the mistakes it has made in its relations with other countries. America has done more right than it has done wrong. This explains the relatively good relations America has had with most countries in the world. Yet, it is also true that America has made several

---

[*] Eleanor Albert, "The Evolution of U.S.-Vietnam Ties," Council on Foreign Relations, March 20, 2019, https://www.cfr.org/backgrounder/evolution-us-vietnam-ties.

unnecessary and painful mistakes, especially with the Islamic world and with Russia.

In short, unlike the Cold War, where a clear majority of countries showed greater sympathy for the successful America over the failing Soviet Union, it is far from clear that a similar outcome will emerge in the new Sino-American contest. Most countries will, in one way or another, hedge their bets. Both America and China will have to learn to play a more sophisticated game if they want to win countries over to their side.

CHAPTER 9

A PARADOXICAL CONCLUSION

THIS BOOK ENDS WITH A PARADOXICAL CONCLUSION: A MAJOR geopolitical contest between America and China is both inevitable and avoidable.

Let's start with the inevitable aspect. This book has explained some of the dynamics driving America and China toward a major geopolitical contest, from China's mistake in alienating the American business community to America's need to find a foreign scapegoat to hide the deep domestic socioeconomic challenges that have emerged in American society.

At the same time, a huge head of steam has been building up in the American body politic against China. After speaking to several establishment figures with decades of combined experience on China, Greg Ip of the *Wall Street Journal* concluded: "Yet if the pendulum swung too far toward accommodating China in the past, it may be rebounding too far toward confrontation now." Ip cites former treasury secretary Hank Paulson as saying: "We have a China attitude, not a China policy. . . . You have Homeland Security, the FBI, CIA, the Defense Department, treating China as the enemy and members of Congress competing to see who can be the most belligerent China hawk. No one is leaning against the wind, providing balance, asking what can we realistically do that has some chance of getting results that won't be harmful to our economic and national-security interests in the long term?[*]

Hank Paulson is absolutely right. Given the poisonous atmosphere toward China, it would be unwise for any American politician or public intellectual to advocate more reasonable approaches toward China. An indication of how strongly the sentiment has swung against China is Roger Cohen's column in the *New York Times*. Cohen is by and large a fair and balanced columnist. Yet, in his column on August 31, 2019, he had hardly anything positive to say about China. Instead, Cohen wrote that "the United States is now in a direct ideological war with China over the shape of the world in the 21st century" and that Xi's message is clear: "We'll . . . one day run the world."[†]

One key message of this book is that while Chinese leaders want to rejuvenate Chinese civilization, they have no missionary impulse to take over the world and make everyone Chinese. China's role and influence in the world will certainly grow along with the size of its economy. Yet, it will not use its influence to change the ideologies or political practices of other societies. One great paradox about our world today is that even though China has traditionally been a closed society, while America purports to be an open society, the Chinese leaders find it easier than American leaders to deal with a diverse world, as they have no

---

[*] Greg Ip, "Has America's China Backlash Gone Too Far?," *Wall Street Journal*, August 28, 2019, https://www.wsj.com/articles/has-americas-china-backlash-gone-too -far-11566990232?mod=rsswn.

[†] Roger Cohen, "Trump Has China Policy About Right," *New York Times*, August 30, 2019, https://www.nytimes.com/2019/08/30/opinion/trump-china-trade-war.html.

expectation that other societies should become like them. They, unlike Americans, understand that other societies think and behave differently.

Sadly, such arguments will have little impact in an America that has convinced itself that China has today become an existential threat. This is why a major geopolitical contest between America and China is inevitable.

To make matters worse, critical decisions are made in silos. When a Chinese official running an industrial park squeezes an American company to share its technology as quid pro quo for a license to invest, he or she is likely not thinking of the fact that this pattern of squeezing American companies would lead to China's biggest strategic mistake: the alienation of America's business community, which paved the way for Trump's widely supported trade war against China. When a New York judge issued a warrant of arrest on August 27, 2018, for the chief financial officer of Huawei, Meng Wanzhou,* he or she was ostensibly making this decision on purely legal grounds. However, what the Chinese saw are the double standards that Columbia University's Jeff Sachs pointed out: when American companies break laws, the US penalizes the companies, not the senior executives. But when Chinese companies break laws, the US penalizes the senior executives. The prosecutor was not trying to send the message that America has double standards, but this was nonetheless the message that China received because the prosecutor and the Department of Justice acted without considering the broader geopolitical implications of the decision.

Also, short-term gains often trump long-term considerations. When the Chinese government applied pressure, directly or indirectly, on the Cambodian government to veto a joint ASEAN statement in 2012 that mentioned the South China Sea, it ostensibly got a short-term win.

* Ian Young, "Huawei CFO Sabrina Meng Wanzhou Fraudently Represented Company to Skirt US and EU Sanctions on Iran, Court Told in Bail Hearing," *South China Morning Post*, December 8, 2018, https://www.scmp.com/news/china/article/2177013/huawei-executive-sabrina-meng-wanzhou-fraudulently-represented-company.

However, it also provided a huge propaganda coup for America, which used this incident to portray China as a bully against its neighbors. This is how Ernest Z. Bower of the Center for Strategic and International Studies (CSIS) described the impact of China's move:

> China has revealed its hand as an outlier on the question of ASEAN unity. It seemingly used its growing economic power to press Cambodia into the awkward position of standing up to its ASEAN neighbors on one of the most important security concerns for the grouping and its members. China's overt role, underlined by leaks about Cambodia's complicity in sharing drafts, seems to suggest Beijing's hand in promoting ASEAN disunity. Thus the most important message coming from Phnom Penh is not the intramural ASEAN spat over the joint statement but, rather, that China has decided that a weak and splintered ASEAN is in its best interests."

Similarly, when US secretary of state Hillary Clinton "ambushed" her counterpart, Chinese minister of foreign affairs Yang Jiechi, with a blistering statement on China's activities in the South China Sea at an ASEAN meeting in Hanoi in July 2010, she won kudos in the American media for having taken a strong principled stand. However, such public attacks also undermined the prospects for America and China to work out a mutually beneficial understanding on the South China Sea that would respect the core maritime interests of both nations. In geopolitical games, short-term propaganda gains often come at the cost of long-term dividends.

Geopolitical decisions, like all political decisions, are driven by personalities, and personalities keep changing—both in America and

---

* Ernest Z. Bower, "China Reveals Its Hand on ASEAN in Phnom Penh," CSIS, July 20, 2012, https://www.csis.org/analysis/china-reveals-its-hand-asean-phnom-penh.

China. The high point of Sino-American cooperation took place in the 1970s, when an unusual combination of four geopolitical heavyweights came together to forge a remarkable partnership: Richard Nixon and Henry Kissinger, Mao Zedong and Zhou Enlai. Without the geopolitical skills of these four leaders, no breakthrough between the two powerful adversaries would have happened. The close relationship between George H. W. Bush and Deng Xiaoping also helped to cushion the severe downturn in Sino-American relations after Tiananmen Square in 1989.

In contrast, relations between George W. Bush and Hu Jintao were not as close or comfortable as their predecessors. Similarly, Hillary Clinton didn't have comfortable relations with her Chinese counterparts during her term as secretary of state from 2009 to 2012. In theory, national interests, not personalities, drive the course of international relations. In practice, personalities do matter. Future historians may well decide that Vice President Mike Pence's speech on China on October 4, 2018, marked a new low in US-China relations. It was a nasty, condescending speech, one that none of his recent predecessors would have delivered. One year later on October 24, 2019, Pence delivered a second scathing speech that again attacked China on all fronts, reiterating his allegations from a year ago about "many of Beijing's policies most harmful to America's interests and values, from China's debt diplomacy and military expansionism; its repression of people of faith; construction of a surveillance state; and, of course, to China's arsenal of policies inconsistent with free and fair trade, including tariffs, quotas, currency manipulation, forced technology transfer, and industrial subsidies."* A

---

* "Remarks by Vice President Pence at the Frederic V. Malek Memorial Lecture," Conrad Hotel, Washington, DC, October 24, 2019, https://www.whitehouse.gov /briefings-statements/remarks-vice-president-pence-frederic-v-malek-memorial -lecture/.

more calm and reasonable vice president would have been more careful and less strident in such speeches.

Domestic politics often play a significant role in geopolitical decisions. It has always been a mystery to me why the Chinese government decided to print a map of China with the nine-dash line prominently highlighted on all Chinese passports. By so doing, the Chinese government gave its own population the impression that all the waters in the South China Sea contained within the nine-dash line were domestic territorial waters. In practice, however, the Chinese government treats most of the waters in the South China Sea as international waters and allows free passage of commercial and naval vessels. By bowing to domestic politics and publicizing the nine-dash line, the Chinese government had effectively boxed itself in, leaving little room for diplomatic maneuvering. Similarly, I was puzzled that President George H. W. Bush, who was otherwise a good friend of China, allowed his desire to win votes to override a long-term American policy toward Taiwan by allowing major arms sales to Taiwan.

Emotions play as important a role as reason in international relations. It would have been easier for America to accept the rise of another power if China had been a fellow Western democratic power, especially a fellow Anglo-Saxon power. This explains why the power transition from the United Kingdom to the United States went relatively smoothly: one Anglo-Saxon power was giving way to another. No dark emotional overtones accompanied this transition. By contrast, China is a very different culture and has always been perceived to be different in the Western imagination. Between America and China, there is a natural and legitimate concern: Will they understand us, our interests and values? Will we understand them?

To make matters worse, there has been buried deep in the unconscious of the Western psyche an inchoate but real fear of the "yellow peril." Since it is buried deep in the unconscious, it seldom surfaces.

When senior American policymakers make their decisions on China, they can say with all sincerity that they are driven by rational, not emotional, considerations. Yet, to an external observer, it is manifestly clear that America's reactions to China's rise are influenced by deep emotional reactions, too. Just as individual human beings have difficulty unearthing the unconscious motives that drive our behavior, countries and civilizations also have difficulty unearthing their unconscious impulses.

It is a fact that the yellow peril has lain buried in Western civilization for centuries. Napoleon famously alluded to it when he said, "Let China sleep; when she awakes she will shake the world." Why did Napoleon refer to China and not to India, an equally large and populous civilization? Because no hordes of Indians had threatened or ravaged European capitals. By contrast, hordes of Mongols, a "yellow race," had appeared at Europe's doorstep in the thirteenth century. As Noreen Giffney recounts: "in 1235, Mongol armies invaded Eastern Europe and the Rus' principalities between 1236 and 1242. [. . .] The Mongol onslaught was followed by a swift and mysterious withdrawal to the surprise and relief of Westerners."*

Giffney has traced how European writers in the thirteenth century constructed the Mongols as "monstrous" beings, following the latter's invasion of Europe:

> Following their invasion of Christendom and its neighboring territories, the Mongols were subjected to much hostile scrutiny in a variety of writings, where they were identified as "lawless Ishmaelites," "accursed godless ones" and "a host of shedders of Christian blood" (Chronicle of Novgorod, 1914, 82, 83, 82). Their employment of a vast array of military techniques that confounded Western armies,

---

* Noreen Giffney, "Monstrous Mongols," *Postmedieval: A Journal of Medieval Cultural Studies* 3, no. 2, (May 2012): 227–245.

coupled with the apparent invincibility of their ever-swelling army, prompted contemporary observers to describe them as "satellites of Antichrist" (Chronica Majora, 1852, 1:469) and infernal messengers of Satan, hailing from the bowels of Tartarus or hell itself.*

The latent fear of the yellow peril surfaces from time to time in literature and art. As a child living in a British colony, I read the popular Fu Manchu novels. They left a deep impression on me. Subconsciously, I began to believe that the personification of evil in human society came in the form of a slant-eyed yellow man devoid of moral scruples. If I, as a non-Westerner, could internalize this ethnic caricature, I suspect that these subconscious fears have also affected the reactions of American policymakers to the rise of China. This is another reason to feel pessimistic about the future of Sino-American relations. Most Americans would protest that racism does not play a part in their foreign policy, but many Asians (and not just Chinese) would agree with me.

Yet, even though the case for pessimism is strong, one could also make an equally strong case for optimism. If we could marshal the forces of reason to develop an understanding of the real national interests of both America and China, we would come to the conclusion that there should be no fundamental contradiction between the two powers. Indeed, there are actually five *non*contradictions between America and China. If wise heads could prevail in both capitals, they should reflect on and highlight these five fundamental noncontradictions.

The word *noncontradiction* is rarely used in Western discourse. The Western mind is used to black-and-white distinctions. One side is right; one side is wrong. The Chinese mind is different. Both black and white can be right. This mind-set of dualism is best captured in the concepts of yin and yang. In the Western worldview, either yin or yang would be right. In the Chinese worldview, both yin and yang can be right.

* Ibid.

It is difficult to explain the relationship between yin and yang. One professor who has tried to do so is Dr. Hong Hai of the Nanyang Technological University. He writes:

> The ideas of yin and yang reflect a dialectical logic that attempts to explain relationships and change. Stripped to its bare essentials, yin and yang are not much more than labels that capture the perception of duality in nature—light versus darkness, hardness versus softness, male versus female. Thus the yin-yang doctrine is a holistic view of the world that places all entities as parts of a cosmic whole. These entities cannot have existence independent of their relationship to other entities. Dualism implies that an attribute like brightness has meaning only relative to darkness, as does beauty relative to ugliness.[*]

He adds: "One of the most basic principles is the notion that *yin* and *yang* oppose each other, but are also interdependent."

With this dualistic view in mind, it is possible to see the five fundamental noncontradictions between the United States and China. First, there is a noncontradiction between the fundamental national interests of both countries. The fundamental national interest of both societies is to improve the well-being of their people. In March 1809, Thomas Jefferson wrote, on his departure from the US presidency: "the care of human life and happiness, and not their destruction, is the first and only legitimate object of good government."[†] Noting this observation, Martin Wolf asked: "How might one measure 'happiness'? What

---

[*] Hong Hai, "Daoism and Management," chap. 4 in *The Rule of Culture: Corporate and State Governance in China and East Asia* (London: Routledge, 2019).

[†] Thomas Jefferson, "To the Republicans of Washington County, Maryland," March 31, 1809, https://founders.archives.gov/documents/Jefferson/03-01-02-0088, quoted in Martin Wolf, "The Case for Making Wellbeing the Goal of Public Policy," *Financial Times* (London), May 30, 2019, https://www.ft.com/content/d4bb3e42-823b-11e9-9935-ad75bb96c849.

promotes it?"[*] As Wolf notes, these are age-old questions. The Western utilitarian philosophers, including Jeremy Bentham, have long been posing them.

Fortunately, contemporary utilitarian philosophers have taken up the challenge of measuring happiness. For example, Professor Richard Layard of the London School of Economics, in his coauthored book *The Origin of Happiness*, has said that self-reported "life satisfaction" can be a good proxy for measuring happiness. As a result, Layard argues that well-being will eventually become totally accepted as the standard way to evaluate social policies. If we can measure and promote well-being, we can also focus on policies that will improve well-being. We can also decide which items should be given priority in national budgets: domestic investments or defense expenditures?

America is a much richer country than China. Its nominal per capita income of US$62,641 is at least six times larger than that of China at US$9,771.[†] Yet, even though America is richer, the well-being of its people, especially the bottom 50 percent of the population, has deteriorated in recent decades. One fact cannot be denied: America wasted nearly $5 trillion on wars in the Middle East since 9/11. Brown University's Watson Institute reported:

> Totaling these expenses and Congressional requests for FY2017, the US federal government has spent and obligated approximately $4.8 trillion on the post-9/11 wars. In addition, by 2053, interest costs will be at least $7.9 trillion unless the US changes the way it pays for the wars.[‡]

---

[*] Wolf, "The Case for Making Wellbeing the Goal of Public Policy."

[†] World Bank, "GDP per Capita (current US$)," The World Bank data, https://data.worldbank.org/indicator/NY.GDP.PCAP.CD.

[‡] "US Federal and State Budgets," Costs of War, Watson Institute: International & Public Affairs, Brown University, https://watson.brown.edu/costsofwar/costs/economic/budget.

If these $4.8 trillion had been shared among the bottom 50 percent of the American population, each American citizen would have received about $29,000. If this amount is laid alongside the statistic that two-thirds of American households do not have access to emergency cash of $500, it shows clearly why it is in America's national interest to put the well-being of its people first. Heidi Garrett-Peltier wrote in a 2017 paper for Brown University's Watson Institute:

> Since 2001, because the federal government has spent trillions of dollars on the wars in Iraq, Afghanistan, Syria, and Pakistan, we have lost opportunities to create millions of jobs in the domestic economy, and we have lost opportunities to improve educational, health, and environmental outcomes for the American public. [. . .] Education and healthcare create more than twice as many jobs as defense for the same level of spending, while clean energy and infrastructure create over 40 percent more jobs. In fact, over the past 16 years, by spending money on war rather than in these other areas of the domestic economy, the US lost the opportunity to create between one million and three million additional jobs.[*]

In short, the American people would be far better off if America stopped fighting unnecessary foreign wars and used its resources to improve the well-being of its people. Since China's per capita income is much lower than America's, it is also in China's national interest to improve the well-being of its people. The argument that both America and China should make improving the well-being of their people their primary national interest should be incontestable. Yet, the fact that the strategic thinkers cannot see this fundamental point demonstrates just

---

[*] Heidi Garrett-Peltier, "Job Opportunity Cost of War," Costs of War, Watson Institute: International & Public Affairs, Brown University, https://watson.brown.edu/costsofwar/files/cow/imce/papers/2017/Job%20Opportunity%20Cost%20of%20War%20-%20HGP%20-%20FINAL.pdf.

how distorted their perspectives have become. It is the good fortune of both America and China that the vast Pacific Ocean separates them. If they can both focus on the well-being of their people and allow the Pacific Ocean to protect their respective homelands, both societies will be better off.

They could also find areas to cooperate in. America is suffering from a serious infrastructure deficit. China has emerged as an infrastructure superpower. It can build high-speed train networks faster than any other country. In 2012, Keith Bradsher of the *New York Times* reported that "China began service . . . on the world's longest high-speed rail line, covering a distance in eight hours that is about equal to that from New York to Key West, Fla. . . . Amtrak trains from New York to Miami, a shorter distance, still take nearly 30 hours."* Common sense would dictate that both countries should cooperate in infrastructure. Yet, given the poisonous political attitudes toward each other, common sense cannot operate. This is why a major strategic reboot is needed in the relationship between the two powers. If the two powers first tried to define what their core national interests were—especially their core interests in improving the livelihoods of their people—they would come to the logical conclusion that there is fundamentally a noncontradiction between their national interests.

Second, there is also a fundamental noncontradiction between America and China in slowing the forces of climate change. If climate change makes the planet progressively uninhabitable, both American and Chinese citizens will be fellow passengers on a sinking ship. It has become a cliché to say that it is foolish to rearrange the deck chairs on the *Titanic*. Yet, this is precisely what the leaders of America and China

---

* Keith Bradsher, "China Opens Longest High-Speed Rail Line," *New York Times*, December 26, 2012, https://www.nytimes.com/2012/12/27/business/global/worlds-longest-high-speed-rail-line-opens-in-china.html.

are doing when they argue over their geopolitical differences instead of focusing on their common interests in protecting our planet.

Some wise soul has remarked that the best thing that could happen for humanity would be for astronomers to detect a distant comet on a collision path with the earth, with no certainty which continent it would land on. Only such a common threat would make the 7.5 billion people on the planet (including the 1.4 billion in China and 330 million in America) aware that their common interests as earth citizens are far greater than their national interests. The simple truth is that as Yuval Noah Harari writes in *Sapiens*:

> Today almost all humans share the same geopolitical system . . . the same economic system . . . the same legal system . . . and the same scientific system. . . . The single global culture is not homogeneous. . . . Yet they are all closely connected and they influence one another in myriad ways. They still argue and fight, but they argue using the same concepts and fight using the same weapons. [. . .] Today when Iran and the United States rattle swords at one another, they both speak the language of nation states, capitalist economies, international rights and nuclear physics.[*]

As our only habitable planet faces a great peril, should we focus on our differences or our similarities? The human species is supposed to be the most intelligent species on earth. This is the apparent reason why we have become the world's dominant species. Yet the most intelligent species is now acting in a suicidal fashion by allowing climate change to gain traction without acting in common to reverse it. Instead, we are arguing about which countries are to blame. Robert

---

[*] Yuval Noah Harari, *Sapiens: A Brief History of Humankind* (New York: HarperCollins, 2015).

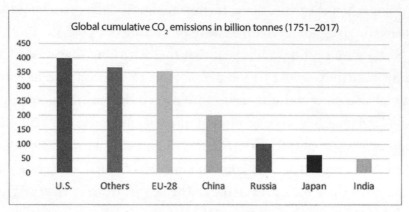

CHART 13. Global Cumulative CO_2 Emissions in Billion Tons (1751–2017)[*]

Blackwill, the distinguished former American ambassador, is right to highlight that China today "generates approximately 28 percent of global carbon emissions and the United States is responsible for only about 15 percent."[†] Yet, it is also a fact that global warming is happening not only because of current flows of greenhouse gas emissions but also because of the stock of greenhouse gases, especially CO_2, emitted by Western countries, including America, since the coal-fired Industrial Revolution.[‡] Chart 13, which documents the cumulative CO_2 emissions by the major powers, indicates that China has still contributed far less than America and the EU. In short, all industrialized nations need to take responsibility for their actions and work together to limit further environmental damage.

---

[*] Hannah Ritchie and Max Roser, "CO_2 and Greenhouse Gas Emissions," Our World in Data, updated October 2018, https://ourworldindata.org/co2-and-other -greenhouse-gas-emissions#cumulative-co2-emissions.

[†] Robert D. Blackwill, "Trump's Foreign Policies Are Better Than They Seem," Council on Foreign Relations, https://cfrd8-files.cfr.org/sites/default/files/report_pdf/CSR %2084_Blackwill_Trump_0.pdf.

[‡] EPA, "Understanding Global Warming," US Environmental Protection Agency, https://www.epa.gov/ghgemissions/understanding-global-warming-potentials.

China and India have been remarkably responsible in not walking away from the Paris Climate Accords when the Trump administration decided to do so in 2017. It is a truly strange world we live in when the relatively poor countries like China (per capita income $9,771) and India (per capita income $2,016) respect their global obligations, while a relatively rich country like America (per capita income $62,641) walks away from them.[*] As Blackwill states, "the U.S. withdrawal from the Paris Agreement has made China an informal global leader on climate change, as the signatories of the agreement proceed without U.S. involvement. This contributes to a widespread international view that the United States, reflected in the policies of the Trump administration, is withdrawing from the world."[†]

Global warming is not the only "global commons" challenge that humanity faces. There are equally pressing challenges in many other areas. The UN has identified seventeen Sustainable Development Goals to "meet the urgent environmental, political and economic challenges facing our world."[‡] These are what the seventeen goals aim to accomplish:

1. End extreme poverty in all forms by 2030.
2. End hunger, achieve food security and improved nutrition and promote sustainable agriculture.
3. Ensure healthy lives and promote well-being for all at all ages.
4. Ensure inclusive and equitable quality education and promote life-long learning opportunities for all.
5. Achieve gender equality and empower all women and girls.

---

[*] World Bank, "GDP per Capita (Current US$)," The World Bank data, https://data.worldbank.org/indicator/NY.GDP.PCAP.CD?.
[†] Blackwill, "Trump's Foreign Policies Are Better Than They Seem."
[‡] Background on the Goals, "Sustainable Development Goals," UN Development Programme, https://www.undp.org/content/undp/en/home/sustainable-development-goals/background/.

6. Ensure availability and sustainable management of water and sanitation for all.

7. Ensure access to affordable, reliable, sustainable and modern energy for all.

8. Promote sustained, inclusive and sustainable economic growth, full and productive employment and decent work for all.

9. Build resilient infrastructure, promote inclusive and sustainable industrialization and foster innovation.

10. Reduce inequality within and among countries.

11. Make cities and human settlements inclusive, safe, resilient and sustainable.

12. Ensure sustainable consumption and production patterns.

13. Take urgent action to combat climate change and its impacts.

14. Conserve and sustainably use the oceans, seas and marine resources for sustainable development.

15. Protect, restore and promote sustainable use of terrestrial ecosystems, sustainably manage forests, combat desertification, and halt and reverse land degradation and halt biodiversity loss.

16. Promote peaceful and inclusive societies for sustainable development, provide access to justice for all and build effective, accountable and inclusive institutions at all levels.

17. Strengthen the means of implementation and revitalize the global partnership for sustainable development.[*]

One fact is undeniable: if the world's two biggest powers cooperate on these common challenges, we are more likely to find solutions. The actions of either one of them can have a major impact. Here is one example. Shark's fin is a delicacy in the Chinese diet. With China having the world's fastest-growing middle class, the demand for shark's

---

[*] UNDP, *Sustainable Development Goals*, United Nations Development Programme, https://www.undp.org/content/dam/undp/library/corporate/brochure/SDGs_Booklet_Web_En.pdf.

fin has grown exponentially. As a result, sharks were going to become an endangered species. Fortunately, the Chinese leadership acted. They banned shark's fin from being served in any meal hosted by CCP cadres. The CCP has ninety million members. When ninety million Chinese stopped eating shark's fin, the demand for it plummeted. It became less lucrative to fish for sharks. One species may have been saved by this unilateral action of China.

Third, there is a noncontradiction between America and China in the ideological sphere. This statement may come as a surprise. It is commonly believed that a key driving force in the Sino-American geo-political contest is a deep and profound ideological divide. There was indeed a time when China promoted communism. I experienced this personally. In the 1950s and 1960s, after the Communist Party took over China in 1949, it actively supported communist parties, especially in neighboring Southeast Asia. It supported the Communist Party of Malaya, which tried to take over Singapore, my home. However, all this promotion of communism ended after Lee Kuan Yew, then Singapore's prime minister, told Deng Xiaoping that communist China could not have peaceful relations with noncommunist Southeast Asia (especially the five founding members of ASEAN: Indonesia, Malaysia, Philippines, Singapore, and Thailand) if it continued to support communist parties in these countries. After Lee Kuan Yew delivered this message, the Chinese Communist Party's support for communist parties in Southeast Asia was gradually withdrawn. This policy shift has implications that American observers of China should reflect upon. Over forty years ago, when China was presented with a concrete choice, it chose to promote China's national interests and sacrificed the ideology of communism. It also stopped promoting communism globally.

The noncommunist countries of Southeast Asia and indeed most countries of the world therefore do not feel threatened in any way by Chinese ideology. Many thoughtful Americans may deem this naïve. Many Americans have become convinced (almost as a matter of religious belief) that the success of Chinese communism inherently poses a threat to democracies. For example, in *The Hundred-Year Marathon*, Michael Pillsbury has written:

> Chinese officials prefer a world with more autocracies and fewer democracies. [. . .] As China's power continues to grow, its ability to protect dictatorial, pro-China governments and to undermine representative governments will likely grow dramatically as well. [. . .] [S]uch efforts have begun with the manipulation of news and information. Part of its $6.58 billion "overseas propaganda" project expressly advocates autocratic forms of government.*

If Chinese communism is an inherent threat to democracies, it should be perceived as a threat by many other democracies. The three largest democracies in the world, in terms of population size, are India (1.3 billion), America (330 million), and Indonesia (250 million). If Chinese communism is a threat to democracies, all three should feel threatened. Some American policymakers feel threatened. Yet, if one were to ask either Prime Minister Modi of India or President Jokowi of Indonesia (or any of their senior colleagues) whether Indian democracy or Indonesian democracy feels threatened by Chinese communism, they would be puzzled by this question. Since both India and Indonesia are geographically much closer to China and have many more links with China, they understand China well. Certainly, the rise of Chinese *power* is a matter of concern to them. But Chinese *communist ideology* is of no concern to them. They see no desire or effort on the part of Chinese leaders to export or promote communism. In this respect, the attitude and behavior of the Chinese Communist Party is the exact opposite of the Soviet Communist Party.

---

* Michael Pillsbury, "A China World Order in 2049," chap. 9 in *The Hundred-Year Marathon: China's Secret Strategy to Replace America as the Global Superpower* (New York: St. Martin's Press, 2016), 177–196.

Unfortunately, even though the behavior of the Chinese Communist Party is the polar opposite of Soviet behavior, many American thinkers have unthinkingly transferred their previous assumptions about Soviet behavior onto the Chinese Communist Party. There is a danger in doing this. The Chinese Communist Party is far more capable and adaptable than the Soviet Communist Party. Unlike the Soviet Communist Party, it is in no danger of disappearing anytime soon. At the 2019 Shangri-La Dialogue, Singapore's Prime Minister Lee Hsien Loong remarked: "The Cold War ended with the total collapse of the sclerotic planned economies of the Soviet Union and the Eastern European countries, under the pressure of enormous defense spending. Even then, it took 40 years. It is highly improbable that the vigorous Chinese economy will collapse in the same way."[*] Why is it more resilient? Unlike the Soviet Communist Party, it is not riding on an ideological wave; it is riding the wave of a resurgent civilization, and that civilization has proven itself to be one of the strongest and most resilient civilizations in history.

Many American strategic thinkers are aware of the strategic mistakes that led to the spectacular conquest of Singapore by the Japanese army in World War II, even though Singapore was supposed to be an indomitable British fortress. The British placed their big guns facing south, in anticipation of an attack from the sea. Instead, the Japanese troops came on bicycles from the north. The defeat of Singapore has become a textbook example of how mistakes are made in strategic thinking.

American strategic minds are making a comparable mistake when they focus on the fact that China is a communist country. Chinese communism is not a threat to American democracy. Instead, the success and competitiveness of the Chinese economy and society is the real challenge. To meet this challenge, American thinkers should focus

---

[*] Lee Hsien Loong, "Shangri-La Dialogue: Lee Hsien Loong on Why US and China Must Avoid Path of Conflict," *Straits Times* (Singapore), June 1, 2019, https://www.straitstimes.com/opinion/why-us-and-china-must-avoid-path-of-conflict-pm-lee.

on ensuring the success and competitiveness of the American economy and society. Interestingly, George Kennan, in his famous Mr. X essay, also emphasized the importance of a strong domestic American society. He used two key phrases that Americans should take note of. The outcome of the forthcoming contest, like the Cold War, will depend on the "spiritual vitality" of America and on America's success in avoiding "exhibitions of indecision, disunity and internal disintegration." In short, it will be domestic factors, not external threats, that will determine how well America does. Sadly, America today is suffering both from a lack of spiritual vitality and from disunity and internal disintegration. Instead of wasting precious resources on a nonexistent ideological threat from China, America should use the same resources to revitalize its own society. There is fundamentally a noncontradiction between American and Chinese ideology, as counterintuitive as this may seem.

Even more surprisingly, there is a noncontradiction between American and Chinese civilizations. Despite Samuel P. Huntington's warning in 1993, there is no imminent danger of a clash of civilizations between the West and China. Here, too, if reason could be the driving force in relations between countries, we would not need to fear the impact of civilizational difference. The arguments of reason and logic, as the great philosophers have taught us, have universal applicability in all cultures and civilizations. There is no reason why different civilizations cannot interact rationally with each other.

Yet just as human beings are heavily influenced by emotions in their personal decisions, they are equally influenced by emotions in their geopolitical judgments. To make matters worse, these emotions are quite often buried in the subconscious. While they may not appear on the surface, they are very much alive.

As indicated earlier in this chapter, over the past two hundred to three hundred years, fears of the yellow peril have resulted in various acts of discrimination against "yellow-skinned" people, from the Chinese

Exclusion Act at the end of the nineteenth century to the internment of Japanese Americans during World War II. The strong anti-China mood that has swept through Washington, DC, may in part be the result of rational dissatisfaction with some of China's policies, probably as a result of the fear of China's unfamiliar culture, but also in part from deeper emotional undercurrents. As the former US ambassador Chas Freeman has observed, "in their views of China, many Americans now appear subconsciously to have combined images of the insidious Dr. Fu Manchu, Japan's unnerving 1980s challenge to US industrial and financial primacy, and a sense of existential threat analogous to the Sinophobia that inspired the Anti-Coolie and Chinese Exclusion Acts."*

Given the psychological reality of this yellow peril undercurrent, American people need to question how much of their reactions to China's rise result from hard-headed rational analysis and how much are a result of deep discomfort with the success of a non-Caucasian civilization. We may never know the real answer, as these struggles between reason and emotion are playing out in subconscious terrains. Still, we should thank Kiron Skinner for alluding to the fact that such subconscious dimensions are at play here. The time has come for an honest discussion of the "yellow peril" dimension in US-China relations. The best way to deal with our subconscious fears is to surface them and deal with them.

Fortunately, we can overcome our irrational impulses. In our modern era, civilizations are not separated from one another like distinct billiard balls. Instead, we have developed into an interdependent human community in a small global village, and our civilizations are deeply connected and integrated with one another. In an article entitled "The Fusion of Civilizations," Lawrence Summers and I pointed out the following:

---

* Chas W. Freeman Jr., "On Hostile Coexistence with China," Chas W. Freeman, Jr., May 3, 2019, https://chasfreeman.net/on-hostile-coexistence-with-china/.

274 - HAS CHINA WON?

The great world civilizations, which used to have detached and separate identities, now have increasingly overlapping areas of commonality. Most people around the world now have the same aspirations as the Western middle classes: they want their children to get good educations, land good jobs, and live happy, productive lives as members of stable, peaceful communities. Instead of feeling depressed, the West should be celebrating its phenomenal success at injecting the key elements of its worldview into other great civilizations.[*]

Instead of fearing a clash of civilizations, American policymakers should be cheered by our observation that "the march of reason, triggered in the West by the Enlightenment, is spreading globally, leading to the emergence of pragmatic problem-solving cultures in every region and making it possible to envisage the emergence of a stable and sustainable rules-based order." We also observed that the overriding dynamic of the fusion of civilizations is also taking place between the West and China. As we wrote:

The second great challenge many worry about is the rise of China. China's success, however, can also be seen as the ultimate triumph of the West. The emperor Qianlong famously wrote to Great Britain's King George III in 1793 saying, "Our Celestial Empire possesses all things in prolific abundance and lacks no product within its own borders. There [is] therefore no need to import the manufactures of outside barbarians in exchange for our own produce." Two centuries later, the Chinese understand that absorbing Western modernity into their society has been crucial to their country's reemergence. It has led to rapid economic growth, new and gleaming infrastructure, triumphs

* Kishore Mahbubani and Lawrence H. Summers, "The Fusion of Civilization: The Case for Global Optimism," *Foreign Affairs*, May/June 2016, https://www.foreignaffairs.com /articles/2016-04-18/fusion-civilizations.

in space exploration, the spectacular 2008 Olympic Games in Beijing, and much more.

Even as Chinese society has accepted modernity with great enthusiasm, however, it has not abandoned its Chinese cultural roots. The Chinese look at their modern Chinese civilization and emphasize its Chineseness, seeing no contradiction. Indeed, China is now experiencing its own cultural renaissance, fueled by its new affluence.*

Chinese leaders have also emphasized that despite China's cultural differences with the West, there need not be a clash of civilizations. Speaking at the opening of the Conference on Dialogue of Asian Civilizations in Beijing in May 2019, President Xi Jinping said: "Civilizations don't have to clash with each other; what is needed are eyes to see the beauty in all civilizations. We should keep our own civilizations dynamic and create conditions for other civilizations to flourish. Together we can make the garden of world civilizations colorful and vibrant."†

One curious aspect of our times is that in the past, it was the Western leaders, not Chinese leaders, who espoused the values of embracing diversity. The one American president who lived through the nightmare of facing a realistic possibility of a nuclear war was John F. Kennedy. He was severely chastened by the experience, and on reflecting on this experience, he provided his fellow Americans with some valuable advice. In his commencement address at American University in 1963, he said, "So, let us not be blind to our differences—but let us also direct attention to our common interests and to the means by which those differences can be resolved. And if we cannot end now our differences,

---

* Ibid.

† Xi Jinping, "Full Text of President Xi Jinping's Speech at the Opening Ceremony of the Conference on Dialogue of Asian Civilizations," China-Pakistan Economic Corridor, May 23, 2019, http://www.cpecinfo.com/news/full-text-of-president-xi-jinping -speech-at-the-opening-ceremony-of-the-conference-on-dialogue-of-asian-civilizations /NzE0MA==.

at least we can help make the world safe for diversity. For, in the final analysis, our most basic common link is that we all inhabit this small planet. We all breathe the same air. We all cherish our children's future. And we are all mortal."* The key words in his statement are: *make the world safe for diversity.*

In short, foresighted American leaders of the past have arrived at the logical conclusion that even though humanity lives in different cultures and civilizations, there need not be a clash of civilizations. If we listen to them, then even in this dimension, where there could be a dangerous divide between America and China, there is a noncontradiction.

Finally, the one area where there appears to be a fundamental contradiction between America and China would be in the area of values, especially political values. Americans hold sacrosanct the ideals of freedom of speech, press, assembly, and religion and also believe that every human being is entitled to the same fundamental human rights. The Chinese believe that social needs and social harmony are more important than individual needs and rights and that the prevention of chaos and turbulence is the main goal of governance. In short, America and China clearly believe in two different sets of political values.

Yet, a fundamental contradiction would only arise in this area if China tries to export its values to America and America tries to export its values to China. Some Americans, who have become obsessed with the threat from China, have begun to suggest that China is trying to undermine the values of American society. This was implied in the famous remark by the FBI director Christopher Wray, who said that there was now a "whole-of-society" threat from China. Sadly, the report put out by a group of American scholars entitled *Chinese Influence & American Interests* also said that China was trying to undermine American freedoms. It said: "Openness and freedom are fundamental elements of

---

* John F. Kennedy, "Commencement Address at American University," Washington, DC, June 10, 1963, https://www.jfklibrary.org/archives/other-resources/john-f-kennedy-speeches/american-university-19630610.

American democracy and intrinsic strengths of the United States and its way of life. These values must be protected against corrosive actions by China and other countries."* Yet, although China, like America and every other country in the world, engages in espionage, and there may be some objectionable activities by some Chinese agencies in America, it is possible to assert with great confidence that the Chinese government has no desire or plan to undermine or overthrow American democracy. Why not? The simple answer is that Chinese leaders are political realists. They would not waste their time or resources on a mission impossible.

Sadly, the same is not true in the American political system. Many Americans believe that they have a moral obligation to support efforts to overthrow a tyrannical communist party system and help liberate the Chinese people from political oppression. Since America succeeded in liberating so many people from the Soviet yoke, it could and should do the same with China. As documented several times in this book, many Americans believe that China is "on the wrong side of history" and America should try to help move China to the right side of history. They also believe that since America is a "shining city on the hill," it has an obligation to promote human rights in China.

Americans are also fair people. They believe that people should practice what they preach. Americans would also agree with the broad principle that a country that violates certain fundamental principles of the Universal Declaration of Human Rights does not have the moral authority to preach to others the virtues of these human rights.

However, while Americans agree with these points in theory, they do not implement them in practice. This can be seen in the reactions of American leaders to the reports that China has incarcerated a million Muslims in reeducation camps in Xinjiang. Many Americans have

---

* Working Group on Chinese Influence Activities in the United States, *Chinese Influence & American Interests: Promoting Constructive Vigilance* (Stanford, CA: Hoover Institution Press, 2018), https://www.hoover.org/sites/default/files/research/docs/chineseinfluence _americaninterests_fullreport_web.pdf.

expressed outrage over the treatment of innocent Muslim civilians by the Chinese government. Americans believe that they have the right to express outrage because they believe that America treats innocent Muslim civilians better.

But which country treats innocent Muslim civilians better? America or China? If the reports are true, the Chinese government has incarcerated hundreds of thousands of innocent Muslim civilians in reeducation camps. If the reports are true, the American government has tortured or killed thousands of innocent Muslim civilians since September 9, 2011. Unfortunately, in both cases, the facts seem to be true. The Chinese government has incarcerated hundreds of thousands of Muslim civilians. Enough media reports have confirmed this. Similarly, the American government has tortured thousands of Muslims. Since 9/11, America has been dropping thousands of bombs on Islamic countries, killing many innocent civilians as a result.

John Mearsheimer summarizes these facts in *The Great Delusion*. Most Americans are aware that torture was carried out systematically in Guantanamo Bay. Fewer Americans are aware that "the Bush administration devised the infamous policy of extraordinary rendition, in which high-value prisoners were sent to countries that cared little about human rights, like Egypt and Syria, to be tortured and interrogated. It appears the CIA also tortured prisoners at its 'black sites' in Europe as well as at Bagram Air Base in Afghanistan and Abu Ghraib in Iraq. This policy clearly violated American and international law, both of which forbid torture."[*]

Torture is a greater violation of human rights than incarceration. Most moral philosophers would agree on this. They would also agree that what is worse than torture is assassination because the most basic human right is the right to live. Few people may realize that in recent

---

[*] John J. Mearsheimer, *The Great Delusion: Liberal Dreams and International Realities* (New Haven, CT: Yale University Press, 2018), 184.

years the American government has stepped up its assassination pro-grams. Mearsheimer describes how it came about:

> Because the Obama administration could neither prosecute nor re-lease the detainees at Guantanamo, it had little interest in captur-ing new prisoners and subjecting them to indefinite detention. So Obama and his advisors apparently decided instead to assassinate suspected enemy combatants wherever they were found. While it is surely easier to kill suspects than bring them to Guantanamo and perpetuate its legal morass, the effects of this new policy may be even more poisonous.
>
> Drones, of course, play a central role in these assassinations. Obama had a kill list known as the "disposition matrix," and every Tuesday there was a meeting in the White House—it was called "Terror Tuesday"—where the next victims were selected.*

Mearsheimer also adds the following observation: "As the journalist Tom Engelhardt writes, 'Once upon a time, off-the-books assassination was generally a rare act of state that presidents could deny. Now, it is part of everyday life in the White House and at the CIA. The presi-dent's role as assassin in chief has been all but publicly promoted as a political plus.'"

Since the records of both the American and Chinese governments in respecting the human rights of innocent Muslim civilians has been less than perfect, it would be unwise for either government to preach to the other the importance of respecting fundamental human rights. A wiser approach for both governments to take is to look at the big picture and acknowledge that both governments face a common challenge of dealing with the threats posed by terrorists recruited by radical Islamic groups. America woke up to this threat after 9/11. China experienced

---

* Ibid., 184–185.

similar 9/11 moments when terrorists recruited from the Xinjiang region went on a killing spree in several cities. Ishaan Tharoor wrote in the *Washington Post* on May 22, 2014: "A gruesome terror attack Thursday morning led to at least 31 deaths in Urumqi. The attack—in which assailants in two cars plowed over shoppers and set off explosives in a crowded market area—is the worst such incident in years, surpassing a horrific slaughter in March, when knife-wielding attackers hacked down 29 people at a train station in the southwestern city of Kunming. As in Kunming, authorities suspect ethnic Uighur extremists."* Most Americans are unaware that China, too, has experienced domestic terrorism. If they were, they would see the long-term value of both the American and Chinese governments cooperating together to assist in one of the largest existential challenges that humanity faces.

This challenge is the massive efforts being made by the 1.3 billion Muslims to modernize and create the same kind of comfortable and secure middle-class living standards that most American and Chinese citizens already enjoy. Fortunately, most Muslim societies are slowly and steadily succeeding, including the most populous Islamic countries of Indonesia and Malaysia, Pakistan and Bangladesh. Over time, these more successful Islamic societies will have a positive impact on some of the more troubled Arab nations in the Middle East. America has already spent a lot of blood and resources trying to fix several Arab societies. Most of these efforts have failed. Yet, America is more likely to succeed if it can cooperate with the successful moderate Muslim societies of Asia and with China. In short, vis-à-vis the Islamic world, America and China should not focus on their differences; they should focus on their common challenges and opportunities.

If a positive growth dynamic develops in all corners of the Islamic world, the result will be fewer human rights violations (incarceration,

---

* Ishaan Tharoor, "Why China's Terrorism Problem Is Getting Worse," *Washington Post*, May 22, 2014, https://www.washingtonpost.com/news/worldviews/wp/2014/05/22 /why-chinas-terrorism-problem-is-getting-worse/.

torture, or assassinations) by America and China. In short, even in the area of values where there are differences of views, there is potential for collaboration. In so doing, both America and China will also be creating a safer future for their own populations.

The common interest that America and China have in dealing with terrorism and with the troubled parts of the Islamic world reinforces the key message of this book. If America and China were to focus on their core interests of improving the livelihood and well-being of their citizens, they would come to realize that there are no fundamental contradictions in their long-term national interests. In 2010, then prime minister Manmohan Singh and Premier Wen Jiabao captured the positive spirit of Sino-Indian relations in a joint statement: "There is enough space in the world for the development of both India and China and indeed, enough areas for India and China to cooperate."* Similarly, there is enough space in the world for both America and China to thrive together.

Equally important, in the face of the overriding challenge of global warming, America and China have a fundamental common interest in keeping the planet habitable for the 1.7 billion people of America and China and the remaining 6 billion people of the world. This pressing and grave challenge to humanity should take precedence over all other challenges.

The challenge that climate change presents for the human species is a simple one: Can it demonstrate that it remains the most intelligent species on planet earth and preserve it for future generations? Humans would look pityingly at two tribes of apes that continued fighting over territory while the forest around them was burning. But this is how America and China will appear to future generations if they continue

---

*"Joint Communiqué of the Republic of India and the People's Republic of China," Media Center, Ministry of External Affairs, Government of India, December 16, 2010, https://mea.gov.in/bilateral-documents.htm?dtl/5158/Joint+Communiqu+of+the+Republic+of+India+and+the+Peoples+Republic+of+China.

to focus on their differences while the earth is facing an extended moment of great peril.

Moral philosophers and religious sages throughout the ages have reminded us that we will never succeed in creating perfection. Nor will we have simple black-and-white options to choose from. At the end of the day, we always have to make trade-offs, including moral ones, figure out what our overriding imperatives are, and learn how to focus on them. At the end of the day, this is what the six billion people of the rest of the world expect America and China to do: to focus on saving the planet and improving the living conditions of humanity, including those of their own peoples. The final question will therefore not be whether America or China has won. It will be whether humanity has won.

ACKNOWLEDGMENTS

The two people who helped me the most to launch this book project are Professor Tan Chorh Chuan, the former president of the National University of Singapore (NUS), and Professor Tan Eng Chye, the current president of NUS. They generously gifted me with a nine-month sabbatical when I stepped down from my role as dean of the Lee Kuan Yew School of Public Policy on December 31, 2017. I'm also grateful that the chairman of the board of the Lee Kuan Yew School, ESM Goh Chok Tong, supported and encouraged the sabbatical. After stepping down as dean, I was happy to be assigned to work with Professor Andrew Wee, vice president of the University and Global Relations, NUS, and his team. Andrew generously gave me the time and space to work on this book. Professor Tim Bunnell, director of the Asia Research Institute (ARI); Professor Maitrii Aung-Thwin, deputy director; and Sharlene Xavier Anthony also extended a warm welcome to me at ARI from July 2019. I was happy to complete this book during my stint at ARI, which has clearly emerged as one of the leading centers of research on Asia in our world.

The 2018 sabbatical was well spent. I was invited to six universities: Columbia University, Harvard University, Fudan University, Sciences Po, Georgetown University, and Oxford University. In each university, I was warmly received and well supported. There are many people to thank, but I would like to thank in particular Professor Merit Janow (dean of the School of International and Public Affairs at Columbia University), Professor Anthony Saich (director of the Ash Center for Democratic Governance and Innovation at Harvard University), Professor Zhang Weiwei (professor of international studies at the School of International Relations and Public Affairs, Fudan University), Eric Li (China Institute, Fudan University), Professor Enrico Letta (dean of the Paris School of International Affairs at Sciences Po), Professor John J. DeGioia (president of Georgetown University), Professor Rosemary Foot (Emeritus Fellow at St. Antony's College, University of Oxford), and Professor Rana Mitter (director of the University of Oxford China Centre). Each went out of his or her way to facilitate and support my research for this book.

At these six universities, I also had many deep and reflective conversations with several leading professors and researchers in this field. Not all of them would agree with some of the arguments and conclusions in this book. Nonetheless, I hope that they will read this book and find in it some of the learning I took away from my rich conversations with them.

I am also grateful that some good friends of mine have agreed to provide generous endorsements. I would like to thank Graham Allison, Ian Bremmer, David Lampton, Michael Spence, Larry Summers, Stephen Walt, Wang Gungwu, and George Yeo.

When I launched this book project, I knew that it would be a challenge to find an American publisher. Hence, I was truly delighted when my old friend and publisher Clive Priddle, with whom I had worked on three books in the past, readily agreed to publish this book. I have always learned a lot from Clive. Hence, it was a real joy to work with him once again. He has done a fabulous job of editing and strengthening this book. I'm truly grateful to him and his wonderful team at PublicAffairs.

In today's messy and complicated world, it is impossible for any author to write a book without good research assistance. I am truly grateful that Yanan Tan participated in this project from its very inception and saw it through to completion. She did a remarkable job of researching and finding facts and arguments that significantly supported the key conclusions of this book. This book owes a lot to her. I am also grateful that a young intern, Ali Lodhi, stepped in to help for four weeks. Jessica Yeo also helped out toward the end. I would never have managed to complete this project without the support of my exceptional personal assistant, Carol Chan. She kept me organized and contributed valuable suggestions and inputs during the way.

My wife, Anne, has brought many gifts to my life, too many to mention. One truly special gift she conferred on me was a close relationship with her family in New Jersey. I have grown to love and admire her family. Her mother, Adele, has been exceptionally generous and warm and welcoming to me. I'm truly happy to dedicate this book to her.

APPENDIX

THE MYTH OF AMERICAN EXCEPTIONALISM

The Idea that the United States Is Uniquely Virtuous
May Be Comforting to Americans. Too Bad It's Not True.

STEPHEN M. WALT

OVER THE LAST TWO CENTURIES, PROMINENT AMERICANS have described the United States as an "empire of liberty," a "shining city on a hill," the "last best hope of Earth," the "leader of the free world," and the "indispensable nation." These enduring tropes explain why all presidential candidates feel compelled to offer ritualistic paeans to America's greatness and why President Barack Obama landed in hot water—most recently, from Mitt Romney—for saying that while he believed in "American exceptionalism," it was no different from "British

This article was originally published in Stephen M. Walt, "The Myth of American Exceptionalism: The Idea that the United States Is Uniquely Virtuous May Be Comforting to Americans. Too Bad It's Not True," *Foreign Policy*, October 11, 2011, https://foreignpolicy.com/2011/10/11/the-myth-of-american-exceptionalism/.

exceptionalism," "Greek exceptionalism," or any other country's brand of patriotic chest-thumping.

Most statements of "American exceptionalism" presume that America's values, political system, and history are unique and worthy of universal admiration. They also imply that the United States is both destined and entitled to play a distinct and positive role on the world stage.

The only thing wrong with this self-congratulatory portrait of America's global role is that it is mostly a myth. Although the United States possesses certain unique qualities—from high levels of religiosity to a political culture that privileges individual freedom—the conduct of U.S. foreign policy has been determined primarily by its relative power and by the inherently competitive nature of international politics. By focusing on their supposedly exceptional qualities, Americans blind themselves to the ways that they are a lot like everyone else.

This unchallenged faith in American exceptionalism makes it harder for Americans to understand why others are less enthusiastic about U.S. dominance, often alarmed by U.S. policies, and frequently irritated by what they see as U.S. hypocrisy, whether the subject is possession of nuclear weapons, conformity with international law, or America's tendency to condemn the conduct of others while ignoring its own failings. Ironically, U.S. foreign policy would probably be more effective if Americans were less convinced of their own unique virtues and less eager to proclaim them.

What we need, in short, is a more realistic and critical assessment of America's true character and contributions. In that spirit, I offer here the Top 5 Myths about American Exceptionalism.

Myth 1: There Is Something Exceptional About American Exceptionalism.

Whenever American leaders refer to the "unique" responsibilities of the United States, they are saying that it is different from other powers and that these differences require them to take on special burdens.

Yet there is nothing unusual about such lofty declarations; indeed, those who make them are treading a well-worn path. Most great powers have considered themselves superior to their rivals and have believed that they were advancing some greater good when they imposed their preferences on others. The British thought they were bearing the "white man's burden," while French colonialists invoked *la mission civilisatrice* to justify their empire. Portugal, whose imperial activities were hardly distinguished, believed it was promoting a certain *missão civilizadora*. Even many of the officials of the former Soviet Union genuinely believed they were leading the world toward a socialist utopia despite the many cruelties that communist rule inflicted. Of course, the United States has by far the better claim to virtue than Stalin or his successors, but Obama was right to remind us that all countries prize their own particular qualities.

So when Americans proclaim they are exceptional and indispensable, they are simply the latest nation to sing a familiar old song. Among great powers, thinking you're special is the norm, not the exception.

Myth 2: The United States Behaves Better Than Other Nations Do.

Declarations of American exceptionalism rest on the belief that the United States is a uniquely virtuous nation, one that loves peace, nurtures liberty, respects human rights, and embraces the rule of law. Americans like to think their country behaves much better than other states do, and certainly better than other great powers.

If only it were true. The United States may not have been as brutal as the worst states in world history, but a dispassionate look at the historical record belies most claims about America's moral superiority.

For starters, the United States has been one of the most expansionist powers in modern history. It began as 13 small colonies clinging to the Eastern Seaboard, but eventually expanded across North America, seizing Texas, Arizona, New Mexico, and California from Mexico in

1846. Along the way, it eliminated most of the native population and confined the survivors to impoverished reservations. By the mid-19th century, it had pushed Britain out of the Pacific Northwest and consolidated its hegemony over the Western Hemisphere.

The United States has fought numerous wars since then—starting several of them—and its wartime conduct has hardly been a model of restraint. The 1899–1902 conquest of the Philippines killed some 200,000 to 400,000 Filipinos, most of them civilians, and the United States and its allies did not hesitate to dispatch some 305,000 German and 330,000 Japanese civilians through aerial bombing during World War II, mostly through deliberate campaigns against enemy cities. No wonder Gen. Curtis LeMay, who directed the bombing campaign against Japan, told an aide, "If the U.S. lost the war, we would be prosecuted as war criminals." The United States dropped more than 6 million tons of bombs during the Indochina war, including tons of napalm and lethal defoliants like Agent Orange, and it is directly responsible for the deaths of many of the roughly 1 million civilians who died in that war.

More recently, the U.S.-backed Contra war in Nicaragua killed some 30,000 Nicaraguans, a percentage of their population equivalent to 2 million dead Americans. U.S. military action has led directly or indirectly to the deaths of 250,000 Muslims over the past three decades (and that's a low-end estimate, not counting the deaths resulting from the sanctions against Iraq in the 1990s), including the more than 100,000 people who died following the invasion and occupation of Iraq in 2003. U.S. drones and Special Forces are going after suspected terrorists in at least five countries at present and have killed an unknown number of innocent civilians in the process. Some of these actions may have been necessary to make Americans more prosperous and secure. But while Americans would undoubtedly regard such acts as indefensible if some foreign country were doing them to us, hardly any U.S. politicians have questioned these policies. Instead, Americans still wonder, "Why do they hate us?"

The United States talks a good game on human rights and international law, but it has refused to sign most human rights treaties, is not a party to the International Criminal Court, and has been all too willing to cozy up to dictators—remember our friend Hosni Mubarak? — with abysmal human rights records. If that were not enough, the abuses at Abu Ghraib and the George W. Bush administration's reliance on waterboarding, extraordinary rendition, and preventive detention should shake America's belief that it consistently acts in a morally superior fashion. Obama's decision to retain many of these policies suggests they were not a temporary aberration.

The United States never conquered a vast overseas empire or caused millions to die through tyrannical blunders like China's Great Leap Forward or Stalin's forced collectivization. And given the vast power at its disposal for much of the past century, Washington could certainly have done much worse. But the record is clear: U.S. leaders have done what they thought they had to do when confronted by external dangers, and they paid scant attention to moral principles along the way. The idea that the United States is uniquely virtuous may be comforting to Americans; too bad it's not true.

Myth 3: America's Success Is Due to Its Special Genius.

The United States has enjoyed remarkable success, and Americans tend to portray their rise to world power as a direct result of the political foresight of the Founding Fathers, the virtues of the U.S. Constitution, the priority placed on individual liberty, and the creativity and hard work of the American people. In this narrative, the United States enjoys an exceptional global position today because it is, well, *exceptional*.

There is more than a grain of truth to this version of American history. It's not an accident that immigrants came to America in droves in search of economic opportunity, and the "melting pot" myth facilitated the assimilation of each wave of new Americans. America's scientific and technological achievements are fully deserving of praise and owe something to the openness and vitality of the American political order.

But America's past success is due as much to good luck as to any uniquely American virtues. The new nation was lucky that the continent was lavishly endowed with natural resources and traversed by navigable rivers. It was lucky to have been founded far from the other great powers and even luckier that the native population was less advanced and highly susceptible to European diseases. Americans were fortunate that the European great powers were at war for much of the republic's early history, which greatly facilitated its expansion across the continent, and its global primacy was ensured after the other great powers fought two devastating world wars. This account of America's rise does not deny that the United States did many things right, but it also acknowledges that America's present position owes as much to good fortune as to any special genius or "manifest destiny."

Myth 4: The United States Is Responsible for Most of the Good in the World.

Americans are fond of giving themselves credit for positive international developments. President Bill Clinton believed the United States was "indispensable to the forging of stable political relations," and the late Harvard University political scientist Samuel P. Huntington thought U.S. primacy was central "to the future of freedom, democracy, open economies, and international order in the world." Journalist Michael Hirsh has gone even further, writing in his book *At War With Ourselves* that America's global role is "the greatest gift the world has received in many, many centuries, possibly all of recorded history." Scholarly works such as Tony Smith's *America's Mission* and G. John Ikenberry's *Liberal Leviathan* emphasize America's contribution to the spread of democracy and its promotion of a supposedly liberal world order. Given all the high-fives American leaders have given themselves, it is hardly surprising that most Americans see their country as an overwhelmingly positive force in world affairs.

Once again, there is something to this line of argument, just not enough to make it entirely accurate. The United States has made undeniable contributions to peace and stability in the world over the past century, including the Marshall Plan, the creation and management of the Bretton Woods system, its rhetorical support for the core principles of democracy and human rights, and its mostly stabilizing military presence in Europe and the Far East. But the belief that all good things flow from Washington's wisdom overstates the U.S. contribution by a wide margin.

For starters, though Americans watching *Saving Private Ryan* or *Patton* may conclude that the United States played the central role in vanquishing Nazi Germany, most of the fighting was in Eastern Europe and the main burden of defeating Hitler's war machine was borne by the Soviet Union. Similarly, though the Marshall Plan and NATO played important roles in Europe's post-World War II success, Europeans deserve at least as much credit for rebuilding their economies, constructing a novel economic and political union, and moving beyond four centuries of sometimes bitter rivalry. Americans also tend to think they won the Cold War all by themselves, a view that ignores the contributions of other anti-Soviet adversaries and the courageous dissidents whose resistance to communist rule produced the "velvet revolutions" of 1989.

Moreover, as Godfrey Hodgson recently noted in his sympathetic but clear-eyed book, *The Myth of American Exceptionalism*, the spread of liberal ideals is a global phenomenon with roots in the Enlightenment, and European philosophers and political leaders did much to advance the democratic ideal. Similarly, the abolition of slavery and the long effort to improve the status of women owe more to Britain and other democracies than to the United States, where progress in both areas trailed many other countries. Nor can the United States claim a global leadership role today on gay rights, criminal justice, or economic equality—Europe's got those areas covered.

Finally, any honest accounting of the past half-century must acknowledge the downside of American primacy. The United States has been the major producer of greenhouse gases for most of the last hundred years and thus a principal cause of the adverse changes that are altering the global environment. The United States stood on the wrong side of the long struggle against apartheid in South Africa and backed plenty of unsavory dictatorships—including Saddam Hussein's—when short-term strategic interests dictated. Americans may be justly proud of their role in creating and defending Israel and in combating global anti-Semitism, but its one-sided policies have also prolonged Palestinian statelessness and sustained Israel's brutal occupation.

Bottom line: Americans take too much credit for global progress and accept too little blame for areas where U.S. policy has in fact been counterproductive. Americans are blind to their weak spots, and in ways that have real-world consequences. Remember when Pentagon planners thought U.S. troops would be greeted in Baghdad with flowers and parades? They mostly got RPGs and IEDs instead.

Myth 5: God Is on Our Side.

A crucial component of American exceptionalism is the belief that the United States has a divinely ordained mission to lead the rest of the world. Ronald Reagan told audiences that there was "some divine plan" that had placed America here, and once quoted Pope Pius XII saying, "Into the hands of America God has placed the destinies of an afflicted mankind." Bush offered a similar view in 2004, saying, "We have a calling from beyond the stars to stand for freedom." The same idea was expressed, albeit less nobly, in Otto von Bismarck's alleged quip that "God has a special providence for fools, drunks, and the United States."

Confidence is a valuable commodity for any country. But when a nation starts to think it enjoys the mandate of heaven and becomes convinced that it cannot fail or be led astray by scoundrels or incompetents, then reality is likely to deliver a swift rebuke. Ancient Athens, Napoleonic France, imperial Japan, and countless other countries have succumbed to this sort of hubris, and nearly always with catastrophic results.

Despite America's many successes, the country is hardly immune from setbacks, follies, and boneheaded blunders. If you have any doubts about that, just reflect on how a decade of ill-advised tax cuts, two costly and unsuccessful wars, and a financial meltdown driven mostly by greed and corruption have managed to squander the privileged position the United States enjoyed at the end of the 20th century. Instead of assuming that God is on *their* side, perhaps Americans should heed Abraham Lincoln's admonition that our greatest concern should be "whether *we* are on God's side."

Given the many challenges Americans now face, from persistent unemployment to the burden of winding down two deadly wars, it's unsurprising that they find the idea of their own exceptionalism comforting—and that their aspiring political leaders have been proclaiming it with increasing fervor. Such patriotism has its benefits, but not when it leads to a basic misunderstanding of America's role in the world. This is exactly how bad decisions get made.

America has its own special qualities, as all countries do, but it is still a state embedded in a competitive global system. It is far stronger and richer than most, and its geopolitical position is remarkably favorable. These advantages give the United States a wider range of choice in its conduct of foreign affairs, but they don't ensure that its choices will be good ones. Far from being a unique state whose behavior is radically different from that of other great powers, the United States has behaved like all the rest, pursuing its own self-interest first and foremost, seeking to improve its relative position over time, and devoting relatively little blood or treasure to purely idealistic pursuits. Yet, just like past great powers, it has convinced itself that it is different, and better, than everyone else.

International politics is a contact sport, and even powerful states must compromise their political principles for the sake of security and prosperity. Nationalism is also a powerful force, and it inevitably highlights the country's virtues and sugarcoats its less savory aspects. But if Americans want to be truly exceptional, they might start by viewing the whole idea of "American exceptionalism" with a much more skeptical eye.

INDEX

KISHORE MAHBUBANI, a Distinguished Fellow at the Asia Research Institute, National University of Singapore, has had two distinguished careers, thirty-three years in diplomacy and fifteen years in academia, when he was the Founding Dean of the Lee Kuan Yew School of Public Policy. He lived in New York for over ten years as Singapore's ambassador to the UN. In 2019, he was elected to the American Academy of Arts and Sciences. He is globally recognized as Asia's leading public intellectual. He has authored several books, among them *Can Asians Think?*, *Has the West Lost It?*, *The New Asian Hemisphere*, *The Great Convergence*, and *Beyond the Age of Innocence* (the last three all PublicAffairs). He travels extensively and lives in Singapore.

PublicAffairs is a publishing house founded in 1997. It is a tribute to the standards, values, and flair of three persons who have served as mentors to countless reporters, writers, editors, and book people of all kinds, including me.

I. F. STONE, proprietor of *I. F. Stone's Weekly*, combined a commitment to the First Amendment with entrepreneurial zeal and reporting skill and became one of the great independent journalists in American history. At the age of eighty, Izzy published *The Trial of Socrates*, which was a national bestseller. He wrote the book after he taught himself ancient Greek.

BENJAMIN C. BRADLEE was for nearly thirty years the charismatic editorial leader of *The Washington Post*. It was Ben who gave the *Post* the range and courage to pursue such historic issues as Watergate. He supported his reporters with a tenacity that made them fearless and it is no accident that so many became authors of influential, best-selling books.

ROBERT L. BERNSTEIN, the chief executive of Random House for more than a quarter century, guided one of the nation's premier publishing houses. Bob was personally responsible for many books of political dissent and argument that challenged tyranny around the globe. He is also the founder and longtime chair of Human Rights Watch, one of the most respected human rights organizations in the world.

• • •

For fifty years, the banner of Public Affairs Press was carried by its owner Morris B. Schnapper, who published Gandhi, Nasser, Toynbee, Truman, and about 1,500 other authors. In 1983, Schnapper was described by *The Washington Post* as "a redoubtable gadfly." His legacy will endure in the books to come.

Peter Osnos, *Founder*